ELGI'

OTHER PEOPLE'S MONEY

OTHER PEOPLE'S MONEY

THE RISE AND FALL OF BRITAIN'S MOST AUDACIOUS FRAUDSTER

NEIL FORSYTH WITH **ELLIOT CASTRO**

Sidgwick & Jackson

Measures have been taken in the illustration of criminal
techniques contained in this publication to prevent misuse

First published 2007 by Sidgwick & Jackson
an imprint of Pan Macmillan Ltd
Pan Macmillan, 20 New Wharf Road, London N1 9RR
Basingstoke and Oxford
Associated companies throughout the world
www.panmacmillan.com

ISBN 978-0-283-07051-8 HB
ISBN 978-0-283-07044-0 TPB

9 8 7 6 5 4 3 2 1

A CIP catalogue record for this book is available from
the British Library.

Typeset by SetSystems Ltd, Saffron Walden, Essex
Printed and bound in Great Britain by
Mackays of Chatham plc, Chatham, Kent

Visit www.panmacmillan.com to read more about all our books
and to buy them. You will also find features, author interviews and
news of any author events, and you can sign up for e-newsletters
so that you're always first to hear about our new releases.

For our mums, Jane Castro and Joan Forsyth

This is a true story. On occasion, names, locations, dates or events have been altered. This has been done to protect the innocent and, mostly, to protect the guilty.

But this is a true story.

CHAPTER ONE

Edinburgh, 5 November 2004

I hate this time, the space between landing and getting off. At least usually I'm at the front of the plane, milling about first class as the stewardess finds my jacket and apologizes for the delay. These short hops just chuck everyone in together and all the hassle in Belfast had left me late to board and scrambling for a seat beside the toilets.

I'd been planning to go to Amsterdam until this morning when I called KLM's central reservations desk while packing my Louis Vuitton duffel bag. *I'm phoning from the Belfast Airport KLM desk, our servers are down, just checking a booking in the name of Elliot Castro, everything OK?* And there it was, 'There's a problem with that one.' So I'd hung up and swore and decided to come to Edinburgh.

Finally, there is a ping and people start clambering from their seats, pulling bags from the lockers and easing themselves into the aisle. I wait until most have departed before rising slowly and picking my bag from the emptied shelves. I smile at the stewardess as I pass but my eyes stay on the ground, I don't give her a face to remember.

The concourse is a mess of passengers, workmen and ladders. A few years ago, when this all began, Edinburgh Airport was a joke. There were a handful of bars and shops and passengers were crowded into a long, depressing waiting area. It was perfect. Now they're getting serious and it's making me nervous as I scan the airline desks. I can't stray within sight of the British Airways people and I need it to be a suitable ... *there*.

'Excuse me.' I select a middle-class Scottish accent. The man is old and local, he needs to hear familiarity but also the impression of authority. He looks up from his newspaper and I smile. 'Hi. I see you have a fax machine there,' I slip the paper from my jacket pocket, 'Could I possibly pay you to send this for me to the number at the top of the page?'

As the machine pushes out its confirmation I thank the man, sliding a twenty-pound note across the desk as I do so, and head for the telephones. I punch in the number and pause, setting myself into character. English, Home Counties. 'Hello there, is that the Glasshouse Hotel? Good, it's David Smith here from Shell Oil. I've just sent you a fax ... ah, great you've got it. Yes, well Elliot will be in touch I'm sure. Thank you.'

A week ago I called the Balmoral Hotel in Edinburgh from my rented flat in Belfast. The Balmoral is a famous and grand hotel but, more importantly, it's very big. This means that when you call and ask to be put through to Mr Smith you have a decent chance there will be a Mr Smith for them to patch you through to. 'Hello?' he answered, and that's when I became David Smith.

I pick up the receiver and hit redial. 'Hello, the Glass-house,' chirps a voice. A different one, though that doesn't matter. 'Good morning, it's Elliot Castro here.' 'Hello, Mr Castro, I believe you're joining us today?' 'That's correct, I was just hoping that I could have my usual ...' 'Number eighty-one? I've already reserved it, sir. Do you require to be collected from the airport?' 'No, I'm already here. I'll be with you shortly, thank you.'

As I walk to the taxi rank I pull out the fax sheets and rip them carefully into shreds, tearing through the middle of the proud Shell Oil logo. I don't have to send these faxes but they help avoid doubt. Doubt is not something that I can afford. The taxi driver leaps from his cab, recognizing the tip potential of my £1,000 suit and fussy luggage set. He is heartened further as we speed across Edinburgh, and he asks the purpose of my trip. 'To spend money,' I answer blankly as I spot the castle behind the rooftops.

I like the Glasshouse Hotel. It's what I've always wanted a five-star hotel to be – expensive, elegant, decadent and fun. Don't get me wrong, I still enjoy the Ritz and the Plaza and the old money stench but I'm never fully relaxed in these environments. I've been humiliated by wine waiters from Toronto to Dubai and in Australia I heard a barman call me vulgar for leaving a $1,000 tip. All I want is somewhere I can spend money in peace.

'Hello, Mr Castro.' I've only ever used my own name here because I knew I'd return. Not just for the hotel but also for Edinburgh, close enough to home without having to go there, to go back. The receptionist's smile is real. When smiles aren't real the eyes are unaffected, you can see it very easily when you know how. My eyes, for example, never really change. 'Can we show you to your suite?'

She hands me over to a small Spaniard in a black suit. 'Mr Castro,' he drawls and leads me to the lift. 'Eighty-one, eh?' He smiles knowingly. A porter had told me once that they call room eighty-one the Celebrity Suite. 'Who's been in there recently?' I ask him, because I know that's what he wants me to do. Along the corridor he lists pop stars and actors, as he opens the door he names a prince.

It is a beautiful hotel room. In the middle is a wooden frame that halves the space, dividing the king-size bed from a large living area. The outer wall is glass and a door leads onto a sprawling balcony that faces a wooded hill. I think about showering but I know I won't. I can feel it grow inside me, the prickly sense of anticipation that quickens my breathing and turns my throat dry. I throw my luggage on the bed and take the stairs back down.

I exit the hotel and turn to my left. Immediately I pass a row of chain bars – *Lloyds No. 1, Walkabout, The Slug and Lettuce*. In my fledgling days, when every nicked quid sent me giddy, I used to love these chain pubs and their card machines. I'd pass them a card and ask for fifty pounds cashback in my most whimsical manner then listen for the wrong beep. If it came, I was out the door.

This is what has happened to me. Shop signs, restaurants and banks mean different things to me than they would to you. To me they mean a lot of things but I can probably boil it down to two, success and failure. In fact no, that's being unfair. I never fail in the end, just sometimes it takes a little longer.

Some are like bumping into an old friend. Look, as I arrive at the top of Leith Walk I can see a cinema, a Bank of Scotland and the John Lewis department store. My reaction is warm, very warm, cold. Some cinema chains want to keep their queues moving so often cards will be swiped through unauthorized to save time. The Bank of Scotland and their competitors you're going to hear a lot more of, and I once had to walk very briskly out of John Lewis.

I pass through John Lewis to enter the shopping centre, exiting through the perfume concessions. I'm going to stop here on the way back and pick up a bottle for posting to my mother. Usually I'd have got her something from the airport but I'd been distracted by the fax business. She follows me round the world from the postcodes on her perfume.

As I pass The Link phone shop I touch the shape in my

pocket. Currently I've got three phones. I've sometimes had more but I've always got two. Next door is a computer shop, which sends a momentary panic as I recall exactly where in the flat I hid my encrypted zip disk. There are two computers back there. I use them for several hours each day and both have entirely empty memories.

Boots the chemist. I once ran from one of their shops in Glasgow after the card was flagged and the manager appeared at the till. His suspicion was understandable as the card belonged to a 75-year-old man who had dropped his wallet on a train, but I was still a thief back then. Ah, they were simple days. Before it became a job and then a life. Before I took these people and inhabited them. Before I realized that I could steal through the telephone, and money could come to me through thin air from the biggest credit card companies in the world.

I like this little street, Multrees Walk. It's a short, zigzag affair behind Harvey Nichols and they built it more in hope than expectation. Now it's nearly full as decent fashion houses, boutiques and other luxury-goods stores have arrived. It reminds me of Bond Street and stretches of Fifth Avenue. I see a jewellery shop has taken one of the remaining units.

The only piece of jewellery I have is a platinum bracelet I bought for £8,000 from Asprey in London. I don't wear it because I don't particularly like it but when you have a high-limit card a day away from being cancelled then you do things like that. Anyway, I don't think you need jewellery if you have a nice watch, and I've always got a nice watch.

The Harvey Nichols doorman nods and steps to the side. I slip inside the double doors, spotting the first of the cameras, and move to the escalators. As I rise through the air above the sunglasses and handbags I try not to strain my neck as I wait for the desk to appear before me. A woman, early thirties. Generally speaking, that's a good sign. I walk towards her and smile.

'Hello there.' Refined Cockney, I'm not sure why. 'I'd like to buy £2,000 in gift vouchers please.' She doesn't really react, just begins to process the order and asks for payment details. I pull out my wallet and open it out of her line of vision. There they are, ranked and ready, but it's not as strong a hand as it looks. I have some others saved in my mind but for this I select the card nearest to me. *David Smith.*

A beep. She reaches for the phone. David Smith's card, my card, is a corporate American Express credit card. The security questions will be full name, address, place and date of birth and mother's maiden name. This information is in my head, along with much more. To keep order in the mess the people are matched to fruit. David Smith is a large juicy pear. As I breathe and bring the pear forward it arrives soon enough, dragging with it names, addresses, dates . . .

I thank the woman and slip the vouchers into my pocket as I make for the escalator. Back in Multrees Walk I wander into Louis Vuitton. 'Hello, Mr Castro.' I'll be honest and say that this catches me by surprise. I'd only ever spent money in here once before, the last time I was in Edinburgh in August. As I consider this the surprise evaporates. That stay, four days in all, had been a blur. I had spent £42,000.

I leave and wander into the Armani shop next door. I'm wasting time here, the vouchers are burning in my pocket but I am trying hard to ignore them. *I can go up a different escalator, she won't see me, and even if she did then I can pay with another card.* I pick up some T-shirts and underwear. I'm always buying underwear. I'm always *buying.*

At the counter I pull out a card from the back of the

rack. It's more humble than the rest, there's no gold or platinum or CORPORATE stamp. It is a debit card from a well-known bank over in Belfast and belongs to my personal account, where my wages go. I like thinking about my wages. This is something I started recently, working as a DJ to fill the hours. They pay me £120 and I leave the bar walking on air.

It's the only money I've ever truly earned and I deposit it in cash the next day into this account. I don't have to, I just want to. My other bank account is in Switzerland and that's not quite so cute. I don't really like it when I send big chunks from the Swiss account to the Irish one, and the bad money dwarves the good. I still do it though. A man's got to live. But that's just bank accounts, they're only a small part of the picture. Most of the money that I spend, that I have spent, comes and goes without record.

I can't wait any longer and I walk round to the front of Harvey Nichols and enter through the other door. I pass quickly through the perfume, remembering again to buy a bottle for Mum, and take a side escalator up to the men's department. As I enter I see Stewart and he sees me. This is why I bought the vouchers.

'Hi, Elliot, good to see you, what can I show you today?' I enjoy the personal shopper system (who wouldn't, really, if they had the cash?) and I particularly like Stewart's style. He doesn't let me leave with anything that isn't right, even if it costs him a few quid in commission. He laughed at me once, when I emerged from the dressing room in a cream suit. That's when I decided that I liked him.

As we walk through the sections he yanks down jackets, shirts, trousers. Anything I dally over he demands a size and slings it over his arm with the rest. We get to the dressing room and it's quite a pile, but first I need to go to the bathroom. I tell Stewart but he's not listening, he's frowning into the distance and mouthing 'What?' to someone else.

Just after I enter the cubicle I hear the bathroom door open and close and someone take a few steps inside. I presume they're in front of the mirror, unaware of my presence. I prepare for a moment of fleeting awkwardness as I pull the door open.

The man is stocky, his face stern as he braces himself in front of me. He's definitely police, even Harvey Nichols' security would have better suits than that. This is genuinely my first thought as I see him, that his suit looks old and from a leaner time. The trousers strain across his thighs and the shoulders are badly pinched.

I move as if to pass him but I do it more to force the issue, the end. When it comes it's with a swing of his arm and sharp pain as he snaps his hand around my wrist. His hand is large and hairy. His thumb is a couple of inches beyond the sleeve of my jacket, his pinkie stretches across the face of my Rolex Oyster President. It cost £12,110 and I bought it on the credit card of an American businessman whom I never met.

My name is Elliot Castro and I'm twenty-one years old.

CHAPTER TWO

The Pheasant Pub, Brill, September 2005

Neil Forsyth

If Hollywood wanted an English country pub with a horror twist, the Pheasant would win the part with something to spare. Little light seeps through the smudged windows and the wooden ceiling hangs low over a lounge of nooks and crannies, including the corner booth where Elliot Castro and I sit huddled over our sandwiches.

Through the doorway we can see a windmill glowering over the rolling fields that encircle the Buckinghamshire village of Brill, which is still recovering from last night's storm. The landlord has been passing through the bar at regular intervals carrying creaking buckets of water from an unknown source and launching the contents into the gutter outside.

For much of the night, I had lain in bed in a small room above the pub as the sky lit up outside and the window frame rattled with the thunder. A few miles away Elliot had finished a game of chess against an inmate from the next hut. It had been a drawn-out affair but a victory all the same, stretching his unbeaten run to thirty-five. Afterwards he had run back to his hut, his trainers quickly drenched through the holes in the soles.

The landlord swoops upon us from behind a pillar and gathers our plates. Elliot orders coffee. On my side of the table sits a jumble of paperwork, on Elliot's a solitary scrap of paper. It is crumpled from being secreted down his right sock and bears a list of questions, the end of which we have now reached. Now it was time for a decision.

*

I first encountered Elliot Castro five months ago while drinking a cup of tea, dressed only in my pants. As I lay on the couch in my Edinburgh flat reading that morning's *Scotsman* I wasn't too hopeful of stumbling across anything particularly life-altering. Certainly nothing that would later have me sitting at my nearby desk and writing the opening chapters of a book.

Yet buried nearly twenty pages into the paper I discovered a two-page spread entitled 'Jet-Set Conman Checks into Prison'. There were five photos, one of the actor Leonardo Di Caprio in a scene from the movie *Catch Me if You Can*, shots of the Harrods department store, a Rolex, Sydney Harbour and a mugshot of a youthful-looking guy that was evidently Castro.

The story was incredible, even through the reserved prose of the *Scotsman*. Castro had duped and deceived and rattled his way around the world displaying an eye for the opulent. The article was patchy, based on official transcripts and quotes from several figures including a detective named Ralph Eastgate who had, apparently, tracked Castro down.

Nowhere in the piece was an answer to the most obvious question – why? It didn't say. Had anyone asked? There wasn't a word from Castro, only an old despairing quote from his mother, Jane. As others – police, the judge, security experts – chipped in all around, Castro sat silent in the middle of their words, staring from the page. And with that I closed the paper and went to get dressed.

A few hours later I was traipsing down Leith Walk. I passed the Glasshouse Hotel and a row of pubs then ducked into a petrol station concourse. In front of the station was a newspaper stand, dominated by the Scottish tabloid newspaper the *Daily Record*. As I passed it by my mind clicked and my feet stopped. Castro was looking at me again – 'Catch Me if You Con', blasted the front page beside that same steady gaze.

*

My first letter to Castro was tentative largely because I wasn't sure if he'd receive it, let alone reply. I had no prisoner number for him and directed my letter to Wormwood Scrubs Prison only on the educated guess of a court clerk. Still, a week or so later arrived a similarly edgy response.

It was a short, noncommittal scribble on official prison note-paper. Although Castro was clearly interested in my proposed inter-view, he offered several reservations. He seemed suspicious of my intentions and what the end result might be. It was childlike in formation and ended with a claim that he was not 'proud or boastful' of what he had done.

Fleeting disappointment passed quickly as I twigged. The letter was written just days after the court case which had now left Castro in one of Britain's most challenging prisons. He was speaking to me with the cagey deference that he would have been employing with lawyers, judges and prison governors. This was bullshit, worth as much in itself as his zero contribution to the case coverage that had by now zipped round the world.

The bare facts had gone out on the international wires and straight into the quirky sections of hundreds of newspapers and magazines. Some British papers had delved beyond the court docu-ments to settle on contradictory accounts of Castro's background and actions. But still there was nothing, not a single word, from Castro. I sent off my reply. Nothing came back.

Eventually: 'I apologize for the delay in getting back to you, but as you can see, I have been transferred to another prison.' Castro, a young man with a penchant for travel and deception, had been afforded Category D status and was now in an open prison. The official prison-issue notepaper had been swapped for a plain pad and Castro wrote in a tight, neat print instead of the cautious block capitals he'd sent from the Scrubs.

He was slowly coming round to the interview proposal but was unsure how we could proceed. I could see his point – with a month between letters the process of asserting visitation rights and photo access looked a thankless task. I did, however, give him my numbers and took this opportunity to notify *Maxim* magazine of my intentions.

When Castro called me, everything changed a little bit. In content the calls were not much more impressive than his letters. He was nervous, questioning, and seemed to place unnecessary importance on what I saw as minor issues whilst not asking questions that I would have considered essential. He stressed repeatedly that he would not want any payment for an interview.

But behind the words I saw two vital signs that drew me to him. In the gaps between his pre-prepared wanderings he would lighten and spark. It was in reaction to my questions that he approached a level of calmness, as if finding inspiration in the opportunity to think on his feet and rely on a natural intelligence. And, vitally, he *knew* how good his story was.

At first this would slip through — 'I know that the story is maybe the kind of thing you'd be looking for.' A couple of calls down the line he would chuckle, 'There's a lot of stuff that wasn't in the papers.' He was taunting me good-naturedly, and that's when I knew I was in. When I came off the phone I called *Maxim* and then looked up exactly where Her Majesty's Open Prison Ford actually was.

On a bright summer's morning, in a car park in the Sussex countryside, I met Elliot Castro for the first time. He was bigger than I imagined, powerful and confident as he strode towards the photographer and me and extended his hand. We drove to Brighton and took him to a greasy spoon, where he devoured a fry-up and led me on a whistle-stop tour of the previous five years in a soft Scottish accent.

I knew I was getting only a sanitized, edited version but it was more than enough. With each twist and adventure I would be freshly astonished. It was hard to match the information with the boyish young man who sat opposite, excitedly slicing and scooping his

£4.99 breakfast while the photographer clicked and whirred over our shoulders.

Afterwards we walked to Brighton Pier, which strained with its fair and the bustling weekend crowd. Castro asked for money to go on the rollercoaster, then the dodgems. He was killing time, this was his first day out of custody for months. He picked out a stall offering computer analysis of signatures. It came back – I swear – 'Spending is something you enjoy doing even when you really cannot afford the indulgence.'

When the magazine came out a month later, it was painful for me to read. There was Elliot eating his fry-up and around him my 3,000-word sprint through his story. Wrestling it down to that size had been a depressing task. It had become a brief glance, serving only to hint at greater glories. I wrote to Castro and proposed a book. He replied vaguely and then all hell broke loose.

Castro had been clear that there were a raft of issues that had to be handled sensitively. There were topics that I could not include in the article and it was agreed that I would avoid sensationalizing events as much as possible, stressing his repentance. This had been achieved to his satisfaction and the book proposal was strengthening when I found myself in Heathrow Airport shortly afterwards.

Keen to read some Scottish football news, I picked up the *Daily Record* and boarded the Edinburgh plane. At 20,000 feet I turned a page and there was Elliot eating his fry-up. It was a splash, an exclusive, a syndication that was perfectly normal but now perfectly terrifying. My article had gone through the tabloid wringer and come out as a bullet-pointed boast of figures, names and places. I felt sick.

When Elliot called, his voice shook with anger. Extraordinarily, he accepted without question my innocence. 'I can read people,' he muttered. But the treatment the paper had given the story, which had been cast widely over his native Glasgow as a result, saddened him. Towards the end of the conversation he changed tack and mentioned that he was under a bit of pressure before signing off hurriedly.

I heard nothing for a few weeks before receiving an unexpected call from Jane Castro. After talking about the book proposal for a while she paused, as if in decision, then explained her son's latest silence. The press attention had ignited tension between him and other prisoners. Elliot had wanted to sit it out but the governor had ordered an overnight move for his own safety.

He was now in HMP Spring Hill, an open prison in Buckingham-shire. He was quite low, Jane explained, owing to problems with his new roommate. 'He's a fucking smackhead,' said Elliot when he called. 'Night and day; it's disgusting, man.' I asked him about the prison, about his thoughts ... he interrupted. 'Come down here, I've got to ask you a few things.'

The landlord is pottering about, opening curtains and plugging in the cigarette machine. Elliot is smoking steadily and leafing through my notes. He shakes his head, 'A lot of this is wrong,' he draws in, holds, exhales. 'There's so much not there.' Suddenly he's alert and involved. The balance has shifted as I watch him scan cuttings, transcripts, phone interviews with people whose lives have touched his.

Finally, he looks up. 'It could be a big story, Neil. What I did, I don't think anyone will have done it before. Not on the same scale, not every single day and not on their own. A lot of people will try and pretend I never happened, they won't want this book to be written. And I'm going to have to tell you about the bad times, because I don't want this to look like fun.'

He laughs, sits forward and rests his mug down. 'I mean, sometimes it was fun, don't get me wrong.' I reach into my bag, and produce my Dictaphone. He sees me rest it on the table and instinctively we both glance at the clock. Two hours and then he has to return. Back to the hut, and the chess, and the waiting.

He leans back, the chair creaking quietly as he settles. He looks me in the eye as a smirk plays across his lips. Short silence, then a nod. 'OK.'

CHAPTER THREE

Why did you buy this book? I'm interested, I really am. Every meeting we've had, every letter I've received, my first question has always been the same – why? It seems that ever since that last trip to Harvey Nichols people have wanted to speak to me. The first letter I got in prison was from a journalist and he was the first of many. I've had interest from television stations and film companies outside the nick and within the walls people who have heard whispers about my story want to know more. I'll be playing chess with some guy whose name I don't know and he'll ask me how I did it. Sometimes a screw will do the same, they love a good crime as much as the next person. Back in Glasgow strangers have stopped my mum in the street and pointed at their newspaper. 'He's some boy, your Elliot,' they say.

Do you want to steal money? You might have read the cover (the stuff I said about Rolex watches and so on) and thought that this could be it, the answer to your problems or the realization of your dreams. Free money. And, you know what? Perhaps it would be, I don't know. You might feel differently by the end. Maybe you want to know about me, about why I did what I did. Well you're not alone there. I'm kind of hoping that we'll find that out together as we go along. Or do you know me? That's the thing that worries me most, that makes me lie awake at night and stare at the cracks in the ceiling of my cell. All those people, all over the world. In bars, hotels, nightclubs and prisons. All those people, and all those lies.

I never meant to hurt you or to make you look foolish, I hope you can believe that. I took no enjoyment from tricking you but I had to do it to get where I wanted to go. Don't be angry with yourselves because, as you will see, you weren't alone. I lied to everyone around me and those closest to me were lied to the most.

I was good at what I did, some people have said that I was the best, and I worked harder at it than anything else in my life. That doesn't make it right and it didn't make it easy but it might mean that you'll at least recognize the motivation behind the lies. What you'll probably realize as well is that you didn't really know me at all.

When people ask me where it all began I'm sometimes a bit uncertain what to say. With the police or lawyers it's easy, we take out my charge sheet and run our fingers all the way to the bottom. With others it's much harder, but now I've had a little bit of time to think about things I know where I would like to begin. It might help people understand when they see how long this has been going on, how long I have been doing these things. I'm going to start with the first lie that I ever told, and how I came to tell it.

The lie began with the birth of my father Carlos in Sicily in 1957. He was the fourth child of a couple from the island's Romany community. As well as occasional persecution from the local authorities, the gypsies were not averse to some in-house bickering and the fact that my grandparents were from different clans was a point of contention that only worsened as the years passed. By the time that my father was four years old it was bad enough for the family to emigrate en masse to a new life in Chile.

They settled in a small town close to the Peruvian border

and my grandfather set up a wine-trading business. If that sounds a little suspicious then that's because it was, and there were reasons behind the proximity to the border. Some wine was getting traded but so was plenty of contraband, and I don't think the Chilean taxman benefited quite as well as he might have done from the family's enterprises. On the few occasions that my father has discussed my grandfather with me he has always lit up at the memory of these roguish endeavours. Along with the mischief came poor health, however, and Granddad Castro passed away just a few years after the move to Chile.

It might have been his father's death that saw my dad leave Chile at such a young age, or maybe it was his nomadic gypsy blood. Whatever the motivation, when he reached the age of fourteen he decided he was ready to see the world and ran off to sea. For the next ten years he rode the ocean waves in a motley collection of rust buckets and creaking tankers, for a collection of hardy souls and ne'er-do-wells.

His temper, which remains very much intact today, would often cause him trouble. Once in Manilla harbour he finally snapped at one captain who was neglecting the cleanliness of the ship to the point of risking its seaworthiness. When the captain refused to listen to his complaints my father walked straight off the ship, leaving him to scour the harbour for days before finding another posting.

If he didn't work then he didn't eat, which meant he would sometimes find himself working smuggling runs around the Mediterranean, scuttling back and forth in the middle of the night with loads of booze and tobacco. Other times he would spend months inching across the Indian Ocean on mammoth oil tankers with only the fear of armed pirates to keep him occupied.

By 1980 he was hardened beyond his years, with long

hair that snaked down his back and a face cracked and darkened from the wind and sun. One night in a distant bar he met some men who told him of the North Sea, a desolate stretch of water between Scotland and Norway where they had found huge oil reserves. Money was being made hand over fist and my father decided to work his way back across the world to the unlikely destination of Aberdeen, the closest Scottish city to the oil rigs that were springing up miles out to sea.

The discovery of North Sea oil had transformed Aberdeen. Almost overnight the factories and fishing industry had found themselves starved of young men as the oil companies called out for able bodies to man their rigs. They were offering weekly pay packets comparable to monthly salaries elsewhere in return for their tough 'two weeks on, two weeks off' working schedule where the men would work fourteen days straight before returning to the city with a pocket full of dough and an eye for diversion.

It meant that Aberdeen had a constant hedonistic sub-culture as the oil workers partied their way through their gains with increasing desperation as the next shift neared. As well as the lucky locals, the work had brought in labour from around the world – from Europe, the Middle East, America and, in my father's case, from Chile. There were certain bars which every night would be rocking to international oil money and it was in these bars that you would find my mother, Jane.

She was wild herself back then, and much more of a drinker than she is today. She lived alone in a small flat in Aberdeen's Logie area and the party would often spill back there at closing time. She befriended the foreign workers, drawn to the idea of an extended family unit, and they took to her as well. When on land they would room in bed and breakfasts, but the industry had yet to catch up with demand and some would always leave it too late. They would often end up sleeping in my mum's front room.

One evening in the bar of the Bell's Hotel a Chilean friend asked my mother if a couple of her compatriots could stay the night. Mum looked over to where she pointed and her eyes fell on a wiry, tanned man with hair strewn over his shoulders. 'He certainly wasn't from Aberdeen,' she once summarized. When he approached he was polite and friendly, though my mum spoke more Spanish than he did English. He looked, she says now, like Robert Redford but as I said she used to drink a lot more back then.

Within a week they were together and so began my father's daily ritual of asking my mother to marry him. She was cautious, having grown up in an area where marriages were made a mockery of, but she recognized that to my father it was much more than that. The clash of Romany and Latin roots made for a pretty intense pride. It was not an invitation he made lightly and he soon wore her down. By the time I arrived they were living in the flat together as husband and wife along with my brother Nicky.

I was born on 10 November 1982. The North Sea oil industry had by then been up and running for nearly ten years and prices were about to climb even higher. Fortunes had been made and Aberdeen wore its disposable income on its sleeve, with flotillas of expensive cars slipping through the suburbs and property prices unstoppable. We remained in Logie and survived comfortably on my dad's generous wage. My mum wasn't working and, anyway, she was busy being my teacher.

It wasn't a post that she had volunteered for. My dad was happy to take the *gringo* pound but he believed strongly in the South American model of the male as provider and female as homemaker. Part of that role was to give the children their first taste of education, and so from the age of three my afternoons were spent in our living room with my mother and a collection of books. It was a revelation.

These are my first memories, my mother and I sitting cross-legged on the brown carpet with a mug of orange juice and a pile of books between us. Maths came quite quickly to me, writing even more so. It was when we began to work on spelling that things really happened. I can't pinpoint the first occasion, and it was only later that I realized mine was not a normal development, but events unfolded a little bit like this.

I was doing a lot of reading from educational books and, being of a basic level, there would be a lot of repetition of short and common words – cat, dog, man, woman. After the reading sessions my mother would go through a spelling test and inevitably these same words would crop up every few days. When she said the words, and I mean almost the second she announced them, they would appear in my head. I don't mean a vague picture, they would literally appear in my mind's eye.

There they would be, written in the font, size, and colour I had last encountered them. I could see the shade of the paper on which they had been written, I could see the way the page would fade towards the paper's edge. If I concentrated some more I could bring up other images, different occasions that I had come across the word; they would flit through my mind like a slide show. I would sit on the carpet watching in awe as these pictures flew through my head, and then I would look up at my mother and I would spell the word.

A photographic memory is a fascinating subject but it

only really comes into play when it is matched with an inquisitive mind. Curiosity isn't something I have ever lacked. Once my mother had kicked off my education, she found she had created something of a monster. I devoured the educational texts she used for the lessons with such a force that she added history books, encyclopaedias and an atlas to the pile.

The history books I struggled through. I liked the dates and the place names but they never really held my attention. The encyclopaedias I used for reference in my daily projects of discovery. My mum remembers car journeys with me at this age with little fondness owing to the constant stream of questions from the back seat – What's that? How do you spell it? What's it *for*? This was the gathering of ammunition for our arrival home when I could retire to the encyclopaedias for additional detail.

My books by now were kept in my bedroom piled beside my bed. In the mornings I would walk gravely downstairs with a stack of them tucked under my chin, announcing my arrival at the breakfast table by placing them with quiet reverence on the spare seat. At night I would lie under my blanket with a torch and open an atlas with my heart pounding.

It was always my favourite. The world had 174 nations. The largest was the Soviet Union. It had seven continents. The largest was Asia. There were nearly five billion people in the world. A billion was a thousand million. Chinese was the most popular language, then English, then Hindustani. These facts hit me hard. I had already gone through the common childhood horror of realizing that my parents would die, and now I was struck by the sheer enormity of the planet on which I lived. Aberdeen was a dot and place name on a single page. It wasn't even the capital of Scotland, Edinburgh was. And Scotland itself was tiny when compared with the world map that only just squeezed across the central pages. I wanted to see the world, to cross those vast oceans and to meet some of these five billion people. Unfortunately I was only four years old, so I was forced to make do with my parents.

My father's years at sea gave me access to a ream of far-flung adventures and these became another part of my daily schedule when he was onshore. He told me about the man-made miracles at Panama and Suez, and of trade winds and tankers that took a mile to turn round. I also had the television, with its Westerns and the weather sections that showed Britain sitting serenely above the European landmass. I used to try and sketch the English border with my finger before the image left the screen and developed a mild obses-sion with the English Channel.

As you've probably deduced by now I was a bit of an oddball, but this love of learning should have meant that when I arrived at Kaimhill Primary School in 1987 I hit the ground running. In actual fact it meant I was doomed from the start. Almost immediately the problems began. It didn't matter what work the teacher set, I found it too easy. I would race through it and run to her desk for her to mark it and give me something further to do. At first she would laugh or praise me in front of the class but soon it became a distraction.

The school put me on the reading books that belonged to the year above but they were just as straightforward. The teacher encouraged me to help the other kids and for a while I was spending most of the day checking the work of my classmates but that caused resentment and I soon lost the few friends that I had made. To make matters worse my mum had been careful to regulate my accent, believing it would help me get a job when older, and this made me stand out to the extent I was afraid to open my mouth.

I began finishing my work and then sitting looking out the window, daydreaming about the bell ringing and releasing me back home to my books. The school complained to my mother about my attitude and she begged them to put me up a year but they refused to do it, claiming that it wasn't in my best interests. In turn they were unhappy with her response and would take it out on me as a frosty relationship developed between my teacher and her star pupil. It didn't help much that I knew the Seven Seas (North Atlantic, South Atlantic, North Pacific, South Pacific, Indian, Antarctic, and Arctic); in fact that probably didn't help at all.

I became isolated and even now I can remember an overall air of despair from that first year of school. I couldn't speak to the other pupils without them making fun of my accent, or my name, or my unashamed interest in any form of trivia. In turn I thought they were boring. All they ever wanted to do was to play games, or run about like headless chickens. None were interested in knowing the capital of Argentina, or the fact that Ceylon changed its name to Sri Lanka in 1972.

And then one day, a few months in, something happened. We were in the playground, and I was alone as usual. Those classmates who did talk to me were quiet kids who would sidle up when they knew they wouldn't be spotted and tarred by the association. In corridors or storerooms they would approach me with their faces strained through a thirst for knowledge – 'Tell me about dinosaurs, Elliot.' 'Tell me about cowboys, Elliot.'

But the playground was wide open and unforgiving, so I stood alone in the corner watching the rest of the school run, skip and play through this hour of daily solitude for myself. I saw them approaching but pretended I hadn't. They came in a ragged line, nudging each other and giggling, pushing the weaker ones to the front. When they arrived they encircled me and began a scattergun goading.

'I'm a wizard.' I don't know why I said it but it came from me in a strange voice. It was deep and authoritative, it sounded just like the voice of a teacher. The other children paused as I scanned their faces calmly, looking into their eyes in turn as I let the enormity of my declaration sink in. They looked shaken, nervous, but more than anything I realized that they were overcome with understanding. They *believed* me.

For the next few minutes we stood in reflection. They fidgeted, looked imploringly at their assumed leaders, asked a few half-questions that I batted away imperiously. I would catch the more impressionable gazing at me in undisguised wonder as I casually related the highlights of my short career in wizardry. Even when one of them, overcome with the occasion, meekly asked for evidence I did not falter.

Even as we decamped to an area of rough grass on the edge of the playground, with me marching them over like an infant Pied Piper, I saw nothing but success in what I was about to attempt. Even as they eventually began to snigger and joke as I ordered the grass for the tenth time to set itself alight, and was gradually left alone as they ran away hooting, I did not lose the rush of enlightenment.

As I stood in the grass watching them go I felt a prickly realization as I reviewed what had just occurred. I had taken the truth, my depressing reality, and twisted it into something incredible. The children's reactions to me had switched from scorn to respect, I had become someone to be looked at and listened to. It sent me giddy with a sense of achievement, and the sudden arrival of possibility. And that was that, the first lie I ever told.

*

It was my father's dream to return to Chile with his new Scottish family. The main obstacles to this were my mum's parents, who lived near us in Aberdeen and were a major part of our lives. Both had worked as labourers in the fish industry, down in the cavernous warehouses at Aberdeen docks where the day's catch is weighed, gutted and washed. Work came and went for them and they were victims of the city's shortage of council housing in the 1960s.

This left my mother and the other children living with their grandparents in an Aberdeenshire village where my great-grandfather worked in the local knacker's yard. When she was four, her grandparents retired to a small flat in the city and again my mum was on the move, this time to a children's shelter in Aberdeen. For four years she and the others were shuttled round various children's homes, much to my grandmother's distress as she waited for the council to find them a family home.

Finally, she decided to take things into her own hands and went along to see Lady Tweedsmuir, the grand old Tory aristocrat who was an MP in Aberdeen for twenty years before being elevated to the House of Lords. The two of them talked for a while, then my grandmother went and caught her bus home. A few weeks later the council mysteriously stumbled across a large flat in the Woodside Estate and the family were finally united.

Woodside was a tough area. 'No one had nothing here then, except for lice,' my mum said to me once as we drove through it. The local school attendance officer would come to the doors and ask to see the children's shoes. If they didn't have any then they would be sent to a local school to collect a pair of what were called tacker shoes, remainders that the council would buy in bulk. Mum liked her tacker shoes so much she was disappointed when she grew out of them. She also grew out of Woodside and moved to Logie, to the flat that my father would ask to stay in.

My mother's parents and my dad got on famously from the start. They were attracted to his exotic nature as much as she had been, and my grandfather enjoyed hearing about the offshore life. At the weekend he would often take me down to the docks and show me the foreign boats, testing me on their colourful flags. We would visit the dockers' bars where he would have a rum with his friends and buy me a Coke and packet of crisps. Afterwards he would take me to the water's edge and point to where my dad's rig was. I would squeeze my eyes until they watered but I could never make it out, even though Granddad said he was waving to him.

By the time I was at school reinventing myself as a wizard, those days out had finished. My grandfather was suffering from thrombosis, a result of the rum and the hard work, and could hardly move his hands. My dad was the only person allowed to shave him, which he would do in the kitchen of their small flat while my mum and grandmother drank tea in the living room and watched *Antiques Roadshow*. My mum was caught between her husband's yearning to take us to our Chilean family to try to carve ourselves a life out there, and the pain of leaving her parents as they began to falter. It must have been very hard for her but they reached a decision and one day she called me into the living room when I returned home from school. I remember the way her face was framed in the sunlight when she told me that we were moving to Chile and I remember walking away, up the stairs and into my room, to find my atlas.

CHAPTER FOUR

There were five of us by this point, my wee brother Dean having arrived two years before in 1986. I was fascinated by my new sibling from the start, always lurking about in the background trying to assist my mother in his care. Mum would arrive back in the kitchen to find me enthusiastically feeding him tablespoons of peanut butter, or come running out the house to stop me wheeling him off towards the horizon in his pram. As he grew into a toddler I recognized his coming potential as a captive companion, seeing as I had so few other options. Worried that he could grow up in Chile without knowing Scotland at all, I drew some pictures of the house and the area and put them in my bag to show him later. This was a more generous gesture than it might first seem as luggage space was very much at a premium.

Once my mother had agreed to our departure for South America she went at the project with a vengeance. The furniture was sold from around us, through postcards in the window of the local supermarket, and huge swathes of possessions would go missing each day to Oxfam or in the heap of binbags in the back garden. She probably took a bit of pleasure in informing Kaimhill Primary of my pending departure, and I wasn't exactly disappointed by that aspect myself. When she explained to me that I would be going to school in Chile with the local children, I started following my father around the increasingly bare house prodding him for Spanish.

When we said goodbye to my grandparents it seemed that everyone was crying. I couldn't understand why they weren't as excited as we were. I thought they would visit us in our new Chilean home. My mum's guilt at leaving was eased slightly by the fact that Granddad's health had improved enough for him to assist with the clearing of the flat, and he even helped to test me on my pidgin Spanish. Still, that didn't make the farewells any easier and it wasn't just to my grandparents that I was saying goodbye.

Looking back, it should probably have struck me as strange that Nicky wasn't going to be joining us, but Mum explained that he had decided that he didn't want to come and, as he was now sixteen, it would be better for him to stay with my grandmother. Even at that age I had picked up that Nicky had a difficult relationship with Dad, and he and I only ever really interacted when we were fighting. Although I loved him as my brother, Nicky seemed to have a lot of anger and I wasn't too unhappy to hear that he was staying behind.

Our first step towards Chile was taken at Aberdeen's train station, where we boarded an early morning train to London. We took a table seat and I slid in beside the window, watching the North Sea glinting behind trees and fields as we raced down Scotland's battered east coast. As we passed through the small town of Broughty Ferry I remember seeing a young boy standing with his bike between his legs watching us pass. I imagined if he knew where we were going, how impressive and impossible it would seem to him.

I watched the cities slip by – Dundee, Edinburgh, Newcastle – and crossed them off the small map on the back of my father's timetable. Dean didn't offer much in the way of entertainment other than occasionally asking questions that I would pounce upon before my parents could react. Still, there was only so much satisfaction in patronizing a two-year-old, and I soon went back to my atlas.

With little luggage allowed it was the only book that I had brought, after an agonizing selection process. I knew the profile of Chile inside out, but I wanted to keep check on our journey there and liked the idea of being able to look at Scotland's profile from abroad. I had nothing else, no toys or suchlike, but that was largely through my own choice. I suppose it wasn't much to start a new life but I was a happy little traveller when we finally rolled up at Heathrow Airport late that afternoon.

If I close my eyes now I can picture the main Departures Hall of Heathrow that day. I can see the bustling crowd, the people bent forwards as they steered their luggage trolleys, the row of airline desks that seemed to go on for ever. More than anything, I can see the departures board. Back then it seemed to be perched somewhere near the clouds, I had to lean back and squint to make out its winking lists.

Amsterdam, New York, Paris, Cape Town, Hong Kong. And on, and on. I laughed and clapped and pointed. My mum helped me find our flight, *Lima via Madrid.* I stood in utter, total awe. The cities, countries and capitals that had ruled my world, that I had pored over on the living-room carpet and under my bed covers, suddenly they were all within reach. I had thought of the airport as just another stop on our journey but now I could see it for what it truly was, an entry point for the entire world.

I looked upon the customers with undisguised admiration. The way they moved with such familiarity through this place of dreams, the way they could yawn and stretch as they waited in line to book their journey to the great unknown. For those who actually worked in the airport I reserved something approaching love. The girl that leant over the desk and asked if it was my first holiday left me beetroot and tying a tied lace until she disappeared. The uniformed security guards who half-heartedly prodded our bags received a muddled salute that my mum enjoys reminding me of to the day, and when my father pointed out a team of flight staff that strode past us in the corridor I looked upon them as I would have done an appearance by Jesus, Joseph and Mary. And all this was before we reached the departure gate and my father called me over to a large window. 'There, Elliot,' he said, pushing his thick finger against the glass, 'That is ours.'

It was enormous. It dwarfed the building we stood in and at first I panicked that it was moving, rolling slowly towards us, before I saw that it had stops as big as buses placed in front of those gigantic wheels. There were people running round below it. Some were feeding a hose into its belly while others threw bags into a hatch that opened like a lower lip from its side. Stairs stretched down from the front and back and a thin strip of yellow circles ran all the way along the body. I gasped as my eyes followed the wings that ran dead straight and outwards above the heads of the brave men that worked down below. I remained at the window long enough for my father to wander off and then reappear. It was time to go.

Dad held Dean in his arms as he led Mum and me towards the plane. My excitement at the discovery of an airport had been replaced by now with a growing fear. A thought had caught in my young mind, a confusion between the hulking mass of metal that I had just seen and what I knew to be its stated aim. I worried quietly to myself as we walked across the tarmac, sneaking a look at Mum who had also never flown before. Incredibly she seemed unmoved by the prospect, busying herself sorting out our tickets.

As we walked up the swaying staircase I was approaching hysteria. Why were these people, even my parents who were the cleverest in the world, walking to certain death with such calmness? I wanted to shout, to scream and, more than anything, to cry, and then we walked into the plane. A uniformed man pointed us to the right and I turned to see banks of faces staring at me. Down the narrow walkway we went until my mum signalled that we had arrived at our row. She and I were to sit beside the window and Dean and my father across the aisle. The seat seemed huge as I settled into it and my mum fastened my buckle.

She leant across me and gestured at the men below. They seemed much closer now, much larger. Relieved, I retrieved my atlas and turned to the section on the Atlantic Ocean. I had a lingering concern over something called the Bermuda Triangle which appeared to lie in our path, but my father had assured me that we would pass to the south of this treacherous area.

The plane filled and the lights dimmed. The man in the uniform was demonstrating something with a large yellow vest but I could only see above his shoulders over the tops of the seats. With a jolt I realized that we were moving and I looked out the window to see tarmac and grass glide past and a row of white lights appear on the ground. The plane paused and there was a charge of raw power beneath my feet. I looked to the floor in confusion as the noise grew and grew.

My mother had a strange look on her face and I turned in my seat to have a better view. I had recently noticed that if I could see someone's whole face then I would seem to know what they were thinking. The plane leapt forward and I was pushed back into my seat. My body felt heavy and not in control. Out the window the string of spotlights had become a white line flashing by. There was a tiny dip and then we were up in the air.

I realized immediately what had happened, I knew why the plane was now tilting back on itself and why everything was suddenly smooth and effortless. We were no longer on the ground, on Planet Earth. We were now in the Atmosphere. I turned to my mum who was examining the switches and lights in the panel above our heads. I looked over at my dad and Dean. Dad was asleep, his stomach rising and falling behind the head of Dean who stared back at me with big eyes.

I looked back through the window but now there was only black and, with nothing else to do and exhausted from my travels and mental torture over aerodynamics, I too soon fell asleep. I was prodded awake shortly after by my mum and handed a small tray of food with a plastic fork and knife. We landed briefly at Madrid but I could only see more tarmac and lights from my window and I soon fell away again.

When I awoke for the second time it felt much later. The rest of my family were sleeping, as was almost everyone else on the plane that I could see. The cabin was darker still and some of the passengers had blankets covering them. I undid my buckle and clambered over my mum. As I stood in the aisle I looked to the right and saw more rows of sleeping people. To the left I saw backs of heads but in the distance was something else, a long grey curtain that blocked the aisle.

My interest caught, I walked towards it, through the snores and the sighs of the shadowy cabin. As I neared the curtain I could hear voices, laughing and the clink of glasses. My heart beat fast as I parted the soft material and slipped inside. It was a tiny cabin, much smaller than ours, and dissimilar in appearance. There were fewer seats in the rows and they were very different from the ones that we were sitting on. They were enormous and with their leather coating and footrests they looked like the chairs in the barber's shop back in Logie.

On our side of the curtain the lights had been dimmed

but here they shone brightly, picking out the gold in the uniforms of the women that seemed to be everywhere I looked. They strode up and down the wide aisle, bending over and smiling at the passengers, or laughing over their heads to someone further away. They poured drinks from a bottle that seemed to be covered in gold paper and the plates that they were gathering were proper china plates like we had at home, with proper metal cutlery.

I turned and saw a man sitting alone in the back row. He was in a suit, like my dad wore when he went to Head Office, and was reading a huge newspaper that was brushing against the roof when he turned the pages. He had glasses and a ring on his finger that were both made of gold, and in a small metal bowl on his tray there was a cigar. I knew what a cigar was because Hannibal from the A-Team smoked them on the television. I also knew that they were made in Cuba, a country that was run by Communists.

The man looked over and saw me frozen in appreciation of him and this secret room in which he sat. He didn't look angry or confused, he just looked at me. Then his face changed and into my mind came what it said – he *knew*. He knew why I was standing there and he knew why I was so transfixed that I was unable to move or to speak. He didn't know, of course, what opening that curtain would mean for my life.

He smiled at me. I looked away – at the lights and the bottles of gold and the laughing – and then I smiled back.

By the time we arrived at the airport in Lima we had been travelling for over a day. Today the airport is a manic, slightly seedy place and back then it was even worse. People called at us from the minute we walked through the customs gate, offering us taxis, hotels, cars, *luca*. My father growled at them and led us through the throng to the main entrance. He was in an unapproachable mood and Mum urged us to keep up but as I trotted along behind I felt a small tug at my sleeve.

I turned to see two Peruvian children, maybe a year or so younger than myself. They were filthy and had no shoes or socks, their feet were nearly black with dirt but they walked across the floor barefoot as if this was normal. Their faces were open and intense and I knew that they wanted something from me. I called to my mum, who took one look at the scene and breathed in sharply. 'Not *now*, Elliot,' she hissed. I looked at the children who were jogging behind us, whispering to me words that I did not know.

We reached the Arrivals Hall and a man emerged from the crowd and hugged my father. 'That's your dad's cousin,' explained my mum, as there was another tug at my sleeve. The children were beside me, one touched my arm and I shouted to my mum. She broke away from her introduction to this new Castro with a glare. My dad scooped me up and I shook the hand of his cousin, then he put me down and did the same with Dean. There was another tug, I called to my mother again as she supervised our bags being placed in the boot of my new uncle's car.

This time she paused, breathed deeply and reached into her handbag. As my dad and Dean climbed into the car my mother handed me two silver coins. 'Hurry up,' she said in a strict voice, but her face wasn't angry. I turned to the children, who were nearly combusting with anticipation at the handover they had just witnessed. Solemnly I handed each child one of the coins, smiling benevolently at them as I did so. They laughed at each other and then turned to me, looking at me the way that my mother did when I surprised her with some new piece of knowledge.

I got into the car and watched them watching me. I

smiled and they smiled. I waved and they waved. As we drove away I looked over the back seat until they were just tiny figures in the distance. They had seen me as some sort of leader, like an adult, just because I handed them those silver coins. Sitting back down I felt light-headed with discovery as we made for the Chilean border. It was the same feeling that I had felt in the playground when I revealed my wizard status. There were now, it seemed, two escapes. Two ways to launch myself beyond reality, to get people to pay me attention and show me respect. Lying and money. Money and lying.

My father's great Chilean dream never really threatened to come to fruition. The illustrations in my atlas, of the Andes and fearsome-looking natives, bore little resemblance to our life in Tocopilla. Sitting on the edge of the Atacama desert, this was the town where my father's extended family now lived. The sun rose early in the morning and seemed to stay stuck in the sky without moving until it got dark. On the rare occasions a wind softened the heat it would carry with it sand that would sting your skin, and these harsh conditions caused varying levels of concern for the immigrant Castros.

My father might have spent the last few years on a frozen lump of metal in the North Sea but he took little time to acclimatize to the old country. Soon he was as dark as his compatriots with only his hair picking him out from the locals. His Latin roots had passed cleanly to Dean as well as me, and we both quickly blackened, but for my poor mother this was a long way from Aberdeen. When we walked through the streets Dean and I would walk in the dust of the road while she hopped between the shop awnings, desperately trying to escape the sun.

Only on sufferance would she leave the house, where

she preferred to spend the days cleaning, cooking and swearing about the climate. She said at the time that she would never again complain about the Scottish weather and I don't think she ever has. Her fondness for remaining inside during daylight hours left Dean and I to explore. I was supposed to be getting placed in a local school but the holidays were approaching and, with Dad disappearing for stretches of work, my mum preferred to have us close at hand. In any case, I was already learning.

Within a few weeks of arrival in Chile I was conversing in basic Spanish with the local children. It would have come even quicker if it had not been for my initial reluctance to approach them. My experiences at Kaimhill had left me nervous and self-conscious and this was exacerbated by the fact that my alien nature drew the locals like moths. Dean would occasionally be with me but he was of little help, grabbing my hand when he saw them coming at us.

At first I would point at objects for them to name and I would repeat the word like a mantra, much to their amusement. The next day I would walk through the streets until they found me and tested me on what they had told me the day before. Then they would give me some new words, and on it went. It got to the stage that I would spend my days talking only in Spanish and every time my father returned from his trips he would be freshly delighted with my progress.

While I was revelling in these daily language lessons my mother was having slightly less fun. She knew Castilian Spanish pretty well but not all the locals could follow the mother language accurately. Mum's fair complexion marked her out as a *gringa*, which meant she never stood a chance of melting into the local population as easily as Dean and me. When she needed cigarettes she would send me into the shop to ensure that she paid local prices.

Her other great luxury was the Spanish-language version of *Time* magazine which she would buy weekly and read a small portion of each day so as not to run out before the next issue appeared. This tiny slice of the outside world probably only worsened her mood, however, and I knew from watching her that Tocopilla was not going to become our permanent home.

My father, perhaps sensing that he had one last throw of the dice to convince my mum about remaining in his country, decided to move us to the Chilean capital of Santiago. From a relatively peaceful existence in Tocopilla we found ourselves in one of the largest, most vibrant cities in South America, home to six million people. This was the beginning of the end. My father found work in the oil industry increasingly hard to come by, and took various pieces of temporary employment that he never really enjoyed.

My mum took a voluntary position in the local Salvation Army hostel, working with abandoned girls, and Dean and I spent our days in there with the orphans. Money was running low and, as we pondered our next move, I began to panic that maybe we wouldn't be able to go home. Although I enjoyed Chile and the novelty of speaking in a different language I had always expected us to ultimately return to Aberdeen.

When I voiced this concern to my mum she sat me down and told me about a place called the Embassy. She explained that if someone from Britain is in any kind of trouble in a foreign country then the Embassy would take charge, and help sort things out. The people at the Embassy were very important, she stressed, and the local people would always listen very carefully to what they said. It was a piece of advice that I would recall many years later, with great effect.

The money for our return was gathered and my parents

explained to Dean and me that we were going home to Scotland. It meant we would see our grandparents again of course, which made us both happy, but there was something else in my excitement. A return to Scotland meant another trip on an aeroplane. As our departure neared I found myself fantasizing about the journey and clinging on to a hope that we would board the plane and be directed through the grey curtain to the special room beyond.

It wasn't to be. When we reached the top of the stairs the man in the uniform pointed to the right and we shuffled down the plane once more. It was time for my trusty Plan B. I ate the meal with the plastic knife and fork, then waited for my parents to fall asleep. I climbed carefully over my dormant mother and walked up the aisle.

I was inches from the curtain, my hand was reaching out to part it, when the man in the uniform leant round the corner. He had a tray of glasses in front of him that he was filling halfway up from one of the golden bottles. 'You can't go in there,' he said flatly. I looked at him but his face was still and set; he was not going to change his mind so I turned and walked back to my seat.

CHAPTER FIVE

How many schools did you go to as a kid? One, two, maybe three? Any more than that and you would be a rarity – maybe your dad was in the army, or a travelling circus. Me? I went to eight schools, or what were meant to act as schools, and one college. That's a lot, I know, and it could be hard for you to keep track as I talk about them now. For that reason, and for your reference, here is my academic career in all its glory:

Kaimhill Primary (left)
Battlefield Primary (expelled)
Yorkhill Hospital Department of Child and Family Psychiatry
   (discharged)
Mount Florida Primary (expelled)
Greenview Special School (left)
Stonelaw High School (expelled)
St John Bosco High School (expelled)
The Keppenburn Unit (asked to leave)
Cambuslang College (left before expelled)

Well we've done Kaimhill so I suppose we'd better start with Battlefield, a small primary school in the Battlefield area of Glasgow. We never moved back to Aberdeen when we returned from Chile; I think maybe my parents had made such a show of selling up when we left that they didn't want to start over there. Whatever the reasons behind it, we moved to Glasgow and after a short stay with friends we found a nice flat in Battlefield. A couple of weeks later I was back within the warm fold of the British education system at the primary school a few streets from my new home.

I was eight years old, and to keep me with others in the same age bracket I had to pass an entrance exam which pitched me in with just a couple of months to go until the summer holidays. For the other kids, friendships and cliques had been formed long ago and a deep-tanned laddie with a weird east coast accent and a propensity to slip into Chilean Spanish wasn't seen as much of a catch. I was interesting though, and their patience with my eccentricities just about lasted to the summer holidays when I slipped effortlessly back into my usual solo status.

Battlefield was more boisterous than Aberdeen and I was still in the feral mindset that I had been forced to adopt in Chile. Battlefield Road and the area around it was hectic and intimidating but then I stumbled across the River Cart, which ran right through the neighbourhood and had a pedestrian walkway beside it. One day I climbed over the wall, slipped through a gap in the trees and found a narrow grassy ledge. This led down to a tiny natural platform that jutted out into the river. Invisible to the outside world I would skim stones for hours on end, or sit in extended contemplation as the brown water eased by. I had read both *Huckleberry Finn* and *Swallows and Amazons* by this point and would daydream about the extraordinary river-based escapades that could spring from that starting point. This was where I spent the long weeks of those holidays, and others to come.

Nicky had chosen to stay in Aberdeen rather than join us down in Glasgow and Dean was not permitted by Mum to accompany me on my daily wanderings. I remember once asking her why and her telling me that there was too much going on in my head for me to look after him as well. It infuriated me. I loved Dean and wanted to show him the secret place that I had found. I had no friends and yet this available and willing sidekick was being denied me.

When school reopened at the end of summer the sudden rush of social interaction meant I launched myself into the new environment with gusto. I craved attention and would do anything to attract it. I would spend entire lessons devising increasingly abstract ways to attract the teacher's interest and then react to the inevitable rebuke with an insistence on debate. The result was predictable. My classmates moved quickly from bewilderment to mimicry and name-calling. The teachers despaired and sent me with regularity to the headmistress, Mrs Terrace.

Mrs Terrace ran the school with what she would probably have called old-fashioned values. If she came into a classroom to speak to a teacher her eyes would spend the conversation coldly scanning the petrified infants for any possible breach of acceptable behaviour. I was another case altogether, however, and she eventually gave up trying to control me and referred me to a school-board psychiatrist for weekly sessions. I would spend an hour answering his questions then go back a week later, when exactly the same questions would be asked in exactly the same order.

Meanwhile I was encountering physical bullying for the first time. When I think about that guy now, I find myself shaking with anger. I want to stand up and go and find him. I want to walk into his house and ask if he remembers me, and show him how it feels to be scared. I'm not the weird little kid who he'd chase every night and punch and kick until he begged for it to stop.

Prisons have made me understand violence. I hate it still, probably even more so than when I was young, but I know

now why it's there and what it's for. Anyway, with a shrink asking me the same questions every session and an older boy giving me a hiding every time he could catch me it's fair to say that these weren't particularly happy days.

Finally, I broke down and told my father about the bullying. At first the gypsy in him demanded that I stood up for myself, that I threw down my satchel and went toe-to-toe with this besmircher of the Castro name. After a few more weeks of bruises, Dad realized that he was going to have to take charge. He dragged me round to the guy's house and knocked gently on the door. The father answered the door in a loose T-shirt that showed the tattoos raining down both his arms. I was terrified but my father was as calm as could be. He said, 'Sort out your son, or I'll sort you out,' and the other man just nodded slightly and pursed his lips. And that was the bullying finished.

Unfortunately, my parents weren't quite so keen to warn off the psychiatrist. They were convinced that there was something deep-rooted to my problems and to be honest most people would have agreed. I continued to excel in my work but I couldn't sit still for more than a few minutes before I would be off – trying to correct classmates' work, asking the teacher a string of questions, producing my own books and suggesting the class work from them. During the school's Christmas party a large decoration went missing from the canteen and was later found squashed into my bag. I hadn't stolen it, some unknown hand planted it there, but it was enough to wrap things up for me at Battlefield Primary and that's when I went to the hospital.

The first time my parents and I went to Yorkhill Hospital I was a little baffled. None of us was obviously sick, and my mum and dad would tell me only that there was someone I had to talk to. When we got into the doctor's office my mum started to cry, which shocked me. I'd never seen her in such a state and it slowly dawned on me that I was to blame, causing me to start sobbing as well. My guilt at causing the hurt was matched by an inward anger at not knowing why I was doing these things. The doctor didn't know either, which was why they decided I should move in.

In all I spent a jolly six months as an in-patient at the hospital's Department of Child and Family Psychiatry. Apart from weekends, I lived in a large ward with around twenty other kids who came and went with alarming frequency. This constant turnover of patients failed to stop a miraculous development – I made a friend. Her name was Kimberley and we would spend the afternoons chatting on her bed as I told her stories or we drew pictures together. One small detail that may have helped develop the friendship was that Kimberley was completely mute.

Every morning her sessions with the residential psychologists would consist of an increasingly desperate attempt to drag a word from her. 'What is your name?' they would start, followed minutes later by a more pleading, 'Just say your name, Kimberley,' which always made me laugh. She had spoken for a number of years before stopping one day without warning. Her parents, school and local doctor had been unable to coax her into opening her mouth and York-hill's finest weren't having much luck either. She just smirked, looked away and kept her mouth firmly shut until the day I was prattling along about one thing or another and she whispered, 'I like you, Elliot.'

I stopped in surprise and, clearly concerned I was about to cause some sort of scene, she added forcefully, 'Promise you won't say.' I promised and I never did. She left shortly afterwards, without speaking again, still in that secret world of hers. After her departure I quickly made friends with a couple of the other kids. It was easy to get on with them as I think every classroom reject that rolled up there realized he or she was on to a good thing. The terrors of conventional education may have left us jumpy and scarred but this new environment with its boxes of toys and absence of bullying mobs opened us up to suggestion.

I became more tranquil and my attention-seeking practically disappeared. I enjoyed my daily discussions with the doctors, which were interactive and engaging, and could follow the advice they were giving me. I loved seeing my family at the weekends but by Sunday I was aching to be back in the safety of the ward. It was a happy time but I ultimately became a victim of my own success as my progression continued right through to discharge and a forced return to normal life.

Battlefield Primary wisely wouldn't touch me with a bargepole so I went to the other local primary school, Mount Florida. It was a disaster. Straight away the old behaviour resurfaced as I wreaked havoc on a daily basis. I was so erratic and my outbursts so severe that the other kids couldn't even raise themselves to bully me. The Education Department had been keeping an eye on me. Within a few months I was out on my ear after they had got wind of my spectacular relapse.

There followed a period when I was no longer in any kind of education. My mum didn't have the time or means to give me any relevant work and it was just a case of waiting for a letter from the council. My days were spent down by the river or reading in the house when the weather was bad. Another couple of months passed by before the letter arrived and I was directed to Greenview Special School. At the age of eleven I settled into the routine of catching one bus to

Glasgow city centre and then another out to the school, a
rambling building in the northern suburbs.

It was a small school that specialized in correcting
troublesome kids, using a reward scheme. With some this
worked well, including myself who, I'm unashamed to admit,
became a bit of a teacher's pet. This was largely due to a
lovely lady called Fiona Mackay who taught me with great
sympathy throughout my stay there. In return I was pretty
quiet in class and enjoyed being back in a learning environment.

My quiet demeanour didn't equate to a peaceful classroom, however, as there were some far bigger bampots than
myself at Greenview. Pupils would lose the plot on a regular
basis, having screaming tantrums or running aimlessly from
the room with Fiona in hot pursuit. They would throw objects
at each other when Fiona was distracted and wrestle on the
floor while she wrote on the blackboard. Compared to them
my idiosyncrasies looked almost twee and I was one of the
students rewarded with trips to Scottish country parks and
camping expeditions.

Away from the school my continual hunt for diversion
was producing less positive results. My bus journeys forced
me to confront the wider world beyond Battlefield and I was
enthralled by the daily exposure to the city centre and, in
particular, the large music stores. I noticed that they had a
fairly unquestioning returns policy and began a ritual of
buying CDs, taking them home and copying them, then
returning them the next day. It was a soft introduction to
crime, but I soon fell into something more impressive.

The electric-shock love of travel that Chile had rooted
within me was reawakened when I discovered the railway
network. My local station, Mount Florida, was a small affair
but as the maps on the walls demonstrated, the run-down

building was a gateway to distant treasures – Glasgow Central, and from there the world. I made friends with the young ticket vendor, Alan, whose daily boredom was probably only marginally alleviated by the regular appearance of a slightly manic schoolboy.

I would visit him in the evenings, weekends or every day in the school holidays. Soon he would let me sit in the booth with him and I was immediately drawn to a huge stack of blank tickets. He was confused when I asked if I could take them but the request was roughly in line with my general oddness and he just shrugged as I stuffed them into my schoolbag. Back at home and sitting on the old family typewriter it took a few trial runs but I soon got there. My forgeries were crude but passable and I was still working my way through that pile of blank tickets a couple of years later, in fact there are probably still some in the house now.

This opened up considerable possibilities for me and I would venture ever further in the evenings and weekends on my trick tickets. I would take a leisurely jaunt up the West Highland line, or down to Ayrshire. Occasionally I'd go through to Edinburgh and wander round Waverley station for a while. Behind the station was a huge hotel called the Balmoral and I liked to stand watching the doorman helping people from their taxis in his kilt. Then I would walk back down the station steps and pull out another homemade ticket for the journey home.

One day at Glasgow Central I decided to try a new line. I walked up to the ticket office and explained that I had just put my money into the machine but neither my ticket to Mount Florida nor my money had been returned. The man took one look at me and pushed the sixty pence under the grille. I couldn't believe it, free money. A couple of days later I returned and, with a roll of the eyes, told the same man the same story. He gave me a strange look and told me to come into the office. When I got in he locked the door and phoned the police.

My parents went ballistic. To have a police car parked outside the house was a humiliation and my father felt my behaviour made it appear to anyone concerned that I was not being adequately provided for. As the policemen delivered their warning and then my parents their onslaught all I could think about was the pile of blank tickets under my bed. *Please don't search my room, I've got another hundred journeys there.* They didn't.

After nearly two years at Greenview I was sent to Stonelaw High School for my secondary education. It was in Ruther-glen, around two miles from my house, and it was felt that I had little chance of running into anyone from my earlier schooldays there. My improvement during my time at Green-view meant that it was a normal state secondary school but I was held back one year owing to the chaotic nature of my primary education. It was a faceless bureaucratic decision and even a glowing academic reference from Greenview couldn't change it. My mother got very angry about it but I couldn't really have cared less.

To all intents and purposes, Stonelaw High School marked the end of my formal education. I scraped through a few months without getting myself into any serious problems, which was largely due to the fact that I encountered language classes for the first time. After the novelty of speaking French and German wore off I began to get bored again and that's when things went a little bit peculiar.

There were two main incidents that led to my expulsion from Stonelaw. The first was the result of my impulsiveness.

I decided one day, for no obvious reason, to start a school magazine. With no friends and a tricky relationship with the teachers this posed a significant challenge. Clearly, support was going to have to be rustled up from somewhere and I soon alighted on a suitably daring plan. Each morning the teachers would print off any memos they had received on their computer workstations and read them out to their respective classes. One day in computing I had spied on a teacher sending out one of these missives from the central computer and had memorized the password and procedure.

As I sat in my classroom that morning listening to the teacher reading out the announcement of the formation of a school magazine I was trembling with excitement. She read it in the dry, clipped manner that all official proclamations would receive and I could see my classmates stiffening at this unusually interesting school decree. It was only when she got to the bottom of the page that things changed. 'If you are interested in taking part please contact...' She paused, frowned, her face flushed and she looked up slowly as she finished the sentence in a different voice, '...Elliot Castro.'

As she led me through the corridors to the headmaster's office, pupils poured out of their morning registrations where they had received similar renditions of my ALL STAFF memo. They laughed, clapped and shouted – *There he is! That's Elliot Castro!* – as I walked coolly through them. It was a truly wonderful moment, and it put me on my final warning.

The second incident is a little harder to explain. I can't put it down to impulsiveness because before I left the house that day I slipped one of my dad's ties into my pocket. I can't put it down to a well-worked plan because even as I disguised my uniform and donned the tie I wasn't sure what I was going to do next. Even as I walked through the classroom door and explained that I was Mr Castro and could they please settle down I'd got no idea what I hoped to achieve.

The pupils slowly stopped talking and slipped into their seats, looking at me expectantly. 'Who are you?' asked one boy, with a threat in his voice. 'Who am I?' I answered, drawing up my teenage frame as high as I could, '*I* am your new teacher. Maybe *you* would like to have my first punishment exercise?' He looked at me. I looked back. I held his eyes and made myself breathe evenly. He looked down and muttered, 'Sorry.' And with that I turned round and saw the real teacher standing in the doorway with a disbelieving look on his face.

Stonelaw High School and I parted company that day but, as I sat on the bus home, I didn't feel scared or nervous about informing my parents of their son's latest setback. All I could think about was that moment when the mouthy kid had backed down, when he had looked me in the eye and his opposition had melted away. It had been worth the expulsion letter I had in my blazer pocket.

I was now fourteen years old and had perhaps four years of proper schooling behind me. The next stop was St John Bosco High School, the local Catholic secondary that was pretty much the only place daft enough to take me. This was a surprising decision but I soon found out that it was not rooted in a religious belief in redemption; rather, I had boarded a sinking ship. A couple of weeks after I arrived I discovered that the school was closing in the summer for good, a fact of which everyone except for myself and my parents seemed to be fully aware.

Despite the tight deadline, I still managed to get expelled. I had been in the headmaster's office on official business a few times and noticed the bottle of whisky on a low shelf beside his desk. When he decided during a final conversation in the office to coldly label me a liar I responded, in what I thought was a perfectly fair trade of insults, that he was a drunk. He might have won the bottle in a raffle for all I knew, but he decided to bring our little debate and my attendance at the school to an abrupt end. So that was St John Bosco.

The Education Department had pretty much given up on me by this point, and I had absolutely no interest in going to another school. I was learning far more from my reading at home than I had in any classroom and my ever-expanding railway excursions were opening my mind to higher aims than these schools could satisfy. I dreamt of going to London and working as an undefined computer whizz in a huge office that looked out over the Houses of Parliament. It would take time, of course, but that was my masterplan at the time.

For now I was still at the mercy of officialdom. Weeks turned into months and I wasn't allocated another school. I would get up most days, pack some lunch and books into my bag and head to the train station. Meanwhile my poor mother was on the phone to the council every few days, until she finally snapped and threatened them with legal action. Their hand forced, they decided I was to take up residence at the Keppenburn Unit. I had been in my last school classroom.

The Keppenburn Unit was an experimental social-work project based in a house near the Ayrshire seaside town of Largs. Over the year or so that I was there, there would usually be myself and two other rogue kids living along with several residential social workers. The Unit was a communal facility in which everyone worked together to keep things ticking along. Bills had to be organized, food budgeted for, repairs made. It was aimed at teaching us responsibility while the overall emphasis was on understanding and improving our behaviour.

I would get the train down to Largs on a Sunday evening and stay at Keppenburn until early Friday afternoon. At first the nearby Seaview School would issue me with some work but I never did it and no one ever mentioned it again. My days would be spent in the company of the care team led by a warm and reassuring woman called Fiona Leith. Often I would be allowed to accompany the staff into town to get something for the house or for them to demonstrate some everyday task. If there was no such expedition available then I could choose to read or write letters for a few hours alone in the living room.

Two evenings a week I went to the local Sea Cadets in Largs where I learnt knots and nautical terms. I was also encouraged by the Keppenburn Unit to spend my own weekly food budget at the local Safeway on a Monday evening, to teach me about the value of money. That was probably my favourite part of the week, prowling the aisles looking for bargains and constantly running through pricing combinations in my head.

The other referrals in the Unit would come and go and the only one I was close to was a guy called Ian. He was a lovely, goofy guy who would make the most unintentionally hilarious comments that would have us all in stitches at the dinner table. During the day he was serving an apprenticeship at the local garage and I'd look forward to his reappearance in the afternoons, covered in oil and always with a slightly warped story to tell.

The ample spare time that life at Keppenburn offered had a couple of effects. The first was that I could take my daydreaming to almost hallucinatory levels. I would sit for hours staring out at the Ayrshire fields imagining that I was far away – on a plane, in the back of a limousine cruising through some exciting foreign city, or checking into a luxury hotel like the Balmoral. Those social workers that had travelled abroad were pumped relentlessly for information and I would throw a tantrum if I was out-voted from watching travel programmes on the communal TV.

One of the female carers, obviously an upwardly mobile sort like myself, had *Tatler* magazine delivered. I loved it and the glamorous world it portrayed. The photos of parties and functions hinted at a life far from Keppenburn or Battlefield and at the back there were clothes and jewellery that cost as much as a car. I told her that she would see me in the magazine one day and she laughed and said she wouldn't be surprised, which left me even more convinced.

The other result of the vacant hours I had on my hands was that my mischievous streak was given free rein. One day I persuaded Ian to skive work and meet me instead at Largs station for a day trip to Edinburgh. We went to Edinburgh Castle, bought ice creams in Princes Street Gardens and lay on the grass staring at the sky. I told him I was going to be rich and famous and he told me about a work colleague who had got his arm stuck in a car exhaust.

On the way back to the station I stopped again outside the Balmoral Hotel. Through the front door I could see the reception area. Men and women with smart suits and shiny faces talked and laughed in a room that seemed to have polished brass and dark wood wherever you looked. I craned my neck to see more and a shadow fell upon me. 'Can I help you?' asked the doorman, but his tone was hostile and I walked away without answering.

We received a rebuke for that little escapade but worse was to follow when I coaxed Ian down to the local off-licence where we blew our food budget on booze. As well as a few bottles of MadDog 20–20, a celebrated alcopop of the time, we bought a large bottle of Drambuie whisky liqueur.

I'd read a cocktail book the day before and so the two of

us returned to the house and spent the afternoon drinking bad Irish coffees and swigging the MadDog. By the time the staff realized what we were up to we were long gone, lying on Ian's bedroom floor listening to hard-core dance music. Fiona hit the roof over that one and marched us down to the off-licence to apologize for tricking the old lady into selling us the alcohol.

So I was on my last chance when one Saturday night in Glasgow a friend and I managed to get into a nightclub. Our jubilation at getting past the bouncers at the age of sixteen left us frantically chatting to fellow punters, who must have thought we were on some form of substance. One group invited us back to a house party, where the two of us drank some more and became even more ecstatic.

I was in the strange combination of joy and self-discovery when I accidentally stumbled into the host's bedroom. As I turned to leave I saw a credit card sitting on a table and I picked it up and put it in my pocket. I can't really say much more about it than that, there was no great ceremony or inward debate before I nicked my first card. The next morning, however, I woke up in a cold sweat. What had I done? I couldn't decide my next move and had no one to confide in. In the kitchen I asked my mum what happened if someone used her credit card and she told me the bank gave her the money back. Suddenly things didn't seem so bad, and a thought entered my head.

Every Friday Keppenburn refunded the cost of my train tickets when I produced the stubs. If this little card could be used for the purchase of those tickets then come Friday the money I would be handed would not be returned to my parents. It would be mine for whatever I wanted – nightclubs, parties, day trips to Edinburgh or maybe even further than that. That Sunday afternoon on the Largs train I felt giddy with anticipation and fear. I was so shaky at Glasgow Central that I had all but decided not to go through with the plan until I found a way to combat my distress.

I took the name on the credit card and repeated it to myself until I had become convinced that it was my real name. By the time the journey had started I had added a job, hobbies, friends to my character. I thought back to the playground at Kaimhill Primary and the classroom at Stonelaw, about these earlier successes and how I had pulled them off through my own certainty. When the conductor came towards me I smiled warmly and handed him the card, ordering my ticket in a flippant manner. Unsmiling and without a word he swiped the card on his machine. It beeped and his eyes flicked to mine, sending a jolt through my body, but then he was reeling off the ticket and handing it back to me with the card.

As he walked away my breathing steadied and I was overcome with what I had just achieved. The piece of plastic in my pocket was busy opening doors in my mind as the train neared Largs. Leaning back victoriously I let my eyes follow the slowing scenery, as the farmlands gave way to the small greystone buildings and the pedestrians battling against the Atlantic wind. The train wound its way through the town as people paid it little attention, unaware of the new master criminal that it unwittingly carried. Then we were easing into the station and there was a platform, and on the platform stood two policemen.

CHAPTER SIX

Glasgow, November 2005

Neil Forsyth

Glasgow has two train stations. Glasgow Queen Street is a small, cosmopolitan depot dumped in the centre of the city, from where it pulls in visitors from across Scotland. The trains spit out of a row of tunnels every couple of minutes to roll into the tightly ranked platforms that sit nearly upon the tiny concourse. Large screens advise travellers that train doors close thirty seconds before departure while others warn that tickets must be purchased before travelling. The displayed schedule is precise, all routes end in cities and the times are neat and regular. The Edinburgh train comes and goes every fifteen minutes, a pendulum swinging between the two cities.

The seating provided for the station's passengers is flimsy and temporary, resting with steel heels on the tiled forecourt. During the rush hours, when this area is hidden under suits and overcoats, they are whisked away to ease the hordes' passage between home and office. Right now, on a winter's late morning, I am the only one using them.

The station is quiet and those present walk quickly and bowed as if ashamed to be here at this dead time. A pair of housewives squawk at each other as they arrive from the east for the Christmas shopping, their voices fracturing the cold empty air. A businessman becomes wedged in the ticket barrier in his haste to be free of this place and a man in a luminous jacket walks silently towards him, his palm held upwards for calm.

I rise from the freezing metal and walk through the station's exit, past two ruined drunks who sleep half-standing, beer cans gripped in fingerless gloves. To my left is George Square, the red expanse ringed with Victorian grandeur. The stern statues – Victoria, Albert, Rabbie Burns, Walter Scott the highest of them all – send forbidding stares as the pigeons flit between them. I walk in the other direction, down a busy street shrouded by the greying sky.

The suggested rain arrives as I turn into a pedestrianized sweep that stretches away across a series of junctions. The ubiquitous High Street pulls of mobile phones, franchise restaurants, clothes and coffee are attracting few shoppers as the rain stiffens and a sharp wind sails across the concrete. Journeys become rationed and necessary, people break into halting jogs while others divert into diagonal marches across the wide street and disappear through sheltered alleys.

Halfway along I turn into a downward spiral of environment. The shops are replaced by low-rent travel agents and take-aways, mixed with tired office entrances and the occasional uncomfortable bank. Some of the units I pass lie empty, decorated instead by fly-posting and doorway litter. A final combination of 24-hour newsagent, Chinese buffet restaurant, fish and chip shop and bookmaker's signal my arrival at Glasgow Central station.

It is a vast, muddled space. Under an undulating glass roof sits a huge, misshapen concourse cluttered with stalls, shops and banks of printed timetables. All around me are people, the old and the bored, and a busy chatter competes with an endless drone of announcements. A row of pensioners sit staring into the mid-distance, a posse of students laugh and shout and everywhere people cluster in pairs and upwards. They have the depressed air of non-workers as they stare unhurried at the never-ending list of routes. The trains are departing at ugly times – 11.43, 12.07 – and to places doomed by insignificance – Corkerhill, Hawkhead, Glengarnock, Drumfrochar. I make for the ticket machines and the windowed booth where a young Elliot had asked for a refund one time too many. That day his phantom ticket had cost 60p, eleven years later it is £1.55.

I find the train lying listlessly beside a quiet platform, my progress unchecked by barrier or guard. The custard-yellow livery is covered in a film of grime and the plastic bucket seats inside are bolted to a filthy floor. The only other people in the carriage are a goth in a Megadeath leather jacket and a Sikh reading the local paper. They don't look up as the train shudders into action and we slide across a bridge over the Clyde and onwards through man-made gullies of steep walls marked with spray-paint and soot. Occasionally a block of high-rise flats flickers over the walls as the rain spatters down the glass, carving thin lines through the dirt. When the stations appear they seem subterranean because of the height of the walls, and gloomy in the blocked light. The first few pass by and then the walls ease back from the tracks and there is more air and space as we roll into Mount Florida.

On a short platform sits a low red-brick building that looks vaguely fortified, an image strengthened by the CCTV cameras bolted to its overhanging roof. Through the window I see an office where a woman gazes at a chart on the wall. As I watch she exhales deeply and casts her eyes to something below her on the floor. There is no one else in the building, on the platform, on the walkway that leads to the station. I turn away and walk up the stairs.

I have a crude map with three points crossed and I head towards the nearest one. Four-storey blocks of red sandstone tenement flats flank the quiet streets, and I see few people as I pick my way around binbags awaiting the truck I see rumbling down a side street. I pass a funeral director's and a fishmonger's then emerge onto a busy junction. The road is wide and hectic and cars splash past as I look through the rain to the large building at the other side. It is a Victorian school house, with *Boys* and *Girls* embossed in the red stonework above separate doors and *Mount Florida Public School* above another. The playground is narrow and ringed with wire mesh, and the school is bordered on three sides by the road. Looming behind it are the floodlights of Hampden Park, the national football stadium.

Past the school is the tail-end of Battlefield Road. For a de facto high street, it is a lonely place. On one side stand two high-rise blocks of flats and on the other a garage, then a long brick wall and then a pub. A low bridge shows the route of the trains as they leave the station, and beyond it the road becomes busier with a bank of parked cars in front of shopping units. A post office, news-agent's and off-licence all show signs of life while two teenage girls run squealing into a tanning studio with their jackets pulled as shelters over their heads. A drayman wheels barrels into a further pub and an Alsatian dog rounds a corner alone and ambles non-chalantly past me.

I turn down a side street and find Battlefield Primary School. The long, low construction is the original stone base topped with a wooden prefabricated shell. It is fronted with long windows and I can see into the classrooms where the teachers stand in front of their classes or walk amongst them, heads tilted to their pupils' work. The windows are too high for me to see the children but in one room a flurry of tiny hands appears just above the window sill, held aloft in straining hope of selection.

I walk on down these narrowing roads, turning this way and that until I find the entrance to the street I want. Cars are hoisted up on the pavement, two wheels on it and two on the road, and I walk cautiously behind the bonnets with my eyes on the other side. I see the number I'm looking for painted on the sandstone. It belongs to a ground-floor flat that stretches over three windows of the block behind a tidy garden. The curtains are closed but as I see this I think that maybe they just twitched. Seconds later the door opens and closes and a figure appears veiled under an umbrella. She walks quickly across the street and past me, nodding onwards as she does so and stealing a quick smile in my direction.

'You're late,' she says.

*

'I'm sorry you couldn't come to the house, but...' She doesn't finish her sentence, just shrugs and pulls a cigarette from the box that sits on the table. The resemblance to Elliot is immediate, the same determined manner and fleeting smile that comes and goes so easily. We are sitting in a café on Battlefield Road, and the old woman at the next table is arching back in her chair. I didn't think Jane Castro had noticed but as she lights the cigarette she whispers.

'Aye she'll be wondering what he's done now.' There's no trace of emotion. 'I don't mind it,' she says. 'I love Battlefield, you'd have to drag me back to Aberdeen kicking and screaming. Up in Aberdeen it would all be Chinese whispers, then they would bullshit you in the street. Here the people are honest, they come up to me and ask how Elliot is, or how he managed to do what he did.

'The people in Battlefield understand crime. They know that sometimes, when you haven't got a lot or you've got a big family to feed, people bend rules. They're not criminals, they're just trying to get by. Now Elliot's a criminal, that's for bloody sure, but some people look at what he did and they say to me, "Jane, you should be proud of him because he beat the system." They say that people from round here shouldn't be going where he went, doing what he did.'

But that's other people. What about her? 'I'm BAC,' she says simply. 'Born Again Christian. I smoke like a chimney and swear like a navvy but that's all by the by. You either believe or you don't and that's it. In Aberdeen Carlos worked with a Kiwi guy who held Bible readings with his wife in their flat, right above ours. One night I went up there and the Pastor walked in the room.' She sits back in her chair and reaches her hand back behind her head. 'The hairs stood up.' She leans forward and points her cigarette at me. 'That man shone, Neil, he *shone*.'

She looks a little uncomfortable, her voice had risen and next to us the old woman was nearly falling backwards out of her chair in response. Our coffees arrive and Jane chats to the waitress about the rain, Carlos, Elliot, Dean. It looks as if she is distracted but the minute we are alone again she picks up the thread seamlessly.

'I know what Elliot did was wrong, and so does he,' she says in a quieter voice. 'The only people I feel sorry for are the ones that got the bank statements because they must have been close to having bloody heart attacks when they came through. I don't feel sorry for Elliot because I know that he's a survivor, he's had to be.'

I mention the schooling and she sighs and shakes her head. I talk about bullying and how the smallest things can give kids years of ammunition, even names. 'Eliot Ness,' she interrupts gravely. 'That's how he got his name. My Dad and I used to watch *The Untouchables* all the time and Robert Stack was always my favourite. So we called him Elliot.

'Now what was I supposed to do?' she continues. 'We had our son being bullied and being sent from one place to another and sometimes nowhere for months on end. I knew he was different and wanted to school him at home but then he would never have got any better with other people. We just had to send him where they said and hope that one of the places would work.'

These problems that Elliot had, that grew within him and sent him out into the world to do what he did. I suppose, I explained, that one of the main reasons I was here was to ask where they came from. She says she doesn't have the answer, but she tries to give it. The education system didn't help, she starts, but she knows they were dealing with a hard case.

'I love him more today than ever, but he's always been a cocky bastard,' she says. 'At school he wasn't afraid of telling a teacher that they were wrong or that he knew better than them and they're not exactly going to take too well to that, are they?' She stirs her coffee slowly and begins again. 'I suppose what has always got Elliot into trouble was that he always believed he was smarter than everyone

else. And if they didn't believe him ... well, then he would have to
show them that he was.'

We walk back down Battlefield Road together, our eyes to the ground
as we weave through the puddles. 'The police used to come to the
house a lot,' she says unprovoked. 'Towards the end they would walk
around the place and anything that looked expensive they would ask
where we got it from. Sometimes they would make little remarks,
"Present from Elliot?" That kind of thing. By then they had given up
asking us where he was.'

She lights another cigarette and nods at a man who appears
from a shop doorway in front of us. He smiles and opens his mouth
to speak but stops when he sees me and stands uncertain as we
walk past. 'The thing with the police is that all they had was our
address,' she says when we're out of earshot. 'It was like they came
round just to feel they were making progress, that they were
somehow closer to Elliot. They would say things like "Tell him to
come home, Mrs Castro, it's the only way." I said, "Look, it's you lot
that keep losing him, not me."'

We turn into the Castros' road. I ask if she's speaking to Elliot
that night. 'Of course I am. Do you know what? The best conversations
we ever have is when he's in prison. I make him laugh and he makes
me laugh. I play him his music off my computer and look up things
for him on the Internet. We talk for hours, when he was in Canada
he ...' She laughs and shakes her head. 'Ah,' she sighs, lifting the
umbrella to look up at me, 'Elliot.'

As she walks away I turn towards Battlefield Road and the train
station but hesitate and look back, further down the road. It runs for
another hundred yards before ending in a row of trees and shrubbery.
Peering into the rain I see another line of trees a little distance
beyond. Something is in between and I think I know what, something
I forgot to add to my map. I check on Jane Castro but she's well

down the road and so I pull my hood a little tighter and head for the trees.

They are sparse though tightly packed and I can't see through them, but further up the pavement is an opening. Here I find a roughly paved walkway with a wall of graffiti to the right and, to the left, the river. It's moving far quicker than I expected, gushing in brown torrents between the trees which stand on top of a grass bank. I follow it along the path looking for something that might tie in with what I know but I am giving up hope when I get to a sharp right turn. The river is turning too, a concrete diverting wall has blocked it and sent it back on itself. The water is calmed and stilled before it collects and swings away towards a distant bridge.

A low wall separates the path from the bank and I climb over it and stand on the sodden grass. The rain is coming down harder now, whipped in sheets across the water and through the bare winter trees. The branches are catching my hood so I push it down and part them, spotting something over the brow of the bank. I force myself through and ease down the slope but the grass acts as a slide and I am carried downwards, then briefly through the air until my feet hit ground and I am standing hunched over my knees. As I right myself I think for a moment that I am standing in the water, so close is it to me, but I see that in fact this is a natural jetty of grass. Behind me the bank closes everything else from view while beyond there is just the water then the concrete. The rain is still falling but the wind cannot catch itself so easily down here, where Battlefield disappears and the river pauses as if in thought.

CHAPTER SEVEN

In the back of a police car in the car park of Largs station I received my first ever interrogation. I was much calmer than I would have expected as I explained that my friend had lent me his credit card, and was that not something that you could do? The words just seemed to come from me without any effort on my part. I sat forward in the seat as if eager to get this terrible misunderstanding resolved, looking them both directly in the eyes as I spoke. They peeked at each other as I did so, wanting the other one to make the decision, and I pushed on with my defence. My friend, I explained with a rueful shake of the head, is from quite a rich family. I shouldn't probably say this but he has lent me his card before, he likes to say – 'Let my dad get it.'

One of the policemen stopped a smile. They exchanged a significant look and then he spoke. 'Well, you won't be using your friend's card again, will you?' I felt the pressure lift from me as the radio suddenly burst into life. The card, it told them in a flat tone, was stolen. A rather awkward silence settled in the car and they looked at me like wronged lovers as I managed only a vague frown in response. 'I think we'd better take you to this school of yours,' the one in the driver's seat eventually muttered as he turned the key.

When we got to Keppenburn, Fiona and Ian stood at the window watching our arrival. Ian laughed and pointed when I emerged from the police car but Fiona looked drawn and defeated behind her folded arms. After a long conversation she and the policemen came and found me sitting in the living room staring out of the window. I was mentally preparing for prison, thinking how best to break the news to my parents and wondering about my pending sentence. Before he'd left for the garage Ian had kindly predicted fifteen years. 'You're a very lucky laddie,' started one of the policemen, and I knew that Fiona had got me out of it. Not entirely, however. I received an official caution and she had agreed to inform my parents. It was also the end for me at Keppenburn.

I felt dreadful leaving the Unit that day for the last time, having let down Fiona and her team one occasion too many. It didn't make the situation any easier having my furious parents waiting for me at the other end of the journey. My father's family may have had smuggling coursing through their veins but that was an old and worthy crime; this was something sneaky and contemptible. Again I had pricked his Latin pride by implying to others that I had been forced into it through lack of funding, and once again a police car was parked outside the house when they came to confirm my caution. A police car outside a house in Battlefield never loses its intrigue to the locals, despite being a common sight, and word was starting to go round the community that I was going off the rails.

My mum's despair was simple – what the hell was I going to do now? This is where I had an ace to play. Fiona had refused to abandon me altogether, even though she had no option but to jettison me from Keppenburn. She had managed to gain me a place at Cambuslang College, a learning centre just outside Glasgow. As luck would have it a course started the following week. 'A course in what?' asked Mum suspiciously. 'Computers,' I replied and she looked even more suspicious. This was to be the last phase of my glittering education, and it would be one of the shortest.

I had owned a computer from a young age. The ZX Spectrum, an Amiga, then a PC had all passed through my bedroom and I'd gradually come to understand how these machines worked and thought. I'd developed a basic grasp of programming, and the running process behind it. It wasn't particularly impressive but it made me Cambuslang College's very own Stephen Hawking. The college specialized in retraining schemes for traditional industry refugees and adult learning sign-ups. When I arrived on the first day I found my study group dominated by older people, some of whom needed help in that first lesson to turn their computers on.

I happily assisted my fellow students at every available opportunity and, stunned by my knowledge and ability to use a floppy-disk drive, they elected me as class representative in the first week. As with my schooldays there was an initial period where my screwball behaviour and constant showing-off was seen as fresh and endearing before it swiftly advanced to irritating. It never reached that stage at the college, however, owing to the arrival of a tutor named Mr Holmes.

At first I thought Mr Holmes had perhaps borrowed a leaf out of my old Stonelaw High School book of tricks and wasn't really a lecturer at all – a bored janitor perhaps, or some weirdo who had just been wandering past the classroom. He had no notes, and looked like he had slept fully clothed in a skip. He knew less about computers than I and a few of my classmates did and spent his time with us locked in a constant battle to conceal his ignorance.

The tactics he employed to achieve this end were varied, his favourite being to talk very quickly about nothing at all and then react with theatrical frustration to questions as if he were a genius surrounded by imbeciles. Another ploy, which I took far more notice of, was for him to hit us with a stream of leading queries that never seemed to end. I was watching him do this one day when I realized what was happening. Through his incessant probing, he was subtly building knowledge for himself. I was quite impressed with that, I must say, and it was something that stayed with me.

Mr Holmes' shortcomings attracted differing conclusions from the students. Some were amused, and would ask him increasingly complex and often fictitious questions to torture him. Others were angered by the wasted time and sat in fuming silence, while a few felt sorry for Mr Holmes, pointing out that he was obviously undertaking his own painful retraining programme. As class representative I felt I had to do something to reflect these varied views and decided, obviously, to produce a spoof newspaper front page on the computer printer at the back of the room.

The result was a joy to behold. 'Lecturer in Know-Nothing Shock!' screamed the headline above Mr Holmes' photo from the college website and a short article explaining the controversial theory of placing both pupils and lecturers on simultaneous retraining schemes. This was a story for beyond our group and I pinned copies of the scoop all over the college on my way home that night. Having already decided that this was to be my parting shot, I never did discover Mr Holmes' reaction.

It was time, I believed at the age of sixteen, for Elliot Castro to enter the world of work. I knew that my parents weren't going to take this latest development particularly well so I disguised it as progress. I described the farcical nature of proceedings at Cambuslang College and followed it up with the news that I had got a job at a call centre. This was, in fact, true. I had gone into a job agency in Glasgow and they had phoned me on the bus home to tell me I was starting the next day at a call centre in Stockwell Street.

Scotland has a well-established call-centre industry because it's thought that the accent is friendly and warm. This explains why I got a job so quickly, but there was nothing friendly or warm about the scene that greeted me in Stockwell Street. In a grimy, freezing room a few dozen miserable people sat in front of their computers with headsets on. They looked like ghosts sitting there under the lights, muttering into their mouthpieces with their eyes stuck on their screens.

Sitting through my day's training I discovered why they looked so shattered. I had been told the work was for a medical insurance company – which it was, but not quite in the way that I'd expected. The job was this: phoning up middle-aged women who weren't expecting our call and attempting to sell them breast-cancer insurance. Jesus Christ, talk about a tough crowd. I did it for three days. On the third day a woman started crying down the phone to me saying that I was too late, she already had it. She sounded a bit like my mum. I put down the phone, put on my jacket and went home.

As I said, you don't lack for call centres in Scotland and so I soon got another posting. This time I was careful to ask what the company did. Telecommunications, they told me, which was all right with me, and I was happier still when I arrived at the offices in central Glasgow. The company (I'll call it Imagine) handled areas of customer relations for a major British mobile phone network. The office was large and bright and filled with a lively young team who larked about between calls.

The training was more impressive also, two full weeks and then I was let loose on the customers. I enjoyed my work at first, not knowing if it was going to be an inbound or outbound call and having to react quickly to unfolding situations. I liked speaking to people and hearing and solving their problems, or matching up their requirements to one of the handsets that we offered. Then I discovered another part of the job and everything else became irrelevant.

Being caught the first time I used a stolen credit card had been a shock, but it failed to dampen the memory of the exhilaration. I had become entranced by the cards and what they offered, but didn't have the motivation or the guts to steal another one. Sitting at my desk at Imagine I started to realize that perhaps I didn't have to steal them at all. Every day dozens of people were using their cards through me to pay for phones. There had to be a way for me to take this information and use the cards myself somehow.

My basic knowledge of the system at this time threw up two problems. Firstly, I knew that you needed a range of security information to back up any significant purchase on a card, not just the data on the card itself. Yet that was all I was being given when customers were buying their phones through me. Secondly, I wasn't being given any opportunity that would lead to me getting hold of the cards that belonged to these people. They were passing through my headset every few minutes and all I could do was helplessly key the numbers in. Hundreds of sixteen-digit runs, expiry dates and issue numbers. These were cards, fresh credit cards just waiting to offer their riches to me and I could look but not touch.

And then one day I received a call from a guy who owned a business. He needed to order ten phones and wanted to pay with his corporate American Express card. This was it. It wasn't prepared and I wasn't even aware what I was doing at first but something had clicked and I moved smoothly into action. I asked the man to hold and lifted my headset from my ears. I sat looking at my reflection in the computer screen, steadying myself and concocting my scheme. Ready to go, I placed my headphones back on my head. 'Are you there, sir? I've got American Express on the other line, I'm just going to ask you some security questions.'

It went like a dream. I asked him every question I could think of, far more than would have been necessary, and he rattled off the answers without hesitation. I scribbled them all down in a notebook along with the original card details, then thanked him and hung up. Soon this was a common practice, whenever someone had a friendly voice and a large order to place, and my notebook slowly filled up.

I didn't know exactly what I was going to do next but that did not stop me becoming convinced that great days were around the corner. I began to live my life in a state of near-constant daydreaming, imagining the life of luxury that I would enjoy as soon as the notebook's role became clear. Such was my conviction that the warnings I had been receiving for my general detachment failed to register and I was sprung back to reality only with the announcement that I was to be fired with immediate effect. The manager walked beside me to my desk and watched as I shut down my computer. He stood over me as I put on my jacket and he saw me pick what I told him was my address book from the drawer and walk out of the office. By the time I got home, I knew what the notebook was for.

The next day American Express received a telephone call from the holder of an American Express corporate account. He wanted to change his address to a new location in Glasgow's

Battlefield area. That was no problem, said the American Express woman, just a few security questions first. Shortly after, the cardholder phoned again, this time requesting another woman to send him a new card because he had lost his original. Having cleared security the new woman said she wanted to check the account's address.

'Battlefield,' confirmed the cardholder, 'Yes, that's us.'

'It will be couriered out tomorrow, sir,' she confirmed.

When I came off the phone I was sweating and breathless. I knew that my position was not perfect but I had found temporary solutions to my concerns. I would have a card in my wallet that I could back up with any security information requested, and I also had in reserve a plan that would hopefully both buy some time and cover my identity. But first I had to receive the card without alerting my parents to this new endeavour of mine. I got up at six o'clock the next morning and sat at the kitchen table, watching the garden path intently. Two hours later I was still there, and still alone, when I saw a man carrying an envelope push open our gate.

I had some pretty emotional moments in my career as a fraudster, and opening that first envelope and seeing the gleaming card is certainly one of them. It was gorgeous, with an empty signature box and stamped with the CORPORATE emblem. I ripped up the envelope and letter and pushed them to the bottom of the bin, closed the kitchen door and picked up the phone. Again there was the background of noise and tapping and voices. After passing security I changed the account address back to the original and hung up. I waited ten seconds, then called back; this was the important one and I was acting on a hunch.

'Hello there. I'd just like to check the address on my account.'

'OK sir, I'm just going to ask you some security questions.'

'Of course.'

After security she read out the account holder's original address.

'That's the one,' I said. 'Actually, you can probably help me here. The other day we changed our address to our new offices in Glasgow but the move is taking longer than we thought and I believe our finance director changed the address back. I need to post something out to the new office, you don't happen to have the address there, do you?'

'I'm sorry, sir,' said the woman sympathetically. 'We only keep one address on file. When your finance director changed the address back, I'm afraid we would have wiped the other one.'

'Oh dear,' I said in triumph. 'Not to worry.'

I was realistic enough to recognize that there was still a live chance the security division of the company could bring up my address as having received the card, particularly if they spoke to the courier service. But I was hoping that things would develop a little like this:

— In the next few days the cardholder's card won't work.
— He calls American Express, who explain that according to their records they have sent a new card out, and they will read out the address they have on file.
— Confused, the cardholder will agree to wait for the new card.
— A few more days and he'll call American Express again, and they will look at the account and realize quickly that someone has been using this new card on the guy's account. This is the vital moment. Do they do a bit of digging and find me or do they look at the situation – an apparently unrequested card has been sent to the cardholder's actual address, that he is confirming, only to

fall into dodgy hands – and quietly buy the account holder off as quickly as possible? The last thing they would want is for a blunder like that to be publicized surely?

I had, I reckoned, a week before I would find out.

I fairly floated down the road to Mount Florida station, the card tucked into my pocket. At the station I saw Alan, still loyally manning the ticket office, but only waved as I walked up the platform. I've moved on now, I thought as I climbed onto the train. My first stop in town was the British Airways shop in Gordon Street where the following conversation took place:

'A first-class return ticket to London, please, leaving tomorrow.'

'I'm afraid there is no first class within the United Kingdom, sir.'

'But ... what's on the left when you get on the plane?'

'Our internal flights will board at the front of the plane sir.'

'Eh?'

'We do offer a club class.'

'Right, yes. OK, club class then.'

'How will you be paying, sir?'

'American Express.'

It wasn't the smoothest of entries into the world of high-class fraud, but it was a start. I told the uninterested woman that I was booking a ticket for a work colleague by the name of

Elliot Castro and minutes later I was out in the street with the ticket in my hand. I bought a few more things in town but didn't want to attract any attention to the new card so decided to wait until the following day before really testing its capabilities.

After a fitful night's sleep I got up and told my mum I was going to London with money I had saved from my wages. She was impressed and told me to make sure I went to see Buckingham Palace, which I assured her was on my list. I told her that when the Queen was at home there were four guards outside the Palace and when she wasn't there were only two, and she replied that I knew an awful lot about very little. I got a taxi to the airport and walked to the British Airways desk.

This was the first time that I had been in an airport since the Chile trip of my childhood and that combined with the thrill of the crime to leave me weak with nerves as I approached the girl behind the desk. She saw me coming and I could see her reaction to this scruffy young kid ambling towards her. Even when I told her I was on the London flight she looked uncertain but when she brought up my club-class booking things seemed to change. 'Thank you, Mr Castro,' she smiled as she handed me my boarding pass and ticket.

I went straight to the gate and stayed there until we were called to board. Every time a policeman or security guard passed by I would be nearly paralysed with fear, but they never even looked over. It was only when the plane began to roll down the runway with me safely on it that I realized everything was still OK, my card was still alive and that meant . . . well, it meant anything that I wanted.

*

At Heathrow Airport I phoned the Park Lane Hilton and booked a room on the card, once again airily referring to my work colleague Mr Castro, then trekked there by train and tube. I had chosen the hotel from the Internet the night before, it looked nice but also wasn't too extravagant. I knew that I would be tense and was realistic enough at this point to see that a sixteen-year-old travelling alone would look a little out of place in a hotel like the Balmoral. I wanted a busy chain hotel, not somewhere that went for upscale, personal service where too many questions were asked.

The checking-in process was easy enough and I took the lift up to my room, declining the porter's offer to carry my sports bag that until recently had been used to carry my lunch and books on my train tours. As the door to my room swung open I was presented with this first victory. It was large and immaculate, with a view across Hyde Park. Below me people hustled through the streets or sold newspapers or drove taxis. They were scratching about for a living down there, working to survive, while I stood in my hotel room in the sky planning my next move.

I smartened myself up as best as I could, left the hotel and hailed a cab. I was a little nervous as I was unsure of the exact whereabouts of my destination, which could have been in another city for all I knew. When I had lain in my bunk at Keppenburn reading *Tatler*, everything had seemed to come from the same street. All the watches, clothes and jewellery that had filled the back section, they all stemmed from this place. I had to get there, no matter the cost.

A taxi stopped and I got inside, reaching into my pocket and pulling out five twenty-pound notes. My mum had expressly told me not to get any taxis in London because of the extraordinary expense. In my hand was all the money I had in the world, except, of course, for the unknown funds offered by my stolen card.

'Will this be enough to get me to Bond Street?' I asked the driver.

The driver looked first angry, then confused. It took a moment before I realized what had happened. I had over-powered him with the money and the exclusive destination. For someone like him, driving about all day with his faded dreams, to see a youngster like myself making such a demand in such a manner must be painful. I tried again, attempting to sound less boastful, without being overly patronizing.

'There's a hundred pounds here, will it be enough to get me to Bond Street?'

'I should think so, son,' he said slowly. 'It's about five hundred yards away.'

I nodded. I didn't move.

'Would you rather walk?'

'Yes please,' I said, sounding about five years old. I exited the taxi and walked to Bond Street, where my humiliation was instantly forgotten. The street was narrower than I had imagined and this made the buildings even more imposing. With their delicate masonry, pillars and flagpoles they stood in stately processions down either side of the road. But my attention soon turned from the architecture.

De Beers, Cartier, Gucci, Yves Saint Laurent, Watches of Switzerland, Chanel, Tiffany, Prada, Daks, Dolce & Gabanna, Bulgari, Asprey, Nicole Farhi, Ralph Lauren, Armani, Ermene-gildo Zegna, Sotheby's, Jimmy Choo, Burberry, Louis Vuitton...

The names pinged through my head, bringing up images from advertisements and magazines. I didn't even know that fashion labels had their own stores; now they were all laid out in a line. I had already decided what my first purchase was to be – a bag that would look a bit more appropriate for trips like this and offer more room than my faithful sports holdall.

I went into the Louis Vuitton store and picked out a large travelling bag, explaining to the sales assistant more than once that I was in town on business as he nodded blankly. At the till, to take my mind off the £700 that was about to be extracted from the card's account, I selected a Filofax and added it to my order. I tried not to look at the machine as I heard it cough into action and push out the receipt, but there was no hesitation and the sales guy barely checked my signature before handing over my purchases.

Out in the street I ducked into the mouth of an alley and pulled the Vuitton bag out of its plastic covering. I yanked off the labels and put them, the plastic and the Filofax in the bag. I swung it over my shoulder and walked into the Gucci store. Having it resting on my back with its logo clearly showing made me feel safer as I sensed the sales girl walking towards me. As I looked up to her my eye was immediately taken by the belt display. I took a shine to a thick leather example and cautiously twisted the price tag to face me: £300. That was good enough for me, I thought as I handed it to her.

By the time I entered Prada, therefore, I was wearing an old T-shirt and jeans with a £700 Louis Vuitton bag across my back and a £300 belt prominently bunching together my waist. I must have looked faintly ridiculous but I felt invincible. I bought a selection of underwear and some plain T-shirts and walked back out to Bond Street. By now the afternoon was turning to evening and businessmen were mixing with the shoppers. I looked around this sudden influx and the street held me in its grasp once more.

They were all strangers, the people on the street, and yet they could have all been related. They had the same certainty and confidence in the way they moved, as if they each owned the little sections of pavement in which they walked. Their hair and skin seemed to glow as they passed me standing there with my stolen bag and belt. They were, well I didn't really know what they were, just ... different. They moved around me as if I were an inanimate object and none of them looked at me as they passed, not even at my £700 bag. I felt a bit deflated then, and I decided to return to the hotel.

Back in my room I lay on my bed and phoned my mum. I told her about the room, and the view, and Bond Street. She asked me about Buckingham Palace and I said that I was going to go there in the morning, but for now I was deciding where to go for dinner. She told me not to waste my money going anywhere too fancy and I said that I wouldn't, which was true, of course.

In the end I skipped dinner. I went for a drink in a bar near Oxford Street that the girl at reception had promised was very exclusive. She'd seen two people from *EastEnders* there the week before. I had also got her to make a reservation for me at a restaurant but at the bar I started speaking to a couple of guys in suits who had clearly been in there for a few hours. From what I can remember they worked for some bank or other, but they weren't making a whole lot of sense.

They invited me to share some of their champagne, which I did, and then I ordered another bottle. They were slurring their words and slapping me on the back and I soon abandoned my questions as the drink and the situation began to take effect. The champagne was costing £200 a bottle and I was soon as drunk as they were. The three of us sat glassy-eyed in our own private worlds, linked only by this steady drowning of money, with hardly a word spoken between us. I remember one scrap of conversation. It came when I was leaning over the bar trying to catch the barman's eye for another bottle and one of the bankers lifted his drooping head with a conspiratorial smile.

'No work tomorrow?' he said, and started to laugh.

On the plane back I bought a glass of champagne and sat back fiddling with my £300 belt. I had never earned £300 in a week at the call centre, now I used as much to keep my trousers from falling down. I had woken that morning with a fuzzy head and a bunch of receipts in my pocket. In all, I had spent nearly £1,000 on champagne in the bar. £1,000. It was incredible. I thought back to the schools I had gone to, all those other kids who had dismissed me and called me names. I wondered how many of them had been to London on their own, drank champagne in bars and bought £300 belts. Most of them probably hadn't even left Glasgow.

I *knew* I was better than them, I thought now. I may not yet belong with the golden people of Bond Street but I was moving towards them, I had no doubt about that. Throughout my childhood I had felt that I was destined for better things, to outgrow my surroundings, and now I finally seemed to have got the proof in the clothes I had bought and the money that I had spent. Those bankers had accepted me as one of them from the moment I had joined them. They saw the way that I ordered the champagne without asking the price, how I had signed the receipts without flinching. How could I go back to working in a call centre, after the two days that I had just had? I wasn't going back to Glasgow to work, I wasn't even going back there to live. I was going back for the notebook and where it was going to take me next, and I was delirious with anticipation as the plane flew back to the north.

CHAPTER EIGHT

I think at this point I will mention the fact that I'm gay. Did you see that coming? Probably not, there's not been much to go on. It's hard for me to know where to add this in so I'm just going to do it now. The important thing for you to realize is that at this point in my story, when I'm back home in my bedroom in Battlefield leafing through my notebook and making a list of possibilities, nobody knows that I'm gay except for myself.

It came to me a few years before this, when things started to get a little bit strange in the way that I looked at the other boys in my class. There was no great eureka moment, it was just a suspicion in my mind that was confirmed over time. If I'm honest with you I have wished ever since that I was straight because it would have made things a lot easier for me. It was hard enough doing what I did without having that corker swirling about my head.

It was a pain, something that I would have daily battles with and would do anything to forget about. Music, reading and boozing would give some temporary respite but it remained a recurring thought that would invade my mind whenever I let it. The thought of telling anyone struck me with fear. The daydreaming, the lying awake at night that I have mentioned before, it also contained the searing issue of my sexuality – how I had become what I was, and if I was ever going to be able to do anything about it.

Upon my victorious return from London, everything seemed a little bit brighter. There was something about the cards, something about what they suggested. I was still gay but I just didn't think it was going to be such a problem any more. Nothing was. These cards, and what they meant for my life, were going to make everything all right. I was sure of it.

Over the next week I leapt up from the kitchen table another four times to intercept couriers outside the front door. My parents were becoming increasingly baffled by my behaviour – I would be up first thing every day to ensure I was there to take the delivery then would retreat to my room for hours on end. They would ask me what I was doing about getting a new job and I would ask them what they *thought* I was doing on the Internet for hours on end each afternoon.

What I was doing was planning my escape. I wanted to find somewhere that I could hide for a while and enjoy the cards that I was stashing under my bed. I was still extremely nervous at this stage about using them, and thought if I did so somewhere away from home then it would give me a better chance of not being recognized. If things went badly, I could slip away and be on the first train home to Glasgow. On the other hand, if the police turned up at my house to find out who had been ordering all these cards then I wouldn't be there waiting for them.

When I read on the Internet about Manchester's vibrant gay scene and their Mardi Gras Festival my mind was made up. London was too frightening for me at this point to consider moving there, and I was a long way from plucking up the courage to steal myself abroad. I told my parents that I had a friend down in Manchester who could get me a job working in another call centre then filled my Vuitton bag with clothes, stuffed all my cards and what little money I had into my wallet and walked to Mount Florida train station.

Alan was on duty in the ticket office and he told me that he'd been down to Manchester once for a football game. It was funny, just as I was leaving he shouted after me, 'Is it one of your special tickets you're using Elliot?' He was laughing but I was surprised, I wasn't aware that he'd known what I had done with that pile of blanks.

When I got off the train in Manchester it was a beautiful sunny day. I stopped a young couple in the station concourse and asked them where Canal Street was, the centre of the city's gay area. I must have looked like the eager young buck that I was but they were friendly enough and told me it was just down the road. I half-ran through the streets and turned into a long road of bars, restaurants and a mass of people.

I'd never seen anything like it. Men were kissing, holding hands and hugging. Straight couples were all over the place too, as well as families and even a few smiling policemen. Everyone just looked so happy, and comfortable with this revolutionary situation. The sun felt much stronger than in Glasgow and people sat round tables that poured from the bars right into the road itself. Dance music pulsed out from the pubs and I could smell hash in the air.

I saw a sign saying Rembrandt Hotel and walked in, checking in under a Visa card belonging to a 22-year-old Imagine customer. The room was small and grimy but I hardly noticed as I pushed the window open and leant out over the street. Below me a few heads flicked upwards and I realized that I'd shouted out with excitement. 'Sorry!' I yelled and they smiled, one guy saluted me with his bottle. I went back into the room and pulled out the cards, lining them up on the small bedside table. I grabbed one at random, jumped up and walked out the room.

The first few weeks of that summer of 1999 are a bit hazy. I was staying in the Rembrandt but only used the room to sleep in. During the day I would explore Manchester's city centre, visiting the clothes shops and record stores where I would spend hours listening to music through the customer headphones. Depending on my mood I would have lunch anywhere from a small café to a posh restaurant where the staff would look with undisguised disdain at this teenager in his T-shirt who was grappling with a lobster or squirting tomato ketchup onto his filet mignon.

At night I would embark on solo pub crawls where I would hover around the bar, trying to catch people's eyes. I would leech myself onto any group that paid me the courtesy of letting me stand next to them, and would wildly order excessive rounds of drinks in an attempt to cement my position. Cocktails, flavoured shots, champagne, jugs of beer – I'd have them all over in a flash before my new friends had a chance to send me on my way. I never had any problems getting served. By now I had filled out and my face was harder than when I was younger. Besides, I was a regular customer and spending money like a madman. No bar worthy of the name would turn me away.

Manchester seemed vast and chaotic. I branched out from Canal Street to different areas – Deansgate, Castlefield, Chapel Street. I would as readily speak to a group of teenage girls, housewives, businessmen or pensioners in my enthusiasm over this new life of mine. They would all receive a different version of my background and obvious wealth, but no one would ever press too much. It was as if everyone understood the deal – they would let me talk to them as long as I kept buying the drinks.

One by one the cards stopped working. At first this wasn't really a problem, I would just look perplexed and say that I was popping out to phone the bank. It just meant there was one less bar that I could visit and one less card on the bedside table. Soon, however, there were only two active cards left and I was starting to worry. Walking past a bar near the hotel I saw a sign. *Bar Staff Required.* I told them I was nineteen and had experience working in a bar in Glasgow. They asked me what cocktails I could make and I listed every one I knew, which impressed them enough to start me that night.

Over the next couple of weeks I worked most nights at the bar, studiously collecting glasses and emptying ashtrays to hide my lack of ability at pouring drinks. It was a novelty and I enjoyed the enforced company of my colleagues a lot more than they did. I was full of questions, of course, and they must have been somewhat baffled by this young Scottish guy who appeared to be working shifts in a bar for less than his nightly hotel charge. They didn't know that I was after more than money: I wanted the company and to have a look at the card machine.

It was only in the previous couple of years that bars had started to offer cashback, a service where a customer paying by card could request cash on top of their order when their server swiped their card through the machine. I had been using it sparingly for those times that I needed actual cash but still preferred to pay for everything on the cards themselves. There was something about these machines that made me hesitate, they seemed less predictable than a standard transaction.

As I got down to my last card, it slowly sunk in that I

was going to have to find new sources of funding as the glory days of the notebook came to an end. I had already sourced some free accommodation in the spare room of The Magic Francisco. Frankie was a karaoke DJ who worked several city centre bars and had taken me under his wing after I told him a vague story one night that hinted darkly at an unhappy childhood.

We were an odd pair. Though he was gay (the stage name may have given a clue), nothing romantic ever developed. I think we just mildly interested each other. For me, here was a nice guy who had done a bit of travelling and offered bawdy stories and a spare bedroom. For him, I was company, willing to sit up until the early hours drinking and swapping tall tales. When that last card stopped working, I soon felt guilty about eating Frankie's food and drinking his beer with no means of buying my share.

I was fully aware that all the cards had now been cancelled, and this would spark off a chain of events that could lead to my arrest. I made a conscious decision not to think about it, after all I had more pressing issues to deal with. I had now been sacked from two bar jobs after each in turn had slowly twigged that I didn't have a clue what I was doing, and was down to my last few pounds.

I considered returning to Glasgow, getting another call-centre job and trying to wangle a similar access to card details. I knew that was a long shot though and I wasn't ready to go back yet. Down in Manchester I had freedom and opportunity, even if the easy supply of money that I had brought with me had gone. I *will* make it down here, I declared inwardly, I just had to get hold of some more cards.

It's strange, but at first I didn't make the connection between this burning need and the act of physically stealing a card. I had done it once before but that had been a spontaneous reaction, catalysed by drink and excitement. At this point I was still thinking about other ways of getting hold of people's personal details and security information. I had just spent over a month living hassle-free from the practice, surely I could find a way of doing it some more.

I was probably pondering these exact thoughts as I sat in a bar in the city centre with a man in a suit a few stools down. He took off his jacket and put it on the back of his chair. It registered with me that he had done this but still I do not believe that I had made any decision. It wasn't a part of me to do such a thing, not in the cold reality of a daytime bar and with the risk of capture all around. I'm not brave, and back then I didn't even have guts. Yet, when the man went to the toilet I walked over and slipped my hand inside the jacket pocket. I felt cold leather and grabbed it, walking straight out of the bar.

Back in Frankie's apartment I emptied the wallet onto my bed. There was thirty pounds in cash, various membership cards and one credit card for the National Westminster Bank. It was a Thursday, late opening, so I put the money and card into my pocket and went back into town. From the moment I got off the bus I was in a terrible state, sweating and panicky as I walked through the streets. This was also the debut appearance of my nervous cough, an excitable bark that has gone on to scrape my throat dry all over the world.

When I had walked about with the cards I had got from my notebook, they had made me grow in strength, not feel like this. They had been *mine*. It didn't matter that the names were strange, the cards had come to my house fresh and clean for me to use. The card I had with me now felt dirty and used. It was alien and dangerous, like a grenade in the pocket of my jeans. I should have gone home at that point, for a cold shower and a consideration if this was really a route I should pursue, but onwards I pushed into a boutique clothes store to try my luck.

I'm not a big believer in fate but what then occurred was a pretty savage twist. After I had calmed down, tried on some clothes and taken them to the counter two things happened in quick succession. I gave the sales guy the card and he held it up to examine. At *exactly* the moment he did that one of the (at most) twenty people in the whole of Manchester who knew my name appeared at my shoulder and said, 'Hi, Elliot.' I looked at my friend and then looked back at the sales guy, who looked at my friend and then back at the card. I turned round and ran out the door, *directly* into a policeman. Not exactly to plan, I think it's fair to say. I can laugh thinking about it now but it brought a suitably painful end to a horrific few hours.

The policeman radioed for a car as my friend walked out the shop looking confused.

'Are you OK, Elliot?' he asked.

'I'm fine. Bit of a mix-up,' I said, trying to look unperturbed as the policeman took my arm and led me away.

Back at the station I broke down and explained that I had run away from home in Glasgow and had done this stupid thing just to try to pay for my train journey back. Remarkably, the police didn't observe that it was pretty tricky to buy train tickets from a clothes shop and they actually took pity on me, much more than I deserved. They cautioned me but explained it wasn't definite that it would lead to anything more and suggested I caught an evening train to Glasgow. I agreed and after being released went straight back to Frankie's and packed my stuff. He wasn't in so I left a note.

Going back to Glasgow for a bit mate, speak soon, thanks for everything, Elliot.

I've not spoken to him since. Sorry, Frankie.

CHAPTER NINE

The crime of fraud, when conducted well, is a fascinating and rewarding pursuit. It's a test of intellect, determination and stamina. It demands a love of self-improvement – it needs you to want to get better because if you don't then you'll stop learning and that's when you're in trouble. It is a floating mess of fact and fiction that you have to carry in your mind for twenty-four hours a day. You also have to distil it into your clothes, your speech and the way that you walk. It's about figures, places and names that should never be written down. It can be used to realize dreams, to slip on any mask required. It's very, very hard indeed and it's also extremely worthwhile.

You will have perhaps seen the potential of all this in the last chapter, the trip to London and the notebook and so on, but you have also seen that I couldn't quite get there. I didn't know how. There were too many things missing, and when I got back to Glasgow I found that I lacked the time and space to work it all out. You see, I had no money, and no job. I had parents who were concerned with me and that meant I had to try and avoid them and their questions as well. So I had to leave the house and I had to get money, and so I became a thief. Being a thief is everything that fraud is not. It's brutal and basic and horrible, but I didn't have any choice. I became a thief.

*

A Thief's Top Ten

1   I was staying at a university hall of residence in Glasgow. It was a large, decaying warren of depressing little rooms but I suppose it suited me at the time. If you were a non-student then you could pay a low nightly rental and they accepted all bank cards with little scrutiny. It was also handy, parked slap bang in the middle of town, meaning it tied in nicely with the new daily schedule that I adopted. In summary this was to get up, have something to eat then spend the time before I went back to bed pursuing two aims – to steal bank cards and to get cashback. For the cards I would ride the underground trains, catch buses that took circular routes, drift round cafés, bars and nightclubs. For the cashback I was slowly finding the bars where things were a bit slacker, where the staff were rushed and lazy and didn't care about signatures or an untidy seventeen-year-old paying for everything on plastic.

It was a junkie's existence. From the moment I opened my eyes in the morning I was thinking about where I could get more cards and whether the ones I had would still work. All day long I was a nervous wreck, half-running around Glasgow away from imaginary pursuers. At night I lay awake trying to remember the bars where a blocked card would only elicit an embarrassed apology from the staff, not a phone call to the bank.

One morning there was a knock at my door and I was convinced that it was the police. It was. I was arrested standing in the dank little room with my clothes strewn over the floor. They took me back to the station, charged me and let me go. As I left, the desk sergeant said that he was sure he would see me again. For some reason, it felt like a win.

2 It was coming up to Christmas and I hadn't been home
for a while, telling my parents I was picking up temporary
work around the country. I'd been staying in cheap hotels in
Glasgow or Edinburgh, but even then I needed to generate
around £100 a day just to survive. It had been a hard few
weeks, but I was slowly scrabbling together some insight into
the cashback system. I had some money in my pocket and a
couple of active cards. I wasn't looking forward to seeing my
parents, as I was sure that the police would have been round
by now to follow up one of my recent misdemeanours.

Deciding the best approach would be a distraction of
some significance, I hit upon the less than logical plan of booking a chauffeur-driven Bentley on one of the cards. A confused
driver picked me up at 8 a.m. from a small hotel in Glasgow
city centre in a shiny monster of a car. The back seat was
enormous and I pulled down a tray and popped my newspaper
on it as I instructed him to drive to Edinburgh. Once there I
got him to loop through the town for a bit before parking up
in front of various expensive clothes shops where I made as
much of a fuss as possible to the interest of no one.

After I had bought expensive presents for everyone I
decided it was time for my glorious return to the family home
and we drove back to Glasgow. The driver didn't know
Battlefield well and I had to guide him through the streets,
where he tentatively chugged past bemused locals. As we got
to my house I asked him to press on the horn until my mum
appeared at the window. I climbed out and, grinning inanely,
held up the shopping bags for her to see. She looked at the
bags, the car and back at me, then shook her head and drew
the curtains back closed.

3 I stood at a bus stop in Southside Glasgow thinking about
where I was going to stay that night. The bus pulled up and I

got on, paid my fare and took a seat beside the window.
There was only one other person on the bus, an older man in
a sheepskin jacket who gave me a thumbs up as I sat down
opposite him. He was wearing a Celtic football scarf and I
could smell beer. His head tilted slowly to his shoulder and
after a minute or so I looked over to see that he was sleeping.
In the side pocket of the sheepskin jacket I could see his
wallet. I got up from my seat, plucked it cleanly away and
walked briskly to the door. I could see the bus stop nearing
the bus – *thirty yards, twenty yards, ten* – when he shouted.

'Hey!'

I watched the driver's face in his security mirror. He
didn't react. *Five yards.* The bus was slowing to a stop.

'Hey, you!'

The driver turned his head, unsure of the source. I stood
to the side of his berth, blocking the view down the bus.

'Thank you,' I said to him.

'No bother,' he answered as he released the doors.

I sprang from the bus and ran down the road but I could
hear the brakes hiss as it rolled away, and I stopped to look
back. As the bus rolled past me the man was standing up with
his fists banging on the window. His mouth was moving but
his face wasn't angry. As he passed by behind the glass he
looked a little bit lost, and a little bit hurt.

4a   I stole a card from a party just outside the city at 6 a.m.,
got a taxi straight to Glasgow Queen Street station and caught
the first train to Edinburgh. I walked up the steps of Waverley
station and stood in front of the Balmoral. Grand-looking
businessmen swept out from it with their leather bags and
suit-holders. I was wearing my jeans and a T-shirt, I hadn't
showered from the night before and had no luggage of any
description. It was early in the day and Princes Street was

full with workers on the pavements and buses and taxis scrapping away on the road. I moved to avoid colliding with a man on his phone and I just kept walking – up the stairs, through the revolving door and onwards to the reception desk. The woman behind it watched my approach with increasing alarm. She went to say something but before she could I announced . . .

'I'd like a room please,'

. . . which made her frown.

'I'll be paying with . . . this,' I said, and placed my new card on the polished glass with great gravity.

Ten minutes later I was sitting in a small room facing a security guard whose skin was red and sweaty under his uniform and whose shoulders rose and fell as his breathing slowly returned to normal. I was tired as well with the running and the panic, and my hand was scraped where it had caught a lamppost.

Twenty minutes later I was in Gayfield Square police station where they charged me and let me go to steal some more.

46   The Balmoral incident hit me hard. I didn't like to think about London, about Bond Street and the people I had seen there. It was supposed to have been the beginning of something extraordinary. It was supposed to signal my lift-off into another world. Yet now I found myself going through a daily hell to get £30 cashback here, maybe £50 there. I was having to steal cards every day, to *see* the people whom I would stalk for hours with my eyes on the bulge in their pockets. I wanted desperately to get back to what I had with the notebook, access to the rewards without dirtying myself with this horrific exposure to the crime. But I couldn't. I just didn't know.

how to do it, how to get the information, and I couldn't bring myself to study it. I was too busy trying to survive.

What I could do, however, was try to look the part. And so it was that I threw caution to the wind and within a few weeks bought a laptop computer, an Armani suit and some Thomas Pink shirts. I had left my Vuitton bag at home as it clashed too obviously with my normal wardrobe but I threw that back into the mix as well and put the whole outfit together one night in the Glasgow Holiday Inn. As I stood in front of the mirror wearing the suit, with my bag over one shoulder and the laptop in its case on the other I was momentarily startled. Where before there had been a young man with shifty eyes stood an affluent young businessman. A go-getter who could be planted effortlessly into any environment. His eyes were still a little shifty, but I could work on that.

5 I was lying in bed in a particularly grim hotel in Ayr, drinking instant hot chocolate and watching a fly-on-the-wall documentary about a hotel in Liverpool called the Adelphi. It was apparently a famous old place that was now a little rough around the edges but still had a glamorous pull for people of a certain age. The next day I caught a train down to Liverpool and checked into the Adelphi's Presidential Suite. I should have stayed in Ayr. The room was stale and murky so I didn't hang about for longer than it took to shower before heading out into town.

I had taken to wearing my Armani suit on the majority of occasions. It made me feel a bit more positive about my miserable existence and it also tied in well with my new cover story that I was a hotel consultant. It didn't make much sense but people rarely questioned me on it and it explained the suit, the travelling and the frivolous use of bank cards. So I was in my suit in Liverpool when I stumbled across a sleek bar where I explained my hotel consultant background to a friendly barman who idly mixed my cocktails. The two of us remained virtually alone for most of the mid-week evening and by the end of the night we were getting on not too badly at all. I left a spectacular tip and told him I'd be back the following evening.

'Good morning, Mr Devine, sorry to inconvenience you but I'm having a problem with your payment details down here, could you possibly pop down for a minute?'

That's the telephone call that I woke up to the next day. Mr Devine's card sat on the bedside table, but Mr Devine had clearly noticed that it was no longer in his possession. I jumped out of bed, put on my suit, bundled everything else together and cautiously opened the door. No one. Lucky, I thought as I walked down the corridor, through a fire escape and, five floors later, out into the alley behind the hotel. I had enough money for lunch but no other cards in my possession and being laden with luggage made the chances of nicking one pretty rare. Panic slowly began to set in as the day wore on with me sitting in various bars waiting for an opportunity that failed to arrive. It was getting later and later when I finally recognized the place from the night before. Luckily he was working again.

I paid for my cocktail and a large tip with the last money I had, then took the call on my mobile in front of the bar.

'He's *what*?' I asked incredulously. 'But he's supposed to be picking me up in twenty minutes for my flight. He's got my credit card with him.'

The barman looked up with a faint interest.

'Well what am I supposed to do?' I demanded angrily. 'Where am I supposed to stay?' I shook my head, ran my

hand through my hair. 'Oh *God*,' I said as I hung up and put
the phone back in my suit pocket, looking thoughtful.

The next day I woke up on the barman's couch as he
stood above me. A woman stood behind him, peering doubt-
fully at the suit and bags that lay beside me.

'Hey, man,' he said, looking a little bit sad. 'We've got to
go to work, so if you could . . .'

'Yeah, no problem,' I said, 'I'm going.'

6 I was in Manchester where I had stolen two cards from
the front desk of a well-known hotel and another one from a
man in an art gallery when he had taken his jacket off to
explain something to his son. I walked to the station and got
on the London train. I pulled out my laptop and switched it
on. The screensaver appeared as the computer warmed up,
showing a photo I had found on the Internet of a desert
island. The sun beat down on a small beach where the sand
was smooth and untouched and a hammock hung between
two palms. As I looked once more at this image it cut away
to the start-up screen and I selected Solitaire.

I played it all the way to London, where I got off and
walked into the busy forecourt of Euston station. I was
standing there thinking about nothing in particular when I
was suddenly overcome with an intense unease. It came as
a barrage of thoughts and pressure that left me reeling. I
dropped my bags at my feet and put my hands over my face.
I could feel a sweat form under my suit as the onslaught
slowed and crystallized. I pulled my hands from my face as
I saw the reasoning, which was just as frightening as the
confusion. As I stood and watched all these people walking
past me – going places, doing things, planning things, talking
to other people on their mobile phones – I could only think
one thought. That I had *nothing* to do.

7   I was in the Spy Bar, which liked to position itself as the most exclusive bar in Glasgow. I had been coming here on and off since my Imagine days, buying gargantuan rounds and being generally irritating. This night I was a bit too drunk and a bit too bold and I ordered three rounds in quick succession and paid with three different cards in three different names. Even in the most laid-back, unassuming venue that was going to be spotted.

As I handed over the third card I realized my mistake, it was the same barman from one of the earlier orders. If I had been a little more discreet then perhaps he would not have noticed the disparity in the names, but I had been anything but and I saw his face in the mirror as he paused on his way to the card machine. He began to turn back towards me but I had already started to run for the door. The bar was busy and I pushed people out of the way as I ran. I could see the door in the distance through the swarm of bodies and I put my head down and barged, squirmed and rammed my way through. I was probably a yard or two short when the bouncer caught me.

Lying in the police cell that night I felt sure that I was to be put in prison. The charges were slowly racking up and I must have missed a court case by now. On my last journey home I had found a pile of official-looking letters on my bed that remained unopened when I left. Yet after breakfast it was the same drill – charge, sign the paper and I was back out a free man. They even gave me back the cash I had had in my wallet. I hailed a taxi and asked for Queen Street station. The driver eased away from the kerb.

'What were you up to in there?' he said, jerking his head back towards the station.

'Visiting a client,' I answered, 'I'm a lawyer.'

'Oh, right, aye,' said the driver in mild acceptance.

'He's been stealing credit cards.'

The driver looked up. 'What for?'

'Drinking, clothes, food, a laptop,' I said, looking out the window at the normal people going to work in the cold morning sunshine. 'Hotels.'

'Hotels!' said the driver, his voice high in surprise. He laughed out loud, looked at me in the mirror, and then laughed again.

'Cheeky bastard.'

8 After grafting away for weeks on end, I had around £3,000 in cash for my bravest outing yet. The first twenty went on the taxi from Euston station where the driver kept nicking looks at me as I tried to appear indifferent to the destination I had given. Then I got out and two men helped me with my bags. As one took them away on a trolley the other leaped in front of me to open the door. 'Welcome to the Ritz, sir,' he beamed as he gestured inside the building.

I had left nothing to chance. It was a strictly cash booking (£650, not including breakfast or tax) in my own name and so I breezed through the checking-in process and followed the porter to my room. It was even better than I expected – ornate, glamorous and elegant. I imagined that this was how Buckingham Palace would look, with the rich wall-paper and antique furniture. I tipped the porter and walked over to the double windows that opened onto Piccadilly. Below me I watched the doorman escort an old man with silver hair from a taxi. I went and lay down on my bed. *The Ritz*. And I was untouchable, safe. There wasn't a card respon-sible that someone would start searching through his or her pockets for at any moment. The clouds were lifting, I began to understand. This was why I had been going through the days, weeks, and months of pain. To bring me to places like this. The world I had seen through the grey curtain on the plane to Chile and then in agonizing glimpses ever since. It was here, it was in my hand. If I could just get a bit better, a bit smarter, then I could have this *all the time*.

9 Just outside Manchester, in the first-class carriage of the Glasgow train, the conductress arrived at my shoulder. I smiled and handed her the card. As I tried to concentrate on my newspaper I was aware that she was pausing, turning the card in her hand. I could feel the tickle rising in my throat when the card was pushed back towards me.

'Thank you, enjoy the journey,' she said simply and walked away down the aisle.

It was shortly after this that the tannoy crackled.

'Would anyone with medical experience please make themselves known to the train staff. We have a passenger who has been taken unwell.'

This amused me somewhat as the card in my pocket belonged to a doctor. Unfortunately for the passenger, I thought, I only had a first aid certificate to back it up. I went back to my newspaper but felt a little peckish. The first-class attendant was nowhere to be seen so I got up and walked through to the buffet cart. I took my place in the queue and smiled at the conductress who was now sitting at a table with a fraught-looking woman. As I saw her eyes thin slightly in thought I was hit with the sickening stream of knowledge – *the card, she's seen it, she read it, that's the sick passenger, you fucking idiot Elliot, now she's going to . . .*

'You're a doctor, aren't you?'

At first things weren't too bad. I used my real name, presuming we would be done in a matter of minutes. I sat facing the passenger and she told me that she had started to feel really panicky, and had struggled for breath. I told her it sounded like she had suffered a panic attack. Two genuine doctors showed up, an older Chinese man and a younger Asian woman. They fortunately agreed with my diagnosis, and the Chinese man suggested that the woman go to hospital. The conductress picked up her walkie-talkie and told us she would get an ambulance to meet us at the next station.

The passenger looked much happier with this, she smiled and thanked us doctors but was especially grateful towards me. The other two drifted off but she started to tell me some more about her situation. She'd been visiting her family in England and was nervous about going back to her boyfriend in Glasgow for one reason or another.

'Is anyone,' she said from nowhere, 'able to come with me to the hospital?'

She looked at me, the conductress looked at me. I couldn't think of . . .

'OK,' I said with a sickly smile. 'I'll come.'

So then we were in the ambulance – the passenger, a slightly suspicious paramedic, and a disbelieving Dr Castro who was looking pretty panic-stricken himself.

'How old are you mate?'

'Twenty-seven.'

'How long have you been practising?'

'Two years.'

'What area?'

'Neurosurgery.'

That shut the nosey bastard up. We drove through the Cumbria countryside in silence the rest of the way, watching as snow began to fall and lie in the fields that we passed by. When we arrived at the hospital in Carlisle the paramedic pushed the passenger on a trolley and I walked nervously behind. The two of us were left in a booth until a breathless nurse shot round the corner.

'There's been a major car accident just outside Carlisle,' she said excitedly. 'Can you check this lady out yourself? We don't have any free doctors right now.'

I explained I was actually a neurosurgeon and, for my own peace of mind, could one of the *regular guys* do it? The nurse went away and didn't come back. The two of us chatted away some more but the situation was becoming a little strained. To be perfectly honest, there was quite clearly nothing wrong with her at this stage and I was expecting to be asked for my full details at any moment. The nurse re-appeared, there were still no doctors. I took a stethoscope and, asking the passenger to lean forward, slid it up her back. I had seen this on *Casualty*, and the nurse looked comfortable enough. After getting her to breathe in and out a bit, and doing a fair amount of frowning I handed the nurse the stethoscope.

'She's fine, could you get us a taxi to the train station please?'

Both of them looked relieved to have the farce over with and soon the stricken passenger and I were at Carlisle station, where we were met with bad news. The snow had meant trains were going no further north. Instead the train company was sending any remaining passengers by taxi to Glasgow. If your ticket was for a journey even further north than that then you would be put up in a hotel in Glasgow for the night. Ever alert, I slipped off to the machine and bought two tickets to Aberdeen.

We shared a taxi with two other men so I sat in the back beside my patient. She was tired now and I think a bit embarrassed about the whole ordeal. I slipped her one of the Aberdeen tickets and explained that she could use that to get a hotel for the night in Glasgow. She looked a bit confused so I added that this would give her an extra night away from her boyfriend. As we drove through the snow to Glasgow I could hear her breathing shorten and I took her hand, squeezing it and telling her to relax, we were nearly home. The last thing I needed was for her to suffer some sort of relapse and my medical non-talent to be called for again. She quietened down but was acting a bit strangely and when we arrived in Glasgow she asked to be dropped off quite suddenly at some traffic lights, pausing only to thank me again.

'No problem,' I said, 'I'm just glad it all worked out.' Which I was.

From the cheap hotel room they gave me that night I called my mum and told her the story, though with my doctoral status replaced by good Samaritan. We hadn't spoken for a while and she was pleased to hear from me but she didn't really seem to be listening. I could tell she was waiting to tell me something or other about the family and finally she butted in.

'They're looking for you, Elliot, the police.'

'I know,' I said. 'It's fine, I've sorted it out,' I lied.

10 It had been nearly eighteen months since the university halls of residence and the first days of cashback and I. Now when I was in Glasgow city centre I could stop and bring up a specific map in my head. It would tell me what bars were in the vicinity, what machines they had and what bank they were with. I now knew that different banks had different cashback policies. For example, HSBC machines would let up to £30 go through without contacting the bank for authorization. Barclays and a few others would check every penny. I knew the machines as well. I knew what every pause meant, every beep. I knew when to hold 'em and when to fold 'em and run like a madman out the door. I knew the bars and shops that I had to cross the road to avoid, where I was a known face and not in a good way.

But I wasn't in Glasgow on this particular day, I was walking through Aberdeen city centre in my Armani suit with a room key in my pocket for one of the city's finest hotel suites. I passed the large court building and decided to pop my head in. I was interested in courts and the legal system, which I guess was kind of lucky considering my line of business. The foyer was bustling with gowned lawyers rushing about and various guilty-looking characters in dusted-down suits following sullenly behind. I looked at the lawyers with admiration, drawn to their gowns and the knowing way they bore their power.

I left and found a local bar where I ordered a large lunch and a bottle of expensive wine. It was a busy little place with a couple of young barmen going about their work happily enough so after eating I settled at the bar and ordered a drink and some cashback. I had two cards in my pocket and both were getting older by the day, I had to get some money off them *now*.

Ten minutes later I waited until the barman who had served me was collecting glasses and made a similar order from his colleague. He poured my pint and ran the other card through the machine but then the phone rang and he went to answer it. The original barman arrived back behind the bar as the machine coughed up the receipt.

I was frozen to my stool watching this unfold, I just didn't seem to be able to move. He picked up the receipt and the card and walked towards me, looking at both intently. He stopped before me and leant forward, resting one palm on the bar as he handed me the card. Behind him the machine started to beep.

'If you want to get out of here, mate, you'd better go right now...' His voice trailed off as he looked over my shoulder. I turned and saw a fat man carrying a large box of crisps and a tray of soft drinks. He had a cigarette in his mouth and a ring of keys in one of his belt buckles. Through the open door I could see an estate car with its boot propped open and more cardboard boxes inside.

'What's going on?' he said, looking at us then the beeping machine.

'That's what I would like to know,' I answered. I said it without thinking and it didn't sound like me. I carried on talking, telling them both that I was a lawyer from Manchester and was using a client's card with his full and legal permission. Was there a problem? The fat man looked bamboozled, then something caught his eye out the door.

'Hey, can you boys sort this out?' he shouted at the two passing policemen, and my heart sank a little.

Those are some examples from hundreds. They didn't all happen *exactly* like that; it's a few years ago now, after all. Some of them might be combinations of incidents or they might not, these things tend to blend together. Some of the cases are bang on because I've got them summarized right here in papers in my cell. If I'm honest with you there are some things I can remember that I would rather not mention, although I do regret them. But that lot gives you a pretty good idea of what life became for me as 1999 turned into 2000 and then 2001 while I ran and stole my way around Britain.

Prison was always coming, the only surprise was how I ended up there. With all these warrants swirling about – from captures and cock-ups and crimes being uncovered in my

wake. With procurators fiscal and the Crown Prosecution
Service in separate cities slowly starting to piece these incidents together. With maybe thirty policemen by now having
my name and description etched somewhere in their note-
books. With staff in bars and hotels all over the place ready
to call the police the minute they saw me. With a few dozen
of my victims going about their everyday business with my
image angrily engraved on their brain. With all that going on,
what did they do me for?

Impersonating a fucking doctor.

Can you believe it?

CHAPTER TEN

It was that fat landlord in Aberdeen shouting out to the two policemen that did for me. They picked up on an outstanding warrant from Glasgow and sent me through there the next day. Incredibly, the duty lawyer managed to get me bail once more and it was while I was pondering the generosity of the system, and planning my afternoon's movements, that he reappeared.

'There's a couple of policemen here from Cumbria, Elliot,' he said, 'wanting to take you down there.' He looked at me blankly. I looked at him blanker.

The two coppers did little to enlighten me, bundling me into the back of their car and driving off without a word of explanation. This bad cop/bad cop routine was slightly dented by the fact that they had to ask me for directions out of Glasgow but they soon regained their composure and answered my questions with stern looks in the rear-view mirror or cryptically foreboding comments.

I remember thinking as we approached Carlisle what a coincidence it was that this was where I had suffered that embarrassing business with the woman on the train. Still I didn't make the connection and I was no closer to realizing my position when the duty solicitor came and found me in the holding cell. They had arrested me, he explained, on suspicion of indecent assault.

'What?'

'Indecent assault, Mr Castro. Do you know what that is?'

I didn't know exactly but it certainly didn't sound great. The solicitor was a nice guy – James McLean was his name – and he studied my reaction. He was a smartly dressed man in his early fifties who had the typical directness of the northerner, and was clearly in the process of sizing up my honesty. I wasn't acting, I had absolutely no idea what he was talking about and said so.

'I think, Mr Castro, we had better go and find out what this is all about.'

We joined two detectives in an interview room. Slowly, slowly it emerged what had happened. They talked about the hospital, and some woman's name I vaguely recognized, then a stethoscope, then something about me holding this woman's hand. It was clear where this was going and I had to reluctantly head it off at the pass. I didn't want to say it, but it seemed the only way.

'I'm gay,' I told them. My face burned and my heart raced. This was the first time I had said it like this, acknowledged it. One of the policemen rolled his eyes and said, 'Here Willie we go.' The other shook his head sadly and James McLean wrote something on a piece of paper. It wasn't quite the reaction I was looking for.

The police charged me with indecent assault and fraud. They might have been way off-target on my indecent use of a stethoscope but they had been pretty smart on another front, tracing the stolen card with which I had bought the two tickets to Aberdeen. 'I'll get bail?' I asked, confidently enough, but James McLean never really answered me.

Sure enough, the next day at Carlisle Magistrate's Court I was refused bail for the first time in my life and realized with horror that I was about to experience prison life for the first time. I felt physically sick as I was led back down to the holding cell and the minute the security guard closed the door

I started crying. Steps sounded from the corridor and I cleaned myself up in time for another young guy to be led into the room.

I stared at the floor, worried that an attempt to make contact would lead to me breaking down again. I was pretty confident that bursting into tears in front of a fellow prisoner wasn't going to be the most effective way of introduction. Another two guys arrived shortly after and then the four of us were led to a police van and driven off. A police officer sat in the back with us.

'Not a fucking word,' he said as he got in, and there wasn't.

Not much time passed until the van slowed and the doors cracked open. There was a glimpse of a modern-looking building surrounded by barbed wire and floodlights before we were taken inside to another holding cell. The door was locked on us and the silence started to build, but I couldn't take the creeping tension and broke first.

'Where are we?' I asked.

The suspense broken, we all started speaking at once. None of us had been in a prison before so there were far more questions than answers and then a guard appeared and called one of the boys out. He came back for the others in turn until there was just me left. Finally, he took me to a desk where two more guards stood. One started asking me if I knew why I was here, and I noticed that he was Scottish.

'Whereabouts in Scotland are you from?' I said with a patriotic wink. He stopped talking and his face darkened.

'I ask the fucking questions here, sonny, got that?' He looked like he was about to hit me. I nodded. His colleague asked me why I was here. I answered politely that I had been charged with indecent assault and he looked at me strangely.

'I wouldn't be telling anyone that in here, son,' he said, looking a little incredulous at my naivety. They made me change into a blue shirt and starched jeans, empty what possessions I had into a plastic bag, then pick up a pillow and some sheets.

'Castro, CC9127. Welcome to Lancaster Farms.'

Lancaster Farms Young Offenders Prison was actually not a bad nick but, being my first, it was always going to be a shock to the system. I walked to my cell with my eyes firmly on the floor and found myself in a room about ten feet by seven. There was a steel bed bolted to the floor, a small sink, a toilet and nothing else. I made up my bed and lay down. Try to think positively, I thought. At least I wasn't sharing with some lunatic who would slit my throat in the middle of the night. And with that cheery thought, I went to sleep.

Waking up in prison wasn't a good feeling and neither was the knowledge that in a week's time I would probably be sent back there. To make matters even worse, indecent assault clearly wasn't going to be a conviction that would make a stay in prison any easier. Just to top things off, I hadn't spoken to my parents in a couple of weeks and was now going to phone them from a prison in Carlisle.

Daylight struggled through the small barred window that was set back into the wall, but there was no way of telling the time. There were noises here and there and then I heard the guards walking down the landing, opening the cell doors as they went. My door swung open and I turned in my bed and stared at this portal into a terrifying new world. As I did so, several bodies rushed past. My interest outweighing my fear, I got up and made my way out to the landing.

I was on the second floor of the wing, which was

contained in a large open space with a walkway ringing the
walls and running past my cell. I leant over the handrail to
see a mob of other boys dressed like me crowding around
one guard. He stood scribbling on a clipboard as they formed
a tense, writhing queue in front of him. Beyond this chaotic
scene was a large area of seating that fanned around a
television, and then a couple of snooker tables. In the corner
hung a sign marked *Shower* with a guard standing in front of
it. I made my way down.

'You on the list?' asked the guard as I approached.

'No, how do I . . .' He stopped me by pointing at the
other boys, and the scrum for the clipboard.

'Is there a phone I can use?' He pointed in the same
direction.

'For the phone?' I said, confused.

'Aye, *furr the fowen*,' he answered, with a terrible Scottish
accent. 'And for the snooker, and for everything else except
sleeping and shitting. And do you know what?' he asked,
nodding over to the others. I turned to see most of the boys
dispersing in various directions. 'You're too fucking late,'
said the guard, and laughed with the abandon of the truly
stupid.

So that day I didn't make a phone call, I didn't have a
shower and I didn't play snooker. Another guard explained to
me that this mayhem was Association, a two-hour period
each day when these luxury activities were allowed. First you
had to get on the list, and the list tended to be full five
minutes into Association. I told him I'd be earlier the next
day and he said I could be as early as I wanted the next day
but it wouldn't make any difference. Tomorrow was Monday,
he imparted authoritatively, and Association was in the evening because everyone would be at Work or Education during
the day. I was only on remand, so where would I be?

'In your cell,' he said.

'All day?' I asked.

'No,' he said. 'You're allowed out to eat.'

For the rest of the day I ached with anger at the hope-lessness of my position. I didn't make any attempt to speak to other inmates because I didn't particularly want to. There was still a chance that my stay would be short and if the other boys would leave me alone then that was fine with me. It was, after all, what I was used to.

The next day I ate breakfast alone at a corner table and then went back to my cell. A few hours later my door was opened. I went downstairs and ate my lunch, then went back to my cell. A few hours after that I did the same for dinner. Then I stood beside my door, flexing and bouncing, ready to run. The flap opened and a pair of eyes looked at me.

'What the *fuck* are you doing?'

'Is it Association now?'

'No, you prick, it's not. We're doing The Count. Association is when we finish doing The Count.'

'When's that?'

'When do you think?'

'When you've finished counting?'

'When we've finished counting.' And he shut the flap.

I didn't move though, I stood right there beside the door until they came back along the walkway and opened it. I flew through the doorway and ran along the landing, down the stairs and towards the guard with the clipboard. Other boys overtook me or came from other angles but I got there not too far from the front. I could feel the guy behind me breathing down my neck as the guard started to work his way down the line and I drew myself up as tall as I could. I was waiting for some form of assault from behind but it never came and then the guard was looking at me coldly.

'Yes?'

'Could I get a phone call and a shower please?'

'You can have a phone call, shower's full.'

It was good enough. I gave him my number and he gave me a time. I didn't want to risk missing it so I went and stood beside the phone where a guard refereed another untidy queue. My turn came and the phone rang and rang and I thought *Oh, Jesus surely not* but then she picked up . . .

'Hello?'

'Hi, Mum, it's Elliot.'

'Where are you?'

'Prison.'

By the end of my week on remand I was dreading my day in court, largely because it had the power to send me back to prison. Over seven days I had not spoken more than a couple of sentences to anyone. Apart from mealtimes and the anarchy of Association, I had stewed in my cell with nothing to occupy my mind other than my pending sentence.

I had managed to make two phone calls to Mum. They had been three minutes long and interrupted by the shouts and obscenities of the other prisoners waiting in the queue. What she had managed to get across was that she and the rest of the family loved me and I had to get myself out of this latest trouble and back to Battlefield. What I had managed to get across was that I would do my best and could she send me some stamps.

When I got to court James McLean came and saw me. He told me that they were dropping the indecent assault case, which was a huge relief, and replacing it with something called common assault. I asked him what that meant and he said it was pretty much the lowest level of physical crime you

could get. For example, said James McLean, if I was to put
my hand on your shoulder without your consent then that is
common assault.

That sounded like a good development, I ventured, in
fact that sounded like a very good development indeed. James
McLean agreed but not too enthusiastically as he also had
some bad news. The prosecution were sticking with the
fraud charge for the tickets purchase and had caught everyone on the hop by rustling up the charge of impersonating a
doctor.

James McLean told me that someone at the CPS had
obviously been in an eager mood when this one came in.
When he had checked the records, he had failed to find
another example of the crime being punished in the last fifty
years. Ordinarily, such a nugget would have been of interest
to me and I'd have met it with a barrage of questions
approaching common assault in itself, but right now it served
only as a rather surreal kick in the balls.

We sat in the small cell contemplating this unexpected
turn. He was a decent man, James McLean, and I think he
saw me as a good kid in hock to some demon or other. When
I asked him if I was going back to prison he looked genuinely
pained. He said that he would do his best and you never
knew, but it was the fraud that was going to be the hardest.
All these things together, he explained with understatement,
looked a little bit off.

Up in the courtroom I stood in a windowed box beside
a security guard. I pleaded guilty to the female magistrate and
then spent the rest of the time adopting various remorseful
and tortured expressions. James McLean put on a fine show,
portraying me as a harmless kid who had got a little bit
carried away. At one point I peeped behind me and saw a

small mob watching proceedings and taking notes. Once James McLean had finished talking, the prosecution had their say before the magistrate announced without much pre-amble that I was sentenced to four months in prison.

Back down I went to the holding cell and, after a quick piece of encouragement from James McLean, it was back to Lancaster Farms. I had accepted in my mind that I'd be making this journey, and the fact that my stay in jail was now given finite definition removed some tension. It was late and dark by the time they processed me again and this time I was sure to announce boldly 'Common assault' when asked for my crime.

That night I enjoyed the best sleep since I had arrived in prison and woke up in a frame of mind that was veering towards the positive. I could be out of here and back into the madness in two months if I kept my head down. Maybe I hadn't given prison a fair crack of the whip.

With this new sunny outlook I signed up for Education the next day, managing to slip into the popular IT classes thanks to a fictional degree from good old Cambuslang College. Over lunch I even made contact with a group of boys, which went pretty well until one of them asked for a burn. The fact that I was unaware this meant cigarette caused great hilarity and they gave me a crash course in prison slang. Most importantly, 'guards' were out, to be replaced with relish by 'screws'. They asked what I was in for and I told them I had hot-wired a car and crashed it into a police van.

'Shame you didn't kill the bastards,' said one of the boys, and I urgently agreed.

That evening I managed to sprint along the landing in time for another three-minute call and, all in all, was feeling not too bad when my mum came on the line and explained to me what the people taking notes in the courtroom had been doing.

....

EXCLUSIVE: GLASGOW CONMAN LOCKED UP
Teenager caged for living out sick movie fantasy
Glasgow Evening Times, 6 April 2001
....
BOGUS MEDIC IS JAILED
Daily Express, 7 April 2001
....
BOGUS DOCTOR PROMPTS REVIEW
Glasgow Herald, 7 April 2001
....
WALTER MITTY MD GETS FOUR MONTHS
Teenage trickster who examined woman in hospital is detained
Daily Mail, 7 April 2001
....
JAIL FOR BOGUS DOCTOR
Scotsman, 7 April 2001
....
FAKE DOC AGED 18 FOOLS 2 REAL GPS
Sun, 7 April 2001
....

Back when I was young and my mum was teaching me at home in Logie, there was an hour in the morning that I hated. After breakfast I would go through to the front room and lay out my books, my paper and pencils. I would read for a while or practise words on the paper, but there was no satisfaction in doing it by myself and every so often I would get up and walk to the kitchen door.

My mother would be sitting on the thin wooden chair, her back crooked as she leant over her newspaper. Even if I walked round the table and stood facing her she wouldn't flinch, though I knew that she could see me. When she eventually finished reading she would look up and smile, or call me through from my sulking in the front room. I would dart to her shoulder and she would leaf back through those vast pages of words and photos.

'Now, where was it now?' she would ask aloud, and then, 'Ah, yes,' and she would point to that day's story. Sometimes it was an exciting tale – a distant earthquake, flood or uprising – other times it would be something more complicated. A black and white face who had either done something very bad or very good, according to Mum. And it was only after we had gone through this daily ritual that we could both head off to the front room and the learning could begin.

It's maybe not surprising that newspapers – with their foreign stories and daily trivia – interested me greatly, but they held other attractions as well. I enjoyed the overpowering feeling of information they contained. From society columnists to business writers, political analysis to thundering editorials. They were written with such confidence and certainty, it made me feel included and trusted to read these things.

When I was scampering about in my Armani suit I would have a *Financial Times* or other broadsheet tucked under my arm, but it was more than a prop. I liked reading about things I had no knowledge of because it gave me the motivation to keep going, to keep trying to improve myself in one way or another. I'd never really noticed that there was another side to all this; that behind all the words and the photos lay people.

That day when Mum told me that I was in the newspapers I was excited at first, until she began to tell me some of the things that they were saying. She had been phoned up herself and given typically straightforward views on my predicament but they had been thrown into a mess of guesswork and some pretty suspicious contributions. Several of the papers had talked about my sexuality but I never knew this until years later as Mum acted as censor and hid those cuttings from my dad.

I suppose I can see the funny side of these stories when I read them now. Some report that I had 'stroked' the lady's hand and suggested that we share a hotel room in such a way as to make me sound like a mix between Sid James and Jack the Ripper. Elsewhere, several of the papers managed instantly to dredge up unnamed friends of mine for suitable quotes, a process not hampered by the fact I didn't have a single friend in the world at the time. Curiously, all these friends gave helpful comparisons to Walter Mitty.

My favourite, and I think it would have to be anyone's favourite, is the daring scoop of the *Evening News*. I can only salute their powers of deduction in their revelation that I was acting out a plot from a movie released in 1990, when I was eight years old. Unbeknown to anyone, let alone myself, I had apparently spent the ten years since roaming the British Isles, looking for an opportunity to act out a scene loosely similar to one from the movie.

(The movie, in case you were wondering, was called *Iron Mask*. I've never got round to seeing it, though it sounds like a cracker.)

They wouldn't have had to do any of that, the wild tangents and the speculation, if they had just listened to James

McLean when they were in the courtroom. I wasn't a sicko, a rampant sexual predator or a wannabe doctor. Maybe I *was* a bit of a fantasist, a Walter Mitty, I wouldn't deny that. The fact at the heart of the truth was far simpler, and perhaps less interesting as a result. I was a thief who decided to visit the buffet cart.

Mum's phone call left me chastened. My mother had been encouraged by the reaction of people in Battlefield, who had assured her that they knew I was a good boy at heart and certainly no nasty pervert, but she was understandably upset about having me feature in the papers in such a manner. I could only apologize once more, not having the time to take her through the quite unbelievable chain of events that had led to this situation.

Hearing Mum upset sent guilt crashing through me and I hated the fact that the people in Battlefield would have read those stories. I wanted them to think of me as the boy who had been driven through the streets in a Bentley, or who was rumoured to have stayed in the Ritz Hotel; not as a loony prowling about with a stethoscope. The only way I was going to wipe out these stories, I decided, was with future achievements that would render them insignificant.

What form these successes would take was unclear but I soon had more pressing concerns as the next day events took a further turn for the worse. Breakfast passed without incident and I enjoyed the escapism of my first IT class that morning. At lunch, however, everything changed a little bit. I went to sit beside the group of boys I had been eaten with the day before and they removed the spare seat as I approached. I stood there with my tray, stunned by the undisguised hostility, and then wandered off to eat alone.

All afternoon I tried to work out what had happened. One of them was in the IT class and I tried to catch his eye as we left. He shook his head as he walked past me. 'What's your problem?' I said weakly, trotting after him like a puppy. He snapped his head round and hissed, 'Fuck off.' At dinner they looked at me with a startling level of disgust and I was relieved to get back to my cell intact.

I was painfully aware of my traditional talent for alienating my peers, but this was a new record by any standards and I had to find out what had occurred. When Association began I stood in my doorway until I saw one of my band of new enemies approaching. He was the smallest and quietest of the group and I stood in the middle of the landing so he couldn't pass.

'What's going on, mate?' I said to him. His eyes were evasive and he took a half-step back.

'Not much.' He looked around us but there was no one else there. He turned back to me sharply and said, 'You're a nonce. He says that you're a nonce.'

'Who does?'

'A screw, he saw it in the paper,' he said and scurried past me.

CHAPTER ELEVEN

Originally the prison term 'nonce' was an official acronym meaning Not of Normal Criminal Element. At one point or another, it was hijacked by the prisoners and turned into shorthand for perverts, rapists, sexual assaulters, child molesters or some gruesome combination of this ensemble. It's a badge of dishonour borne by those wretched inmates who spend their sentences looking over their shoulders, with beatings and stabbings round every corner.

Fortunately or unfortunately, 'nonce' was one of the slang terms that I had picked up and so I was uncomfortably aware of the danger that I was now in. I tried desperately to reason with the inmates who had heard of the anonymous screw's labelling of me. Only aggression and vague threats came back and my protestations just seemed to act as another form of confirmation that the story was true.

I had discovered a prison reality – that if an unflattering rumour grows around you, then you are in a bad situation that will only get worse. It may have been a young offenders' prison, but they knew their prison protocol and the other boys sent me to Coventry in a clinical and determined manner while the screws knowingly watched the whole business unfold.

I could handle that – inhabiting my own world was not exactly a new phenomenon for me – but it was the constant presence of physical danger that haunted me. As I walked about the landings and corridors, ate my meals at my single table and sat in the IT classes I could feel unspoken threats all around me. The speed at which I was fulfilling my class work meant I was soon spending much of my time typing out memos for the screws. If it was possible, this made me hated even more.

I stopped calling home unless I desperately needed something sent down because I knew I wouldn't be able to hide my troubled mind from my mum, whether she acknowledged it or not. My only real escape was the books I could borrow from the prison library, but this was limited for some strange reason to three copies a week. I would be unable to stop myself from racing through them, which then left me with a gaping period of anguish at the end of each week.

It was moving towards summer now and it was still light outside when we were locked up for the night at 8 p.m. My cell faced west and so I would watch the sky redden and the bars stretch as shadows across the floor of the cell. The days when I had no books to read I would lie on my side and watch the progress of the shadows as they moved over the stone. When it grew dark I would turn onto my back and try desperately to empty my head. Then sleep would be followed by morning, and the danger of a new day.

Two things saved me from this torturous cycle. The first was the passage of time, and the growing realization that physical attack was becoming less likely as a result. The screw that had passed on my undeserved nonce status had perhaps been considerate enough to insert me at the lower end of the pervert scale. Between the inmates and myself there seemed to be an unspoken agreement that I would be spared as long as I made no attempt to engage anyone in any way.

The other salvation was the arrival of a letter from James McLean. In what was a generous and unprovoked gesture, he wished me well and suggested that I used my time inside to plan towards a more positive future. I'm sure he meant for me to look around prison and see the error of my ways, which in a way I did. I looked back on the year or two of thieving and the things that I had done and I realized where I had gone wrong. I had got caught.

Suddenly I felt energized again. I had all this secret time on my hands, where no one could get to me or harm me, nearly twelve hours a night. This was what I had kept telling myself that I needed when I was justifying that horrible existence to myself. Some space to develop a system, something that would remove the inevitability of eventual capture.

Rather than dread my cell door being swung shut at eight o'clock and leaving me with my thoughts and the shadows, I began to spend my days typing prison memos looking forward to the privacy and opportunity of my empty evenings. In my cell I would sit in the bunk as the sun set beyond the bars and run through what I had done – right back to the first card, and the police on the platform at Largs station. I'd lie in the dark and go through the Imagine days and then right down to the dirtiest, grubbiest bits of stealing I had committed.

I picked out occasions at random and ran them in my head, trying to see what went right and what went wrong. Some mistakes were easy to spot and some successes could be put down purely to luck. The Imagine cards pulled the hardest. They were the closest to a form of system, some advancement over simple stealing and the limitations that it brought.

Still I was blocked by a lack of knowledge. The card system itself had been revealed to me only in snatches of discovery – the failure of the banks to follow up the wrongly delivered cards, the inner workings of a card machine. I needed to get stronger and more specific information, I needed to get closer to the process.

The other thing I needed was to give myself more protection – I needed the banks to take longer to work out what I was doing. The harder it was for them, the more time I got with the cards and the greater the chance that, somewhere along the line, someone would give up chasing me.

There had to be safety from random checks. I could not relax and enjoy the life that these cards could offer me when they all sat in my wallet bearing strange names. And that was when something came to me. It was a phone call that I had made to a credit card company from a bed and breakfast in Dumfries. I had been attempting to order a replacement card for a man whose details I had appropriated from reception while the old lady went to get my key.

It hadn't worked, but that's not what came to me that night in Lancaster Farms. Rather I recalled the rolling recorded message I had heard when the woman put me on hold, and one particular sentence that leapt out to me now. *Why not order an extra card on your account for family, friends and colleagues?* That's what it had said. Friends and colleagues meant different surnames. Friends and colleagues, therefore, could mean Elliot Castro.

As some of you may know, prisons don't like to see you leave. The first four hours of my release day were spent sitting in a waiting area in my own clothes while the screws did their best to suggest that I was invisible. They were clearly rattled by the fact that I was now back in an expensive suit and I enjoyed the switch of power, leaning back triumphantly on the bench and making it clear that the delay was not affecting my satisfaction. When I did catch a screw's eye I made sure to smile at him. He looked confused.

'You looking smart for them, aren't you?'

'Who?' I said, but he just laughed. *My family, they're here.* That was a surprise, I had called my mum just the day before and she had certainly hidden this one well. The day was getting brighter and brighter. Still the screws ignored me, chatting amongst themselves about football and women or wandering about their office doing nothing at all. Finally, one of them picked up a phone and spoke into it while looking at me. It was hard for me not to laugh at him, trying to intimidate me when he was about to have to open the doors and let me walk out. He came over.

'Ready?'

'Yep.'

'Good for you, son,' he said and led me out the door towards a gate. When we got there he told me to move forward and I caught something in the corner of my eye as I passed through. I looked up to see that he was pointing at me and, turning round, I saw who the target was. I was now standing in a long wire tunnel that led to another gate, beyond which were two policemen standing beside their parked car.

'What do they want?' I asked the screw but he was already walking away.

They hadn't really needed to make it hard for me to leave the prison, because I clearly wasn't going to be leaving after all. I felt drunk with worry as I walked reluctantly down the tunnel. When I got within earshot one of the policemen said, 'Just take it easy, come on.'

I passed through the gate and they turned me round to apply the handcuffs.

'Elliot Castro, we are arresting you on suspicion of fraud . . .'

It was a sunny day on the trip down to Manchester. I got them to open the rear window slightly, just enough to feel the sun and the wind on my face. I asked them what the charge referred to and they said they couldn't go into detail but it was possibly quite serious. That was all I had to hear to know that I wasn't going home that day.

I wouldn't get bail and would be on remand for this new charge in some new prison within a few hours. I felt numb, as if my mind was too fearful to form a response to this new downward development. All I could think about was my mum sitting in the front room in Battlefield and watching for the gate to open and me to walk through. The image gripped me with anger and frustration as I was hit by a general fury. I pushed my mouth to the open window and shouted with rage into the motorway wind.

It was June 2001 and I had been picked up for one of my greatest successes. Amongst the blur of running and stealing back in 2000 I had found myself in the bar of the Malmaison Hotel in Manchester. When I saw a businessman stagger off and leave his jacket on a chair I picked it up, meaning to shout after him. It was only when the lop-sided heaviness told me the inner pocket contained a wallet that I stopped myself.

When I saw the two American Express cards I was momentarily taken aback. The idea that someone would have two – one personal, one corporate – hadn't occurred to me. What did, however, was that this fortuitous find was very fortunate indeed. I left the next morning for London and a £500 balcony room at the Langham Hilton on Regent Street. Then there were three days of Bond Street, restaurants, champagne, and swinging velvet ropes.

I had no idea how much I had spent until I sat, back

once more in the police holding cell at Manchester City Centre station, and the female duty lawyer looked up with a frown and said, 'A little over eleven thousand pounds,' as if sure it was a mistake. At first there was a bit of a thrill there, a charge from within that I had been drifting away from in prison.

Eleven thousand pounds. During the days I had concocted my outfits for the evenings; during the evenings I had left half-empty bottles of champagne in bar after bar. The sense of accomplishment rushed over me but it didn't dispel the somewhat less glamorous reality. This was a sizeable fraud, with repercussions on both the likely sentence and the possibility of bail.

Some hidden electronic eye in the Malmaison bar had picked me up and a matching set of pixels was available from the Langham Hilton. I was bang to rights and my lawyer didn't help matters by predicting two years' imprisonment and a rejection of bail, leaving me wallowing in that prospect as she went to negotiate with the police.

My pain was exacerbated by the manner of its arrival. To be reminded of the Langham Hilton trip, and all that it represented, in a doubleact with a further period of incarceration was heartbreaking. However, the legal system (as you have perhaps spotted already) is a very unpredictable beast and my worries vanished with my lawyer's reappearance. The police had asked her if I had a record of turning up for sentencing. She had answered in the positive and, from nowhere, I was free on police bail.

Within ten minutes I was walking towards Manchester Piccadilly station, dazed but delighted. Such was my distraction that I wandered right onto the Glasgow train without realizing that I was still armed only with my Prison Service travel warrant from Lancaster. My bad luck was compounded by the fact that the ticket inspector was an idiot who decided that I had to disembark in Lancaster for no apparent reason.

I was in no position to cause trouble, however, so I got off the train at Lancaster's tired little station. Bored by the wait for the next Glasgow train, I joined the line for the ticket office. I felt emboldened with thoughts of my surprising escape, the Langham Hilton and my pending arrival home. My turn came at the counter and I decided that I wanted a taste, however slight, of what I had been missing.

I explained with great patience to the man behind the desk that I was an employee of the Prison Service and had been handed a permit that should have been for first-class travel to Glasgow. Somewhere along the line, I added with an understanding shrug, that didn't seem to have happened. He looked at me. He saw the earnest and polite young man in a nice suit jacket, not the black bin bag of belongings sitting at my feet, and handed me a new first-class ticket.

In Battlefield my family greeted me warmly, but there was soon concern after I explained my detour to Manchester. I had to explain why I had arrived back so late, and it was best that I prepared them immediately for what might follow. I tried to reassure them as best I could but I couldn't deny the possibility that I would be back in prison in the next couple of months.

For now, though, we were a family again and chatting away over dinner like we used to. Dean pressed me for prison stories and my parents tentatively asked me what my plans were. I explained that I would have to wait and see how the Manchester business panned out, but that I would be looking for work in the meantime. In a way, that was true.

The next day I left the house with the intention of

stealing a card but within an hour I was back sitting in our front room. I had ridden a couple of bus routes, walked in and out of a couple of pubs, and then caught another bus home. The appetite for thieving wasn't there any more, and I couldn't bear the thought of being back in a cell so soon. Yet, as ever, I couldn't put off my yearning for advancement, which meant money first and foremost.

I was keen to try my theory about ordering named cards on someone's account. As well as making my wallet's contents look legitimate it would also help me with ID concerns. As I considered this I realized that the biggest ID concern it would tackle would be matching up to my passport. That meant travel, international travel, and made me even more desperate to get back on the credit card trail.

For a few days I hung around the house agitating my parents. My father's health was suffering by now and neither of them was working so the three of us got under each other's feet quite quickly. I ended up lying in my room for hours on end, as if I were back in my cell, trying to tackle this new problem. I took it back to a basic level. I needed a card, the type of card carried by people with a lot of money.

Although I may not have understood those people, and my attempts to join their world had so far been met by failure, I realized that I did know one thing about them that was important. It was something that I had known for a few years now, since I first set eyes on the Balmoral and the men and women inside it. What I knew was this – that rich people stayed in hotels.

I was halfway there. Now I had to find a way for the details of a cardholder staying in a hotel to be somehow transmitted to myself. I pondered this a while and then concluded that the easiest way to achieve this would be simply to ask the cardholders themselves. And with that I got up, walked through to the front room and closed the door so my parents couldn't hear me.

I pulled out the phone book and chose an expensive hotel in Glasgow that I had once casually jogged away from while a wine waiter stood over a beeping card machine. The receptionist answered and I asked for Mr Smith. There was no Mr Smith staying there. I apologized and hung up. Ten minutes later I asked her for Mr Campbell. She didn't answer, there was a pause and then a different ring.

'Hello?'

'Hello, Mr Campbell,' I said flatly into the phone. 'This is John from reception. We've just tried to process your card down here and were requested to call for authorization. I've just been on the phone to them and they've asked me to check some security details with you.'

'Oh, OK.' He almost sounded embarrassed. 'On you go.'

That was the arrival of my hotel phone trick. Over the years to come I would change aspects of it, sometimes by design and sometimes through reaction to the guest's personality. It wouldn't always work and it would on occasion require some quick reshaping as the call was taking place. Yet Mr Campbell saw it off to a glorious start as he handed over full details of his Diners Club International credit card. I thanked him and told him to enjoy the rest of his stay and shortly after I ordered a card on Mr Campbell's account in the name of his nephew Elliot Castro.

The two moves had come together beautifully and, with revolution in the air, I packed up my Vuitton case in anticipation. When the card arrived a couple of days later it was the signal for me to get back on the road. I told my parents it was easier for me to be based in London to deal with the Manchester business, and that there was the possibility of some unnamed work down there. It felt bad leaving Dean again so quickly but I promised him I'd return with a gift or two and with that I was away.

In London I booked into the St Martin's Lane Hotel, a place I'd read about on the travel website Expedia. They had rated it very highly and said it was popular with celebrities and an A-list crowd, which was good enough for me. I made such a fuss at reception with my luggage and questions that they upgraded me to one of their corner suites, a palatial set-up with strip windows looking down to the street. I was so entranced that I couldn't bear to leave it that night, ordering a huge array of room service and serving myself up all manner of drinks.

So I was in a pretty ambitious mood the next day when walking down Regent Street. That, I presume, was the main reason for what happened next. I saw the British Airways sign and walked into the shop. It was packed with customers who were queuing in one of those zigzag rope systems but off to the side was something else. At a desk sat an unoccupied blonde woman beneath a sign that read *First Class ONLY*.

For me, of course, this was like a red rag to a bull and I marched over to explain that I wished to book a first-class ticket. The woman was up from her seat in a flash, making me a cup of tea and spouting various inane remarks about the weather and suchlike. As she prattled on I was scanning a poster behind her desk and when she finally got round to asking me for my destination I was ready.

'Toronto, please,' I told her.

It had looked the most attractive on the poster and, more importantly, Niagara Falls had been a great atlas favourite of mine. The woman was nothing but friendly as she announced that the price of the ticket would be over four grand and, caught in the moment, I handed her the card without much consideration. As she took it to the machine I looked around the shop. Any problems and I could be back amongst the street shoppers within seconds.

There was no escape necessary though, and I walked out revelling in the jealous glances of the unfortunates waiting for their economy bookings. The flight left the next day and so I went and bought my holiday wardrobe that was dominated by warm jumpers and a thick ski jacket.

Back at the hotel I packed my bag and then phoned my mum from the bath with a glass of champagne in my other hand. I told her about my forthcoming trip and she went a little quiet and sighed a bit but I gave her something to cling on to by describing it as a work opportunity. She asked if I was going to visit Niagara Falls and I told her that I was.

After I climbed out of the bath a thought occurred to me. Other than a couple of hundred pounds, I only had the one active credit card. With that knowledge I took some of the hotel stationery and a pen and went and sat by the phone. By the time I went to sleep that night, I did so next to a piece of paper with five full sets of credit card details, for use in an emergency. Lucky, lucky boy.

CHAPTER TWELVE

In all the time that I did what I did, there were many moments that showed me what I did it for. There were purchases, and evenings out, hotel rooms and restaurants. I think the best physical representation, though, was flying first class. *It's only an aeroplane journey*, you may say with some justification. But no, it wasn't just that, it never was.

It was something that connected with me from the past, from that first flight to Chile and my infant's walk up the plane's aisle. And when I got there myself, it managed to live up to those childlike expectations. Not only was I part of a moneyed and exotic group that was clearly elevated from the rest of the great British public, but also that fact was constantly acknowledged.

When I checked in for the Toronto flight, I did so in a tiny line next to a vast queue of others who confirmed my status by their bustling presence. They were just normal people – families, young couples, even some businessmen. Yet I had been instantly hoisted clear of them. They knew it too, I could see them pretending not to look at this dashing young man who leant over the desk and laughed with the counter staff who smiled so much more than usual.

I walked tall through the airport, my first-class ticket held open in my hand as if by accident, to the First-Class Lounge. It was like a hotel lobby. Everywhere were leather couches, hushed TV screens and banks of complimentary bars. I mixed myself a drink and took a seat near the windows so I could watch the planes, but soon I had turned to watch the people instead.

There were the senior businessmen in pinstripe and cashmere, muttering into phones or enveloped in newspapers, but it was not they who interested me. Neither was it the few families present, who sprawled over couches with the confidence bought by a £10,000 joint booking. Rather my attention was taken by a handful of others, those who were younger and casually dressed. Where did *they* get their money from? I had to stop myself from trying to find out, such was my fascination.

On the plane a fawning stewardess guided me to the left. I settled into one of the enormous seats while she took my jacket, which I was only slightly uneasy about, and returned with branded toiletries and champagne. She gave me a menu and told me to order anything I wanted at any time, then returned again to remind me of this. At the time I was probably in wonderment at the attention to detail but, evaluating it now, my obvious delight at the surroundings had probably led her to believe I was a little simple.

The first thing I realized when I got to Toronto was that I had made a serious error in my travelling wardrobe. I walked off the plane looking like I was about to tackle Everest and it was seventy degrees in the shade. I peeled off what I could and then got the taxi driver to roll down all the windows on the way into the city.

I had called the city centre Hilton from Heathrow, purporting to be from a British company booking a room on behalf of Elliot Castro. Castro would be paying, I explained, with his Diners Club International card. By doing so I was both ensuring there was accommodation available and hopefully winning some trust in advance. My thinking was that if there seemed to be a problem with my card, this added detail would encourage them to call my room rather than the bank.

When I got to the Hilton I was bold from the flight and the champagne, and I got them to swipe the card through for the full amount. It was an unnecessary move but the card passed through fine, and I therefore convinced myself that I had seven days free from worry.

I embarked on the tourist trail with enthusiasm, bowling up Queen Elizabeth Way to Niagara Falls the next day like the excited kid that I was. I stayed there for hours, skulking around the observation deck and then to the restaurant, from where my eyes could stay on the sheets of water. There were a lot of tourists about and I wondered what they made of this sole traveller in their midst – drinking cocktails at the Top of the Falls Restaurant, jumping in a taxi and calling out for the Hilton back in Toronto.

That week I wandered Toronto's summer streets, carried by the permanent thumping knowledge of how far I was from home. I loved paying for things in foreign notes, and I revelled in that instant when a local clocked my Scottish accent. It was a beautiful, brilliant experience and come the last day I didn't want to leave.

I put on my suit and decided on a final foray to the malls to pick up some souvenirs, taking the usual precaution of slipping my passport into my jacket pocket as I left the room (I'd formed this habit in my early hotel days, in case a cleaner spotted my passport and saw a different name to the room's booking). A couple of hours later I sauntered back to the hotel with my shopping, having decided to try and extend my stay.

My first-class ticket could be switched about without any great hassle and so it was just the hotel that could be a problem. I had struck up a loose relationship with a female receptionist who had been giving me nightlife pointers and I was pleased to see that she was working.

She looked distant, as if she hadn't recognized me, but there was a strain in her neck when she looked the other way. Her cheeks flushed as she spun and disappeared through to the back office when I drew closer to the now empty desk. Rebuffed, I made for the elevator, where a suspicion started to build.

In the corridor I deliberately slowed. My door was near when the muffled voices came and I stopped. I held my breath and strained to hear more, and then everything was obliterated by the crackle of a walkie-talkie from behind the wood. My hands opened as I turned, and by the time the bags hit the floor I was yards down the corridor towards the service stairs.

A door opened behind and there was a shout but I was away, haring down the stairs in long leaps with my arms fanned out to catch the banisters. At the bottom, I threw myself through the door. It was the kitchen and I was running still – past bemused chefs and then through hot steam to a chink of daylight.

An alley. One end was a wall, I ran for the other and then I was in the afternoon crowds. I continued my panicked dash but I was sweating heavily and attracting attention so I turned into a quieter road. A solitary car prowled towards me and instinctively I ran in front of it with my hand raised.

It rocked to a halt and I ran to the driver's window. An old man, I saw with relief. I flashed my wallet in his face.

'Canadian Secret Service!' I shouted, jumping in the back seat of his car. 'Let's go!'

He stiffened in shock, and turned to me with a willing expression.

'Wow, Secret Service, OK, where are we going?'

'The airport,' I said, sliding down the back seat until I was hidden from view.

'Drive.'

It's fair to say that the next twenty minutes presented a pretty odd scene. In the front seat of the car sat a good, patriotic Canadian driving as fast as he dared to Toronto's Pearson International Airport. In the back was a Scottish fraudster wedged virtually upside down, sweating profusely and occasionally shouting out encouragement in a weak Canadian accent.

This was a matter of national security I would yell from the bowels of the car. I had noted his registration, I shouted, and would be commending him for his service to the nation. Perhaps he should slow down a bit, I added as I tried to pull myself back up on the seatbelt, we don't want to attract too much attention.

'I'm ex-army,' he called back. 'Just pleased to be able to help.'

We were free of the city now and I sat up straight in the back seat, gulping for air and trying to ease the fear that was threatening to consume me.

'Shall I take you to the police station at the airport?' he asked.

'*No*,' I yelped. 'No, just the main entrance, thanks.'

'No problem, sir,' he said, and I caught a view of his face in the mirror, alert with excitement. At the airport I thanked him profusely and sidled nervously into the building. I was completely, totally, terrified. Not only was the airport a likely destination for a foreign criminal, but also they would have realized by now that my passport wasn't in the room. They'd spot me any minute, I had to *go*.

The next flight to depart was to Chicago. Maybe they

would only be watching European flights, I thought. Suddenly I was hit by a fresh wave of alarm. *How would I pay?* I pulled out the Diners Club card; it had obviously now been blocked and I wasn't going to take the risk of trying to use it. Other than that I had only $100 and about the same in pounds.

I went to the bathroom and sought to compose myself, drying off the sweat as well as possible with paper towels. My legs felt weak and heavy and every time the door opened or closed I looked for uniforms and handcuffs. As things stood, the only solution meant a phone call to my mum and persuading her to book me a flight. There was no way I could use my return ticket now, paid for as it was by the marked card.

I *couldn't* phone Mum. It was almost as daunting as being caught. I could come up with a cover story, of course, but it would be a terrible thing to do and it would also mean a considerable delay before I got out of here. I stared at myself in the mirror. Why had I not taken more precautions? I had. *I had.* My heart pounding, I slid my hand into my pocket and felt the paper. I pulled it out. Under the logo of the St Martin's Lane hotel was scrawled the card details I had gathered in as that late, late afterthought.

I walked back out to the terminal and stood behind a pillar in the corner. I noted the airline for the Chicago flight and then studied the advertisement hoardings that hung down the wall behind the desks. I found the right airline and could just make out the telephone booking number. Over in the phone booth I booked myself onto the flight, explaining that I was a work colleague of Mr Castro phoning from a convention in Toronto.

The police would flag my name. I had to shield myself somehow and, amongst the panic and the pressure, I added a touch. I made the booking in the name of *Ellot Castrro*. I hung up the phone and shut my eyes. I made myself wait one long minute, then walked as confidently as I could over to the check-in desk. A work colleague in the UK, I explained casually, had booked me a seat on the Chicago flight.

The woman took my passport and typed something in. She frowned and, without looking from the screen, said, 'Nothing here in that name.'

'Are you sure?' I asked, but I could already see that her attention had fallen on my planted booking.

'Oh, yes, there you are, they got the spelling wrong,' she explained apologetically.

'Did they?' I said with a manic laugh. 'Not to worry.'

Through security and the airport gates I went, resigned to a tug that just didn't seem to come. I was the first passenger to board the plane and sat staring from the window as it filled behind me. Only when it moved, then quickened, then lifted clear of the runway did I dare to believe in my escape.

They might see through my spelling scam, I conceded, but the complications of having to liaise with the American authorities should cause enough of a delay for me to get away again. I was going to catch the first flight I could clear of Chicago, and would hopefully be back in the UK by the time that anyone who was interested had worked out my route away from the hotel corridor.

It wouldn't be the end of it. The details of what happened would surely find their way to the police in Britain, but that was not a pressing problem. After all, there was a definite prison sentence on its way anyway, courtesy of the Manchester charge.

For now I had to get out of Chicago, which I did – to New York, and then on to Heathrow using other card details from the emergency stash. Seven days after my first-class trip across the Atlantic, I flew back exhausted and drained by fear in a cramped economy seat, with no luggage other than my passport and a crumpled piece of hotel notepaper.

Back in Britain I retreated to Glasgow, where I spent a few days recovering from my ordeal and trying to avoid my parents' baffled questions. As the shock of my bolt from the hotel lessened, it was replaced with elation. I had achieved my goal of international travel. Even better, I had made it past the grey curtain. When things had got hairy, I had amazed myself with my reaction. I had been like a younger, gayer James Bond.

James Bond, however, didn't live at home with his parents in preparation for going back to prison. I had no idea what was happening with the Manchester charge, other than my mum wearily informing me that a lawyer had been trying to get hold of me. I promised her that I would be returning the calls as a matter of urgency but one thing led to another and I decided to go to Edinburgh for the night instead.

I booked a nice hotel with a set of details from the St Martin's Lane notepaper. I would have one night of enjoyment before handing myself in. Well, maybe a few nights. Or maybe I wouldn't be handing myself in at all. In the end, I didn't have to decide and there was no last night out either.

I walked into the foyer and told the girl that I was Elliot Castro. She looked over her shoulder at the plain-clothes policeman standing there and he took me off to a police station in Edinburgh. The St Martin's Lane numbers had finally failed me. That night in the holding cells, and the next day on the way to Manchester, I didn't think about what was going to happen to me. There was an uncomfortable meeting with my lawyer – where I sat with a suntan and wondered aloud how I had missed her calls – but still I wasn't really paying attention.

Even in the van on the way to remand at HMP Forest Bank in Manchester I wasn't consumed with the fact that I was destined for a prison cell, because I still hadn't come down from the weeks before. The van was filthy and smelt of other men but it didn't seem to matter. I was thinking about first-class lounges, foreign money, and phone calls to expensive hotels.

This distraction was enhanced when I got into my cell at Forest Bank and found, to my astonishment, a small colour television in the corner. It took me a couple of hours to tune in, and would sometimes lose reception for no apparent reason, but it added another avenue of escape to my usual dreaming and scheming. Predicting a fortnight or so of remand, I slipped effortlessly back into prison life as anonymously as I could.

One characteristic of Forest Bank that did grab my attention from the start was the fighting. They *all* seemed to be fighting at one time or another. During Association in Lancaster Farms, the cells had been locked and all the inmates had been forced to congregate in the central recreation area. When conflict did occur it was usually far more about shouting and posturing than anything else.

In Forest Bank, where cells were unlocked during Association, there was a new and sinister edge to conflict between prisoners. Inmates were ambushed in their cells and the first anyone would know about it was when the wardens would carry out their broken bodies.

It wasn't a very attractive sight, particularly if you were eating, but I didn't feel endangered. I wasn't exactly threatening to overthrow the power structures in place amongst the prison population and as such no one was going to bother with me unless I slipped up. On the thankfully rare occasions that people spoke to me I had the slang, some prison experience to embellish and the far more acceptable crime of credit card fraud behind me.

I was eighteen and so still amongst the young offenders, but there was also a wing of adult prisoners at Forest Bank. They were a depressing sight. While the young offenders irritated me constantly with their bullshit hard-man routines and rowdiness, at least they had a bit of spirit. Their adult counterparts were a desperate bunch – grey and fatigued in appearance with hunted expressions. The older ones amongst them looked like ghosts as they passed us by.

I looked at these defeated specimens as I did the whole prison process, as an outsider and interloper. I may have been back behind bars amongst this grisly crowd but it was a hangover from another time. Canada had changed everything for me. There was no longer going to be a series of short bursts of success followed by these horrific spells of detainment, which could only grow longer and longer.

I had the foundation of a method for gaining cards that was thrilling, and even improved on the success I had enjoyed from my unconventional Imagine career. My days as a thief, scouring the streets as both hunter and prey, were over. I had found a clean and impressive technique that took me far beyond even the possibilities I had previously dreamt of. Heathrow and London had once been the limit of my ambitions, now that was where they started.

As my court case neared, my usual dreams and nightmares about the sentence were framed by a concern – how long before I could be on the phone to another hotel, to another Mr Smith? Every day I would construe another international itinerary, and decide on another famous sight that I would soon be detailing to my mum back in Battlefield from a hotel room far away.

I got eighteen months. It seemed harsh but my lawyer explained that it was my second offence and, lest I forget, I had disappeared with no explanation for a couple of months. Back at Forest Bank I was moved from the remand wing to the offenders' wing and suddenly things were a bit colder and real. With time spent on remand combined with parole I could be out in seven months, but even that seemed impossibly distant.

In the remand wing of the prison, beneath the standard air of prison despondency, you could just about pick up a hint of optimism as those who were innocent clung to the fact that the law might get round to agreeing. On the offenders' wing everyone was guilty, whether they had committed the crime or not, and they all walked about with their own personal clock ticking in their heads.

A week in, I woke up to a screw banging my door.

'You're moving,' he shouted. 'Hindley, half an hour.'

I was annoyed far more with the short notice than the move and grabbed my stuff together as quickly as I could. Wherever this other prison was, I concluded, it couldn't be much worse than here.

HMP Hindley was a young offenders' institution on the outskirts of Wigan, and it gave me a pretty poor welcome. After a couple of hours of processing I was led to my cell. Although I was still to be kept on my own, the cell had a metal bunk bed that filled half the room. In the corner was a steel box topped with a small sink and with a toilet bolted onto the side.

The toilet bowl was caked with shit and the whole cell reeked with this and the sweat of the previous prisoners. Other than the electric glare, the only light was a dull greenish glow that fought through the grime on the window as best as it could. In summary, it was fucking disgusting.

A year earlier this scene, and the thought of being a part of it for at least seven months, would have made me burst into tears. Instead I put my stuff on the bed and got to work. I did the toilet first, holding my breath and scraping away the shit with toilet paper. It was hard and stuck to the bowl like limpets but I managed to clear it from the surface and eventually the steel began to brighten and shine. I did the sink next and the small mirror, both of which had been filmed with dust.

I even managed to wipe a layer of dirt from the window and found the plastic was actually clear beneath it. I took the skin off my knuckles from scratching against the stone that the window was set into but I continued to wipe and scratch until the light strengthened and I could just about make out a view of various buildings.

I compared the two thin mattresses that lay on the bunks, then combined the two and lay them on the bottom bunk with the surface bearing the fewest stains facing upwards. I lay the starched sheet over the two and tucked it tightly underneath, then put my blanket on top along with the hard pillow.

After dinner I placed my few possessions on the tiny desk in the corner of the room and then spent an hour tuning in the different channels on the television. I followed this by going down on my hands and knees on the stone floor with more toilet paper and began to wipe the dirt from the cold stone. The dust was too thick to make much of an impression and I decided instead that this would be an extended project with the grid of the stones giving me a divided daily chore.

One of the big choices you make in prison is how to fill those days that the state has decided to take from you. In brief, you get a job or you enrol for Education. The jobs come from a fairly narrow spectrum that usually involves some degree of cleaning or kitchen work. I once met a surgeon in prison, for example, who had been told he was tailor-made for dish-washing.

Being someone who might accurately be described as a non-manual worker, I decided to take my usual trusty route into IT classes. Once again, the classes had little relationship to IT other than the fact that there happened to be computers in the room. Sometimes the computers would not even be turned on and so we would just sit and talk about computers, in a room full of computers.

After a week of suffering I decided to politely approach the two ladies who ran the classes and ask if there were any alternatives. It paid off spectacularly the following day when they called me aside and offered up a role in the prison library. From the next morning I began spending my days sorting books, handling returns and even suggesting titles to some of the more cautious of the prisoners.

It was a great job, other than the fact I had to go to prison to get it, but I had made a serious error. I may have known the lingo and the basics of prison life by this point but I clearly hadn't picked up on a very important lesson – that a new prisoner being awarded one of the cushiest jobs in the place arouses considerable attention and suspicion.

The conclusion that will generally be drawn in such a

situation is that the prisoner is either a grass or under some form of protection. So while I was innocently stamping books in the library, trouble was brewing. It came to a head when I was waiting for my shot on the pool table during Association and another prisoner jumped in front of me.

A shouting match broke out between us and, from the way that unaffected bystanders suddenly swarmed round, it was clear that this was not a spontaneous incident. The screws arrived quickly and broke things up but the next day on the way to the Education building, the same guy came at me through the crowd.

He swung at me and missed and I instinctively swung back at him with the raw force of my fourteen stones, catching him hard on the mouth. He fell to the floor and rose to his knees with blood seeping through the hand that covered his face. I kept walking and was ten yards down the path when the screws finally appeared, running blindly past me.

After that I never got any more than semi-aggressive banter from the other inmates about my plush appointment. As they stood at my desk waiting for their books they would jokingly ask me which screw I'd slept with to get the job. I elected not to inform them that there were a few of the screws that I would have quite happily taken on.

That was another of the reasons that I couldn't really join in the prison conversation, which broadly speaking would centre on moaning about being in prison or sex. For me, prison was an unfortunate by-product of the activities I had chosen. Moaning about ending up there didn't make any sense.

When it came to sex I had the twin concerns of having little to offer and the experiences that I could have shared probably not being designed for an audience of male prisoners. I was once again left to enjoy my own company but that was fine with me, especially when I had unlimited access to books.

As the months passed by, I tried a few different areas of self-improvement in HMP Hindley. First I tried tackling psychology. I thought it might give me an edge over other people, and help me understand myself, but it didn't do anything for me. I didn't need to try and arm myself with science, I decided, I had enough confidence to trust my judgement. Instead, I became entranced by the Roman Empire, about its dramatic rise (up to Scotland at one stage) and fall.

I was only getting to grips with Rome's eventual collapse when I was moved onto the cleaning detail and forced to give up my role at the library. I'd landed on my feet again though, being given the task of looking after three administrative screws who shared a large open-plan office.

I would make them tea and coffee, clean the office and the toilet, empty the bins and so on. When there was nothing to do I would retire to a small room through the back that I jokingly referred to as my office. The three screws grew to like me, or tolerate me perhaps, and sometimes the four of us would chat away as if we were four colleagues doing our 9 to 5. One of them, Gordon, was a particularly approachable sort and it was to him that I went as my release date neared.

I was terrified of being gate-arrested again but he came back to me the day before my release and gave me the joyous news that there were no warrants outstanding for me. Plenty of screws would have lied to me about this, but Gordon wasn't a hard guy to read. After I had said my farewells to the others he followed me out to the stairs.

'You're a smart guy, Elliot,' he said. 'I hope you've got something constructive planned for when you get out.'

'Aye, I do Gordon, don't you worry,' I assured him.

CHAPTER THIRTEEN

The first time I was released from prison I had found that I wasn't able to thieve any more; this time I initially found that I couldn't do *anything*. I thought I was going to emerge ready to embark on a campaign of fraud like nothing I had ever dared dream, but instead I felt disorientated and vulnerable. I even briefly flirted with the possibility of at least attempting to go straight.

I soon mastered such idiocy. The dread of returning to prison had to be handled, and it was. Rather than producing uncertainty, I shaped it into a motivation to enhance my methods above the risk of capture. I once again cast my mind back to the recent past, sitting in my bedroom in Battlefield and noting what it taught me.

A week later I was checking into the Clarence Hotel in Dublin. It was a slick, lavish place owned by U2, the biggest rock band on the planet, and sat centrally in this new city of discovery. I was immaculately groomed and running on a confidence that had been reinvigorated far beyond any previous level. One of the reasons was the victory over the prison fear, another was my adopting a few more rules.

A Few More Rules

Check-in   When I booked a flight fraudulently (and, frankly, when would I not?), I would call the airline shortly before the flight. The purpose would be to discover if the crime had been spotted and I was to be picked up when I attempted to check in. The best way of me making this call, I soon realized, was to phone the airline's central reservations desk and explain I was from the check-in desk at the airport. *I'm phoning from the (insert relevant airline desk), our servers are down, just checking a booking in the name of Elliot Castro, everything OK?*

Cash   Wherever I went from now on, I would do so with enough hard cash to get myself back to the UK. I was still too nervous to attempt to gain cash advances from banks themselves, even though I technically had the means to do it with any card that was in my name. Instead, I found a willing source of ready money in bureaux de change. Not only were they used to people drawing thousands on the strength of a card and a passport, they could be visited in busy airports minutes before I boarded one of a hundred departing planes.

Phones   I bought an untraceable pay-as-you-go mobile phone from a shop in Glasgow and ensured it was internationally compatible. I would use hotel phones only if absolutely necessary. Before, I had been staying in hotels for only a night or two, but my new plan involved longer stays and I was wary of a hotel operator catching one of my work calls.

Security (1)   I was proud of this one. I wanted to know if the cards that I had were still active, and if they weren't I wanted a safe system of discovering this. A simple way was to try and use the card in a phone booth, or something similar, but even then there could be other reasons for a card to fail.

My alternative was to call the card companies directly, pretending to be a shop looking for authorization. I had stood on the other side of the counter enough times to know the format of these calls, and I was also aware how little information the shop assistants were required to give. All they really needed was a merchant number, and these were usually on display on the sides of their card machines. I'd hesitate at shop counters, pretending to check my phone as I entered these codes.

Through this basic trick, I was able to wake up each day and find out within ten minutes which of my cards were still active.

Security (2)   I would never, ever walk into my hotel room without knocking on the door and saying 'Housekeeping'. Any policeman or security guard hiding inside would be quick to tell a lowly male maid to piss off. That's what I figured anyway.

I still got the cards the same way – phoning hotels, asking for common surnames and then trying to extract as much information as possible. Sometimes I got lucky, sometimes I had to work the phones for a while before everything came together. I was happy enough with this side of things, other than the fact that I was still having to get the cards delivered to Battlefield and get up early for the postie.

The cards I was using at this time would have a lifespan of anything from a few days to a couple of months. They would all be cancelled eventually but for some reason the logical next step – for the police to follow up the fact that they had been delivered to my house – never seemed to be taken.

I suspected that this was because the banks weren't passing on this detail to the constabulary for their own reasons.

Despite this, it was a fairly considerable flaw to have my home address being offered up with every move I pulled. This was something that I planned to remedy in Ireland, after I took possession of a final flurry of cards in the days before I left Battlefield once more.

First I had to familiarize myself with my new surroundings, which was no great stretch as I took to them immediately. Dublin, a busy, compact city, was perfect for a wealthy pedestrian visitor like myself. The shopping was good, and the bars and clubs were even better.

At the Clarence I upgraded to a suite that soon filled with full shopping bags and empty bottles as I planned my next move. I quickly fell into my usual approach of dallying in boutiques, chatting to anyone who would have me in bars, and buying drinks liberally in nightclubs.

It was after such an evening out that I returned to the Clarence and spotted Bono sitting drinking in the residents' bar. He was having a quiet chat with a few friends, and I was over in a shot. To his credit, he managed to hide his irritation well and seemed genuinely impressed that I was staying in one of his best rooms.

I managed to trap them with a round of drinks and chatted away about music, Glasgow and the lonely life of a hotel consultant. As I remember, some of the trickiest questions I ever received about that fabricated line of work were probably from a rather bemused Bono. I shifted the conversation into less taxing areas before causing noticeable relief all round by staggering off to my bed.

After the initial excitement over my Dublin flit started to fade, I set about activating my new method to take delivery of my cards. I began moving regularly – staying in one hotel for a week or two before moving on to the next one. As I did so, new credit cards followed me thanks to my new cover story for the card companies.

I had become a benevolent uncle, keen to help my nephew Elliot Castro who was stranded in a Dublin hotel having had his wallet stolen. I wanted a card to be sent to him immediately, on my account, to help him out of the bother he was in. The next day I would take a call from reception and then wander down to the lobby, sign the courier driver's form, and retire back to my room with new card in hand.

Once I had received a couple of cards in this way, I would either move hotels to avoid suspicion or indulge in some of the foreign travel I had spent prison nights planning. At first I settled for short breaks to Europe – Berlin, Madrid, Paris and elsewhere – which usually involved changing at Heathrow. These were enjoyable little jaunts that I regularly booked through the Expedia website.

I would sometimes take the opportunity to nip up to Scotland from Heathrow, and started using Edinburgh airport for the purpose. I found its smaller size somehow more comforting than Glasgow, and enjoyed spending an afternoon or night in the capital before a quick visit home to Battlefield.

My ambitions rising, I booked myself a pricey package to Dubai and flew from Dublin to Heathrow filled with anticipation for the trip and the first-class passage that would take me there. It was supposed to be my first significant journey since Canada, but when I arrived at Heathrow I found it was not to be. At a phone booth in view of the check-in desk I made my cautionary call to the reservations department.

'That booking is the subject of a security hold,' said the woman. Then, more urgently, 'Is the passenger with you just now?'

'No, he's not,' I said sadly, and ended the call.

I flew straight back to Dublin on the next Aer Lingus flight, reassured by the success of my system but deflated about my aborted trip. Bored, I picked up the in-flight magazine and found my next destination. I had been desperate to go to New York but was worried that my criminal record would cause US Immigration to take too close an interest.

However, the magazine helpfully informed me that immigration checks were actually carried out at Dublin Airport, before passengers even boarded the plane. On arrival in the USA, I would simply be waved through. I decided this was worth the risk and, after landing in Dublin, went straight to the Aer Lingus desk and spent several thousand euros using my most recently acquired card. I booked a premier-class return flight, leaving the next day, then retired to one of the airport hotels. The following morning I sailed through the immigration checks and once again I was on a plane, carried aloft with those magical slivers of plastic in my pocket.

The small Indian driver who picked me up at JFK Airport was a bubbly little sort. He helped with my luggage, asked about my flight and told me of his love of the movie *Braveheart* as we negotiated our way clear of the car park. By the time we were amongst the canyon streets of the city, however, I had bled the poor guy dry.

My questioning had intensified the closer we got to Manhattan. I had probed him on the skyline (he told me to wait and see it for myself), the geography (he knew marginally less than me), and his memories of the previous year's terrorist attacks (limited – he had been in the JFK Airport car park at the time).

I elected to take charge of our onward route in a frenetic attempt to incorporate as many sights as possible. I would shout them out intermittently and the driver would swear and jerk his head to his mirror and try some sideways slalom through the traffic. My excitement at the surroundings and the incoming charge of the riches that the next few days would bring was uncontrollable.

I booked into the Hudson Hotel, which the Expedia site had told me was part of the same chain as my great pal the St Martin's Lane, and reserved a deluxe studio. The time difference meant it was only early afternoon and I practically ran back to the front of the hotel for another taxi to Fifth Avenue. I was on my way to another stage of my social climb, armed with cards, money and a nervous cough.

It's hard to piece it together now, but I reckon that in the three days of that first trip to New York I spent around $15,000 in Fifth Avenue stores. Every brand or label that I had ever aspired to – through magazines, newspapers, or billboards – and which I knew were touched with luxury had a home there.

The clientele comprised the rich and the dreamers, and I was there as a member of both. I stood and pointed out my choices while outside yellow movie cabs beeped at limousines that swept to a halt to discharge their moneyed loads. The sales staff looked like actors and pop stars, and yet they smiled and flattered me relentlessly as I pulled one card after another from my wallet.

Initially, the daytime left my nocturnal New York outings looking pretty amateurish. The first night I was blocked at every turn by ID requests, a factor I hadn't bargained for. Here I was, an international fraudster with a new designer wardrobe, and no one would sell me a beer because I was only nineteen. I ended up in a Village dive called the Idiot where a transvestite barmaid poured me free shots and I sat at the bar glumly chewing monkey nuts.

This, clearly, wasn't how I had pictured evenings in the

city that never sleeps. The following day I slipped the concierge $100 on my return from shopping and asked him to
sort me out. When I arrived back in the lobby that evening he
presented me with a list of three clubs, all of which I had
heard of through airline or style magazines. He also asked me
if I would like him to arrange a limousine, a suggestion I
agreed to emphatically.

That night I was ferried around Manhattan by an eager
young driver who latched on to me as I left the first two
clubs. *Whoodyasee?* He begged me as I clambered back in,
explaining the glittering crowd that each attracted. I had been
too taken with the whole experience to try and recognize any
of the faces. Both were filled with people who held some new
form of glamour, they looked like the club should be paying
them to stand there and emitted a confidence that had left me
lurking in the corner.

By the third club I had downed a few cocktails, so when
a woman called out that she loved my shoes I instinctively
went over and sat down. Whenever I catch an episode of *Sex
and the City* I think of the three ladies that I joined at the
table. All were in some area of fashion and we talked about
clothes, and Scotland, and the increasingly confusing profession of a hotel consultant.

They were effortlessly classy but I felt protected by my
foreign status and the shaky shield of my fictitious job. I
bought a bottle of champagne for $1,000 with a fresh card
and they didn't even react. I was flying with the company and
the setting, and when they asked if I wanted to go to a party
I shouted, 'I've got a limo outside,' and one of them smiled
and said, 'Cute.'

The party was in an apartment that would have looked
over-sized anywhere else in the world. In New York, where
I had read that morning that studio flats could cost a million

dollars, it was a raging sign of financial might. A huge window looked down onto a mass of trees that I realized with a thrill were in Central Park. I asked someone who owned it and they laughed and said, 'The Man.' It's not the kind of thing you can say at a party in Battlefield, but there it sounded just about acceptable.

A DJ played in the corner and waiters in white tuxedos circulated silver trays of cocktails and more champagne. I followed a few others up a long staircase and found myself on a rooftop. It ended with a low wall that looked down once more on the Park and all around was the sweep of the city, lit by neon and moonlight. In the corner was a table occupied by a smiling fat man and two beautiful blonde women.

The minute they heard my accent they had sat me down, ordered me a drink and were already running through their favourite British spots. Almost every name they dropped – hotels, bars, nightclubs, boutiques – allowed me to contribute a new, discerning turn to the conversation.

I made a disparaging comment about the room service in a famous British hotel and one of the blondes opened her mouth wide. 'Yes!' she said, 'I *always* say that.' High on acceptance, I decided not to rock the boat and wandered off around the apartment. Every time I caught someone's eye they would smile or nod or just look, I don't know, kind of *OK* with me. When I got back down to the street I had to pick my limo out from a shiny line, and I found my driver bouncing on his seat.

'Look, man,' he said, pointing at a guy I had seen in the party walking to the car in front of us. He wore a nice suit that I recognized as Armani, and on his arm was a woman with the body of a mannequin.

'You recognize him, man?' said the driver, his voice infantile in amazement.

above. With Mum, Dad, Nicky
and the newly arrived Dean.
left. Taking care of wee Dean.
below. Xmas Day 1986,
being spoilt by Mum.

above. 9 November 1987: my fifth birthday.
below left. At Aberdeen train station, bound for Chile.
below right. My first brush with the law (with Dean).

Dinner, in Chile, with Mum and Dean.

Enjoying a sit down with Dean in Chile.

above. Dad introduces me to champagne. Bet he regrets that!
below left. Looking slick at Edinburgh Zoo in 1992, aged nine.
below right. 1995, my first £100 note. I remember it well.

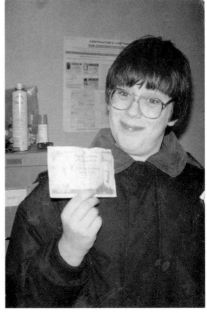

In Chile, again, with Dan, Dean and relatives.

The loneliness of the long-distance fraudster.

Outside court, 2001, with a pocket full of cards, as I remember.

(Photo: Iain McLellan/Spindrift)

On my decks, Belfast 2004. Weeks from the end.

Neil springs me from Ford Prison for the day, summer 2005.

(Photo: James Burns)

Telling him what I trusted him with at that point.

(Photo: James Burns)

The pay off – fry up and a cigarette.

(Photo: James Burns)

Brighton, summer 2005.

(Photo: James Burns)

Free and going straight.
Glasgow, 2007.

Who says fighting crime
doesn't pay? Ralph Eastgate,
Draguignan, 2007.

I didn't, but that wasn't important. There was something else, as he came closer and opened the door for his companion. I looked at the way he moved, the manner in which he seemed to charge the air around him with an easy control. I looked at his clothes and the way he wore them, and then his head turned slightly and I saw his face with those gloating eyes. That was when I saw it. It wasn't physical, but more the way he used everything that he had. He looked like me.

On the flight back from New York I read a men's magazine interview with a former MI5 operative. He explained that an active MI5 agent would often explain to friends that he worked for the Ministry of Defence, in the belief this would stop him feeling guilty for lying to those around him.

I had never felt any guilt for lying to those around me, but the hotel consultant line tended to attract a series of follow-up questions. So when I sat in a bar in Dublin and got chatting to a nice guy called Dermot, and when he said that he ran a security company, I of course chipped in . . .

'Well, that's interesting as I work for the British Ministry of Defence.'

Sitting in a bar in Dublin and dropping heavy hints that you're a British spy is not the wisest of moves, but Dermot accepted the line without any sign of misgiving. He was a likeable and entertaining chap who was desperately trying to get his new business off the ground. Being a committed sympathizer of the upwardly mobile, I threw myself into his plans with customary enthusiasm.

Soon I would leave my €900 room in the morning, have breakfast and then walk over to Dermot's small office. He and his mother would greet me warmly and I would lend them my great security experience for a couple of hours. I would make suggestions here and there, or ask to look over various documents that I would lean back with and read with a furrowed brow before announcing my learned opinions. After a while I would get bored, and take myself away before meeting Dermot in the pub for a post-work debrief.

This arrangement, believe it or not, never seemed odd to any of us. I had explained that I was being paid to be in Dublin for research purposes but had very little to research. Dermot seemed to enjoy my company and I was occasionally of genuine use in the office, specifically the method of cleaning keyboards that I had honed during my office position in HMP Hindley. For me, it created company and killed some time. It also let me play with the idea of a normal life, before going to look at Rolex watches in the afternoon.

One morning in the office, Dermot's mum mentioned that she was going to Dublin Airport later that day to buy a ticket for a trip to Manchester in October. It was only August at this point, but she explained that she didn't have a credit card and wanted to buy the ticket in advance. I sprung into action, pulling up various websites and telling her I would book the flight without delay. I booked it for her and then she opened her purse and gave me the cash equivalent.

I took the money from her and . . .

Here I want to slow to a brief stop. **This moment** *is something that I have often tried to rationalize, always without success. Along the meandering path of my criminal journey there are many sparkling waystations of guilt, but this one perhaps glitters most brightly. To this day I don't know exactly what possessed me, but I do know what happened later. Anyway . . .*

*

Dermot and I continued to get on well both in and out of work and talked often about our respective ambitions. He wanted his business to grow and I wanted to leave the Ministry of Defence and become a hotel consultant. It was an enjoyable little period of fantasy but soon my mind wandered and I decided that it was time to go further afield again. I was running low on luxury hotels and didn't want to raise suspicion by revisiting those I had stayed in already. Telling Dermot, his mum and the various barmen I had befriended that I was off travelling for a bit, I flew to Heathrow.

I decided to go home for a couple of days before setting off properly, and so booked a business-class flight to Edinburgh on British Airways. I was reading my newspaper on the plane as it taxied from the stand, then swayed to a halt moments later. It remained stationary and I could sense frustration growing from those around me until an announcement from the pilot temporarily calmed things down.

'There is a small operational problem,' explained the pilot in the usual comforting tone, 'with an item of baggage.'

The other passengers sighed themselves into resignation, but it wasn't a concern for me with my newspaper and flexible schedule. It became slightly more concerning a few minutes later with the second announcement.

'Would passenger Castro please make himself known,' said an over-friendly female voice.

I was the renegade baggage. My whole body seemed to seize. I pulled the page very slowly to the side and saw two policemen and a stern-looking man in a blazer standing at the front of the plane. I eased the newspaper back over and was oddly reminded of a scene in *Indiana Jones and the Last Crusade* when Sean Connery hides himself behind a newspaper in an unsuccessful attempt to avoid discovery by the Nazis. It combined with my nerves to take me close to laughing but the presence at my shoulder of a policeman, looking up at the seat number and then down at me, soon put a stop to that.

When we didn't go to the police station I knew something was up. Instead the four of us stood in some anonymous corridor in the depths of Heathrow. The man in the blazer, which I could now see bore the British Airways insignia, was whispering to the policemen through some paperwork on a clipboard. I could only make out the odd snatch but it was two words that added a bit of light for me: *Dubai* and *Barcelona.*

These were destinations that I had attempted to travel to in the past few months with British Airways. In both cases, I had arrived at Heathrow only to find through my new method that the bookings had been sprung as fraudulent. (I mentioned the Dubai case earlier; the Barcelona incident was similar.)

The policemen searched me and opened my wallet. I had four credit cards in there, luckily all in my name. The policemen turned them over, put them back into my wallet and handed it back to me. They asked me where the other cards were, the ones I had been using to book all these flights. They asked where I had been stealing cards from, and then they asked me again where those cards were.

I told them that I had no idea what they were talking about and asked if I could go to the toilet. One of the policemen followed me in and, while I was at the urinal, began to ponder aloud about how disappointed my parents must be with me. If I was to just tell him what I'd been doing, he said gently, he could ensure that things went as smoothly as possible from here. I smiled at the tiles. *They didn't know.*

Back in the corridor the police took the British Airways man to the side and I guessed that they were explaining to him that I was free to go. He went red and hurriedly made a muffled call on his cell phone. When he hung up I could see his shoulders move to deep breaths and then he walked smartly over to me, forcing a smile and pulling a slip of paper from his files.

'Mr Castro, I would like to apologize for all this inconvenience,' he said.

'That's no problem at all,' I said, trying and failing to not sound mocking. 'I just hope I was of some help in clearing this whole matter up.'

His face sharpened in anger but he managed to somehow keep the plastic smile in place.

'Yes, I'm sure,' he said. 'However, it's getting late and you've missed your flight to Scotland.' He handed me the paper. 'I would like you to accept this. It's a voucher for a complimentary night's accommodation at the Renaissance Hotel.'

I looked at him and he misread my mystified response.

'It's right beside the airport,' he said helpfully. 'Why don't you stay there and then come back in the morning and ask for me. We'll get you home then.'

There was a tiny bead of sweat above his eyebrow, on the edge of his forehead. His eyes were hopeless – narrowed and twitching with the pressure of the lie. I thanked him and folded the paper and he turned away with the policemen. I watched bewildered as they walked away, their bodies slightly twisted as they tried to hide the fact that they were talking.

'They must think I'm fucking stupid,' I said to the empty corridor.

CHAPTER FOURTEEN

A week later I sat in a bar in Sydney, drinking a coffee and looking out at the rain lashing down onto the Opera House. I had left Britain on a summer's day and spent twenty-two hours to arrive in winter at the other side of the world. Still, it was another sight to be ticked off – the building that my mum had told me had been built to look like shells.

The day of flying had been made more than bearable by the prestige, attention and soft leather of first class. I had sat and read a guidebook, then a novel, pausing regularly to press the service button above my head. After a while I was doing it out of habit, with no idea what I was going to ask for until the stewardess arrived. Much to their relief, I finally fell asleep somewhere over the Indian Ocean.

Needless to say, I didn't fly with British Airways. The curious incident of the men in the corridor had left me slightly unsure. It was understandable that the airline was after me, but it was surprising that the police had been unable to chip in with some information of their own. It seemed unlikely that my antics over the previous few months had failed to produce a single warrant, and it led me to conclude that they must be working their way through the system.

There was no doubt that other parties would be joining British Airways in the hunt soon enough. It was inevitable but, with my new methods of protection and the heightened confidence that my recent travels had given me, I accepted this as simply another indication of my progress.

After they had let me go at Heathrow I had travelled into London and stayed at the St Martin's Lane again. The next morning I took the train back to Glasgow and spent the journey trying to decide on my next destination, only to find that my family had been planning a trip of their own. My father and Dean, it was announced over dinner, were going back to Chile for a month, where they would spend time travelling and visiting various branches of the Castro clan.

I could feel my dad staring at me.

'Would you like to come?' he asked eventually.

His face looked tense and challenging; this was a question he had agonized over. He was challenging me to prove that I had the means to back up my story of a successful career, but more importantly it was an attempt to pull me back in.

I wanted desperately to accept, to alleviate some of the unspoken worries that he and Mum had, but I couldn't. Although my operation was getting slicker by the week, I never knew when a twist of fortune would leave a brief void of means or I would be forced temporarily to go to ground. I mumbled something about work commitments and that I would let him know, and he looked straight back down to his plate.

With the atmosphere still difficult the next day, I made my escape and flew back down to Heathrow and then on to Australia, where I now sat contemplating the rain and what I would do next. I stayed in a smart hotel with views up towards the Harbour Bridge but the weather and the jet lag had taken away some of my usual excitement at being abroad. I still went out at nights and spent money like a man possessed, but during the days I slept or sat around considering the last two weeks.

I decided that I would go to Chile. The only area of my

life that concerned me at this point was the unease within my family. I had never been more content or secure with regards to the fraud, and I had certainly never enjoyed such levels of success. A month in Chile with Dad and Dean could make the whole picture complete.

That evening I sat on my balcony watching the drizzle falling over Sydney Harbour and called Battlefield. My dad answered and I explained that I was in France for a work meeting but had juggled a few things about to make the Chile expedition. He tried to sound matter-of-fact about it but I could detect the pleasure in his voice that deflected down the line.

After speaking to him I took out my laptop and hooked up to the Internet. After a bit of searching I found what I wanted – a flight to Heathrow and an onward connection to Chile that gave a window of just a couple of hours at the airport. The place could still be used without any great risk, but there was no point in hanging about there for too long.

I had explained to my dad that their flight was full but in reality I had no intention of joining them for the journey. Something could go wrong and I could be yanked off the plane again. Although they would find out eventually if I got picked up once more, it would be preferable if they didn't have to witness the process.

Equally, I knew Dad would disapprove of my new first-class status. He had yearned to make this journey to the Castro homeland for years, and would have been saving for it religiously. He viewed such a trip as a pilgrimage and something to be treated with honour and reserve. The thought of me lying prone on a first-class seat while he stewed through in economy made me chuckle, but it wasn't a scenario I was willing to create.

Their flight left before I arrived back from Australia, but

it wouldn't have been possible to see them anyway. I spent what time I had running around bureaux de change and pulling cash from the remaining cards. Two of them had been active when I boarded in Sydney but cancelled on arrival in London, and I became nervous about producing enough money for the month ahead.

As often happened in these spells of mild hysteria, all measurement of proceedings was lost as I flung myself into action. When I eventually responded to a final call for my flight, I walked down the tunnel believing that $2,000 had been gained from maybe five successful trips to bureaux. I felt almost undeserving as I took my seat in first class for take-off. I had wanted to arrive in Chile without requiring any more backing, and started to have nightmarish imaginings of being arrested in a Chilean bureau de change with my dad and Dean sobbing in the corner.

It was only when the plane aligned after take-off and I pulled out the mass of notes and receipts that things became clearer. In fact, I can recall them now with an exactness that had been lost in the buzz and the rush. In around an hour, I had hit nine bureaux for $12,560.

We met up at Santiago Airport where we hired a minibus, loaded it up with our luggage and set off northwards. Chile is the longest country in the world, a thin streak on the western edge of South America wedged between the Pacific and the Andes, and the 900 miles to Tocopilla didn't look too long a journey on the map. Besides, we had plenty to do along the way with Castros, or people who know Castros, or someone Dad may once have worked on a ship with at some point to be visited along the way.

We crammed into their houses at night for dinner and

stories and the great Chilean ritual of looking at family photographs. We'd leave early in the morning while the air was still cool and Dad would wave and beep the horn before setting off up the endless *autopista*. Dean and I would chat and swap CDs for our Discmans, or I would pull out the map to quiz Dad.

He was in his element, leaning on the open window with a heavy arm while he pointed out the sights that we passed. He told us stories of the trips he had taken as a young man on this road, when the country had been under military rule and the *carabineros* would stop you for a bribe if they were feeling bored. This was rare for him, to speak unprompted of his childhood, and there was a closeness in the car as we approached Tocopilla that I had not felt for a long time.

This mood was maintained through our stay in the town, as my dad revelled in being back amongst his family and childhood friends. My grandmother, whom I only remembered through childhood eyes, was a kind and mischievous soul who I think approved of the gypsy she recognized in me. I told her a sanitized version of my life since we had last met but she cut me off eventually with,

'*¿Eres contento?*'

'*Sí, abuelita, soy contento,*' I told her and she looked wise and *contento* herself.

The amount of money that I had with me made me feel awkward and crude. I wasn't in my usual environments, where a show of spending power met approval or at least grudging envy. Here, where people had little and society seemed to run on theories of loyalty and respect, a loud *gringo* flashing his wad about would not have been a welcome sight.

I had come to associate happiness purely with spending money, and it was confusing for me to see the satisfaction of the Chileans. In my warped mind, I concluded that their happiness stemmed solely from the fact that they knew no better. If they had stood in Bond Street or Fifth Avenue with money in hand, or walked into grand hotel suites, then they would have had more to judge life by.

From when we left Tocopilla for the journey back down to Santiago, there was a new hint of animosity between my father and myself. He was obviously saddened by his farewells to people he might never see again, but there was something else. I knew what it was – our return to the UK and the paths that we would both be taking when we got there.

He tried a couple of times to touch on what my future might hold, but I batted him off with little information. My guilt at this situation turned into hostility and the two of us sat in our own private depressions for much of the journey, while Dean tried manfully to keep the holiday spirit alive. I don't know what was going through my father's head as he silently gunned the van south, but I had my own concerns.

I was going to go back to Dublin for now, but everything else was uncertain. Most pressing was the fact that I had effectively taken a month off from the cards, and the checks and balances that made me feel secure. I wondered what had been going on in my absence, in unknown offices of unknown people.

After a subdued farewell at the airport I slept much of the way back across the Atlantic to Heathrow. There I caught the first plane to Dublin, where I took a room in a central hotel and crashed out again. I could hear my phone ringing at various points during the next morning and eventually I stirred and picked up my messages.

They were all from Dermot and the first one gave a decent summary.

Elliot, what the fuck's going on? My mum's being held by the Garda at the airport. What's … just call me when you get this.

And on and on they went, getting more frenzied and aggressive each time. That stupid, spontaneous booking I had made two months ago for his mum to fly to Manchester. It had come back to me on a few occasions in the period since and I had made some faint plan to book an alternative flight nearer the time, but it had been blown away by my sojourn to Chile.

Now Dermot's dear old mum, who used to make me tea in the office and blether away about the Edinburgh Royal Tattoo, was banged up in a prison cell at the airport. Because of a dodgy ticket that I had *sold* her. Oh dear God. I felt awful, but I couldn't afford to get in touch. She would have told them by now that I was responsible for the ticket, and quite rightly so, and they'd have found that I was in Dublin if they had checked through the airline passenger lists.

I grabbed my things together and went and found an Internet café. I booked a room beside the airport for two nights in the name of Elliet Castra. I jumped in a taxi and went straight there, where the receptionist ignored the typo and flashed through my card. I had three active cards left at this point, and I had to get myself to a place where I could start the process of gaining more.

That was a minor concern, of course. Actually getting out the country was the larger issue. My thinking was that I would hole up for a bit and then hopefully slip over to Glasgow without drawing any attention. And so, after two days of takeaway food and hotel movies, I walked over to Dublin Airport and booked on the first flight to Glasgow.

I called my mum and told her I'd be home that evening, and then I tried to call Dermot but I just couldn't finish entering the number. He might guess I was in the airport and alert the Garda after all. At least, that's how I justified it to myself.

I made it to the airport gate and still there had been no uniforms, or signs of suspicion. There was a newspaper lying abandoned and I tried to read it until boarding was finally announced. I joined the queue with relief, and wasn't even irritated when another passenger tapped me lightly on the arm. I moved to let him pass but he stayed still, and then I turned and saw that he wasn't a passenger at all.

At first my dealings with the Garda seemed slightly unreal. The policeman who had picked me up at the gate was a short, friendly guy called Declan Farrell who led me down to his office. He was carrying a few extra pounds and had twenty years on me but the thought of making a run for it never occurred as I plodded along beside him.

When we got to his office he eased into his chair and started to talk about my recent flights and hotel stays as if we were comparing holiday notes. It was all a little unsettling and I was trying to decide on my tactics when he turned his notes to face me. He had a fair proportion of my recent exploits mapped out in print.

He was missing a lot but I was impressed by his police work even though the implications weren't too positive for my freedom. I asked as politely as I could about the bail situation and he told me without reservation that there was a good chance I would get it. He then nipped out of the room and came back with my possessions, which had been bagged during processing.

'These,' he said, holding up my remaining cards, 'I believe to be fraudulent cards and will be holding here.' I didn't answer. He held up the passport. 'I'll be keeping a hold of this as well, Mr Castro.'

He knew what he was doing. I might have been on

course for bail, but he certainly wasn't going to make it easy for me to get away. When I was granted bail as predicted, Declan Farrell was waiting outside the court. He handed over the name and address of a bed and breakfast and told me to stay there for the two days until the court case.

I left him with an assurance that I would see him in court and set off with my directions. There was no way I was going to be foolish enough to go to court, but it was not going to be easy to slip out of this one. I was going to stay one night at this B&B and then hitchhike to Northern Ireland, stealing across the border if passport checks were in operation. I'd then be in the UK, and able to fly to Glasgow without my passport.

The plan failed immediately, as I arrived at the B&B to find the place was a glorified halfway house. They wouldn't let me in for some reason, and those inhabitants who did appear at the window were useless drunks who shouted unintelligibly at me. I wandered back through the city trying to work out my next move, which was limited by my sudden reduction in means.

All I had in the world on that day in Dublin was paper and a pen, the address of the B&B, thirty euros and Declan Farrell's phone number. As an escape kit, it was somewhat limited. If only, I thought despairingly, I had one of the cards. I pictured the card I would prefer, the one that I believed to be the safest bet, and it came straight into my mind.

I tried harder, stopping and sitting on a bench. I took the pen and paper and readied my hand, waiting and hoping for more. Slowly it all came through – numbers, dates, and a name. My photographic memory was something that I had ignored for so long I had forgotten it existed, and I was thrilled with its timely return.

I scribbled all the information down and dived once

more into an Internet café, where Expedia soon provided me with a hotel room for the night. Things were very definitely on the up and up. I had a long bath, ordered room service and looked forward to the following day's onward journey.

As I slipped off to sleep I almost felt sorry for Declan Farrell, but he would be impressed by the manner in which I had tricked my way clear. I slept soundly that night, until around five o'clock in the morning. There were noises, and footsteps, and there seemed to be lights on all around me and then I was awake and looking at Declan Farrell.

He was smiling as he stood looking at me and the room that I had been sleeping in.

'It appears that you got the wrong place, Mr Castro,' he said as I squinted at him from the bed.

They had no choice but to give me bail again but this time it was so loaded with conditions that I was shipped off to Dublin's Cloverhill Prison in the meantime. It wasn't too much of an ordeal. I knew that bail was going to come through soon enough and I was put on the foreign nationals wing, a relatively relaxed area of the newly built prison.

My frustration with the red tape that was holding up my bail managed to consume most of my energy, and there were a few guys on the wing who I got on pretty well with. Even so, this was a prison and it hadn't been part of the planned escalation of my blossoming fraud career to be back inside one within five months of release.

I celebrated my twentieth birthday in Cloverhill on 10 November 2002 with an extra portion of pudding and a pretty desperate call home. I'd had to tell my parents about my detention because I needed Mum to book me some accommodation in Dublin as part of the bail conditions. My dad hadn't been to the phone since that first call but he came on to dryly wish me Happy Birthday. He managed to keep his anger just about contained, which I appreciated.

In late November I was told that I was to be released in two weeks and my mum booked me five nights in a B&B, after which I was to be sentenced. The lawyer assigned to me in Dublin suggested that I would almost definitely be looking at further jail time and that was all I needed to hear. This time there could be no hitches with my escape.

From Cloverhill I went and booked into the B&B, my prison paranoia suggesting that Declan Farrell could be following me. After satisfying myself that I was without company I made my way into town. I was penniless and didn't want to incriminate my mum by having her send the finances for me to get away. I was going to have to dip reluctantly back into thieving.

It was coming up to Christmas and Dublin was wintry and full of decoration. I only had a thin jacket and was bitterly cold as I walked through the streets, looking for some suggestion of opportunity. I tried a few bars without success and then spotted a bustling hotel lobby.

Inside, a coach party were preparing to leave and so people were everywhere, looking for staff with some query or another. The check-in desk had been temporarily abandoned and I scanned the contents as I walked past. There were a small pile of forms sitting beside the keyboard and, on my way back round, I swiped these up and tucked them under my arm as I walked back out the door.

I turned the corner and found a phone box where I looked through my haul. Other than a bag of money, I couldn't have done better. These were administrative check-in forms, with full cardholder details and even home addresses. The possibilities offered were beyond what I had hoped for and I picked up the phone, pushing in one of my few coins and asking the operator for a hotel I knew near the train station.

Half an hour later I walked into that hotel reception in a distressed state. The man behind the desk was an approach-able-looking sort, but I didn't let my pleasure show behind my discomfort.

'Excuse me,' I said nervously, 'I think that my father may have called. Sorry, I might have the wrong . . .'

'Mr Thompson?' he said, eyebrows raised.

'Yes, yes, that's me,' I answered, letting some hope break through into my faltering voice.

'Don't worry about a thing, Mr Thompson.' He looked as if he wanted to embrace me. 'Your father has booked you a room and authorized us to give you a cash advance. He's given a couple of security questions to ask you, if you don't mind?'

'Oh, thank God,' I said, and rolled my eyes heavenwards.

'It's OK, son.' He reached over the desk and placed a hand on my shoulder. 'The Garda will catch the bastards.'

I steeled myself and held his gaze.

'I hope so, sir, I hope so.'

That night I was in celebratory mood but chose not to leave the room. The false name and the cash for my onward travel settled my worries about another Declan Farrell wake-up call, but I wasn't going to take any chances. The next morning I checked out of the hotel and bought myself a hat and scarf both for the cold and as a partial disguise.

I walked to the station and caught the Belfast train without seeing a single Garda uniform. I thought there would be a passport check of some nature during the journey, and had a complicated story of misfortune ready, but it never came. When the train rolled into the first station after the border, I knew that I was away and gone.

I was back into the exhilarating world I had been forced to vacate temporarily during my stay at Cloverhill. Being unable to return to Eire was a small price to pay for once again opening up the globe for exploration.

I flew to Glasgow and arrived a few days before Christmas, which meant the usual tension could be artificially banished. I went first to the passport office and managed to score an emergency replacement, explaining with an element of truth that the original had been stolen in Ireland. The holiday post meant it was over a week before I managed to have some new cards delivered, but the Castro house never dipped below civil as the four of us ate, drank and visited friends to eat and drink some more.

One night I came home from a party and slept late and heavy. I woke up in the early afternoon and wandered through to the front room where my dad was sitting watching the television. I sat down opposite and he looked at me with his eyes hooded and hard. I saw the envelope just before his arm opened up to send it flying into my lap.

'It's for you,' he growled.

I looked down at the bank's crest on the envelope and my father's signature on the special delivery slip. It was probably time to move on.

I suppose it must seem strange that I chose Canada again, but I guess it just demonstrates my cock-sureness at the time. Ireland had been a pain, but it had only arisen due to one stupid error that had obviously led Declan Farrell to dig up some other information.

In Canada, whoever had been waiting in that hotel room had nearly got me for maybe a few grand. It was hardly Most Wanted material and, besides, I had loved Toronto. In Battlefield I looked on Expedia and my mind was settled when I read about the splendour of the King Edward Hotel. I was going back to Toronto, first class of course.

After a comfortable journey I arrived at the airport and booked a limo to the hotel. Sipping champagne in the back, I laughed aloud thinking about the return journey I had made to the airport last time I was here, as an upended Secret Service operative. What I should have been doing instead was making phone calls and checking if the cards I had were still active.

When I got to the hotel, the first card I tried to use to check in sent the machine into a flurry. The receptionist looked unsure, and turned to look behind her as if to ask for assistance.

'Hang on,' I said quickly, pulling out my wallet, 'I'll pay cash.'

The momentary hitch over, I dropped off my luggage in the room and went to look at the second-floor shrine the hotel has to its famous clientele. I walked down the row of photographs and autographs with satisfaction. Elvis *and* the Beatles can't be wrong. It was a good club to be in and I headed out to the shops with a spring in my step.

At first I was trying on clothes with little intention, but soon I had accelerated into a kind of insanity. I had a pocket full of money and cards and I *had* to use them. My nervous cough came out to play and I felt clumsy and obvious, but I couldn't make myself stop. Shop assistants looked at me in confusion as I grabbed and pointed, ignoring their polite suggestions of alternatives or measurements.

The stores began to close around me, sending the welcome

message that my expedition had reached an end. My heart pounded as I walked back through the streets weighed down with the bags. There was still mostly joy and achievement, but that manic edge – it was my first experience of it and it had caught me unawares. I decided that it was the feast after the famine, retail indigestion, nothing more. I would soon be levelled.

I concentrated on the opulence of the hotel to relax me. The lobby was stunning and polished, the elevator smelt of cologne and cigars and the carpet in the corridor was the thickest I had ever seen. My shoes ran through it as if they were parting grass. The bags of shopping were heavy and entangled and so, when I reached the door to my room, I just squeezed the keycard from my pocket and slid it in the slot.

Do you remember this?

Security (2)   *I would never, ever walk into my hotel room without knocking on the door and saying 'Housekeeping'. Any policeman or security guard hiding inside . . .*

CHAPTER FIFTEEN

Heathrow, March 2006

Neil Forsyth

In a small room at Heathrow police station DC Ralph Eastgate is talking about retirement. He and his wife have bought a house in France, down in the Var region near the village of Draguignan. It's got a swimming pool, a large garden and a view across the trees and vineyards. You can wander down one road to the local shops or you can drive ten minutes in the other direction to the golf course. And still, his wife worries.

'She says, "What are you going to do all day?"' Eastgate tells me. 'I just say that I'm going to wake up every day and think, "What will I do today?" It's not that bad a way of life.'

This isn't our first conversation, it's not even our first conversation about Draguignan, but things have progressed. When we talk about it now I am lost in the world of intrigue, and a retiring fifty-year-old fraud detective talking about houses with swimming pools can't help but appear twisted. Eastgate's paid to second-guess, though, and he does so.

'I married late and rich, Mr Forsyth,' he says with his handsome grin. 'Her last husband was a wealthy man but luckily she had the better lawyer.'

Pre-marital life, he volunteers, didn't lack female company and this is easy to accept. He's tall and athletic and carries himself like a sporty teenager, ranging along the corridors of the police station. He's impish and careless in conversation (he will later casually tell me of an affair between a policeman and a famous British aristocrat), which might be the retirement calling but I suspect it's always been this way.

When he talks in that drawled Surrey accent, in fact with everything he does, he has an inherent certainty that goes far beyond the badge in his wallet. To grab and hold his attention someone, or something, would have to show depths of subtlety. Maybe it would help if everyone else wanted them too.

I take him back to Draguignan. What happens when the day draws in and they are back in the big house with the swimming pool?

'Then I tell the wife to stick her jacket on and we walk down to the village,' he answers. 'We go for a nice dinner or a couple of drinks, and talk to the locals. We're both getting French lessons now so hopefully by then we'll be chatting away to anyone who'll listen.'

What about?

'I don't know,' says Eastgate with a shrug, 'tell them stories.'

We laugh, because we know the suggestion. In confirmation, he reaches down and lifts a pile of paper with both hands and places it on the table. It's a wild stack of different colour and size, roughly bound by elastic and topped with a stamped label. Amongst the numbers sits the name. *Castro*. Eastgate looks down at it significantly and he smiles in concession.

'This,' he says, softer than before, 'would be the first one that I would tell.'

Twenty-six years before the lives of Ralph Eastgate and Elliot Castro came together, Eastgate sat drinking with friends in a bar in Purley, Surrey. Since leaving boarding school he'd been working in shops and bars and chasing women, and that was all right by him. Now he was twenty-one though, and suddenly the girls wanted men with a few quid in their pocket to go with the looks and the attitude.

His drinking partner told him that police wages had just received a massive hike. Eastgate wasn't sure about the job but he joined anyway and found out quickly that it wasn't for him. He was a bobby on the beat in south London, driving about looking for crime and then handing over to the CID whenever it got interesting.

Eastgate was the man left after the ambulances went, speaking to secondary witnesses and filling in forms. He was thrown as a rookie into the 1976 Notting Hill riot, where he and his colleagues were told to go and find dustbin lids to act as shields against the bricks. It was amateur night for the capital's coppers and Eastgate wanted out.

He applied for the CID and was eventually put on the Crime Squad, the first step on the crossover. He was in plain clothes but still on the front line and when Brixton rioted in 1981 he was there again. Eastgate arrived for the midnight shift and the DI called them together and said that they had lost control of the streets. They had to stop the looting but lacked the men to make the arrests.

Eastgate wondered what he meant and then a cupboard was opened and they were being handed pickaxe handles. That night, he and others leapt from Bedford vans to tackle the looters against a backdrop of smashed glass and endless fires. As he tells me this now, in a nice suit and with his hair neatly combed, it seems as unreal to him as it does to me.

'Something had to be done,' he says definitely. 'But imagine if that was to happen now?'

It was the final straw for him to push for CID and a step back from the madness. He made it the following year and was posted to Belgravia, the jewel in London's crown and home to England's great and not always good. Eastgate the detective was born, and Eastgate the bachelor didn't do too badly either.

'It was heaven,' he says wistfully, 'heaven. You're talking about the aristocracy here, and they love a man in uniform. I had a very nice relationship with a titled lady who lived in Sloane Square. For a young guy, it was a great place to be and I was starting to love the job.'

There was one case that Eastgate enjoyed more than most. A

youthful impostor was working the area's banks with a well-worked trick. He would stand in an expensive suit in the foyer and introduce himself to customers as the branch manager before relieving them of their chequebooks and escaping out the side door.

When Eastgate caught the scammer he found him to be a charming and respectful young man fresh from Eton who had graduated with a £2,000-a-week cocaine habit. There was something about the civility of the offence that Eastgate respected.

'It was a crime, he was a criminal and I was glad to catch him,' he clarifies first. 'But he was a very interesting chap and I had a certain respect for what he'd done, and the way that he'd done it.'

Belgravia was followed by Richmond, a leafy semi-suburb that was quieter but had its share of council estates. Suddenly drugs were no longer something to be encountered behind closed doors and their effects were showing in every area of crime. Instead of pitting his wits against criminal masterminds, Eastgate was trying to question raving addicts and finding bodies blackened by abuse.

When he moved to Tooting he was freshly disgusted. The troubled estate down the road from Brixton was freefalling through the early 1990s. Back in the day, Eastgate's uniform or badge had made hooligans freeze in deference but now the police were targets. The locals, particularly the African and West Indian gangs, saw the police as an invading force into the concrete sprawls.

There was the case of the Tooting rapist, whom Eastgate once sat opposite in an interview room. The man had dragged women into the shrubbery of Tooting Common and destroyed their lives for ever, but Eastgate couldn't muster the consuming hatred of others.

'He was nicked,' he says simply. 'That's the important thing. You get guys that want to go and take these people apart in their cells, but what good is that going to do other than probably help his case? He was on his way to prison for life, and when he got there he was going to be a nonce. That's enough punishment for anyone.'

And then he says something else. 'Life has a habit of catching up on people.'

The move to Heathrow was a dodge. The Metropolitan Police Commissioner at the time had declared that experienced detectives were going to be forced back into uniform to pass on their knowledge for the greater good. *Fuck that*, thought this experienced detective, and he spotted the autonomous Heathrow command as a way out.

In London's police stations the joke had always been that Heathrow detectives investigating a wallet theft would fly to Greece for a week to get a statement and when in the country, would spend afternoons playing golf or getting pissed in the first-class lounges. In one of these lounges, they said, the Portuguese ambassador had interrupted a female copper granting one of her colleagues a blowjob.

Eastgate arrived in 1996 to find that a new DI had swept the place clean. The CID unit was filled with expertise and professionalism, and he knew instantly that this was the position he had long been looking for.

'I also found out,' he adds, 'that the blowjob story wasn't accurate. The ambassador was Spanish.'

When Eastgate arrived for his shifts at Heathrow, he found that there were no muggers, robbers and rapists to be processed. Instead he found that he was given both freedom and responsibility. This detective constable wasn't interested in becoming an office-and-meetings man to rise higher. Instead he wanted to solve crime and at Heathrow he found a new type.

The Airline Ticket Fraud Unit had been formed in the 1970s to deal with forged and stolen tickets. It was a time when bedroom hucksters could distort tickets this way and that to fly *gratis* all over the world. Technology both won the war and created a new threat with the spread of credit cards. By the time that Eastgate joined the unit, 99 per cent of the work was credit card fraud and running a paper trail on behalf of the airlines and credit card companies.

'You're not relying on an old lady pulling someone out of a line-up,' Eastgate enthuses. 'Everything you need is there in black and white and it's just a case of rolling your sleeves up and getting on with it.'

He was drawn to cases that held throwbacks to old-time daring, to men cast from similar moulds as the fresh-faced 'bank manager' ten years before. He caught an American antiques dealer flying Concorde on jumbo jet economy tickets, modified by a machine he had built himself.

'He denied it to the bitter end, and put in such a performance that the bloody jury let him go,' Eastgate can now laugh.

That story, about the antiques dealer and his ticket machine, was the one that Eastgate used to tell when people asked about his job. Then he came across something else. Twenty-six years after he had joined the police, and four years before he would leave, he found the case that he says he was probably always waiting for.

'I got a call in the summer of 2002 from a woman called Cathie Walker at British Airways,' says Eastgate. He's donned glasses and his voice is infused and official as he starts to unravel his prize file. 'She's been in their security division for years, a lovely lady but I don't think she can speak to you.' *(I will later call Cathie Walker. She is a lovely lady, but she can't speak to me. In fact, she can't speak to me to such an extent that her name is not really Cathie Walker.)*

'She told me that they had this guy called Elliot Castro who had been flying with them through the first-class desk at Edinburgh Airport. He was only a kid, she said, and was flying at all different times of the week. They just weren't too sure about him and she was passing that concern on to me.'

It wasn't much more than a courtesy call. Eastgate noted the name with little interest until another call came in. And then another.

'A couple of credit card companies got in touch about this guy who was ripping them off. A lot of his stuff was going through Heathrow, and so they came to me. I was writing down all the details and then they said that same name again, Elliot Castro. So, OK, I'm interested.'

Eastgate started to spend free hours and quiet mornings toying with this new case.

'British Airways would be forever telling me about these journeys he was making. He seemed to be getting braver, going further afield.'

There is no system at Heathrow that allows a computer search of all future flight bookings. It seems incredible but this is the case as Eastgate and I sit in the station today, and it was the case in 2002 when Eastgate opened the file that now sits bloated between us. Information on Castro was coming in from airlines and card companies, but it was retrospective and seemingly inaccurate.

'There were a couple of times,' reveals Eastgate as he sorts carefully through his notes, 'when British Airways had picked up that he was due to fly and I would go down to the terminal to wait for him.' What happened? 'He never showed.' Where was he going? 'Dubai once, I think. I'm not sure.'

Eastgate pauses as he remembers. 'There was one occasion,' he says, 'when British Airways called me to say that he was staying at the Renaissance Hotel.' His eyes narrow as he tries to order his thoughts.

'I think, I'm sure this is right, that British Airways had actually put him up for the night. I think his flight had been cancelled. So the next morning I get this call from them to say that he's in the Renaissance Hotel. When I get there he's nowhere to be seen, he hadn't even checked in.'

It was shortly after this incident that Eastgate entered Castro on the police national computer. His file was filling with faxes and transactions and pressure was growing on the detective. Yet for the detective, there was nothing but frustration.

'I could only hope that he slipped up,' he admits. 'We didn't have a photo of the guy, and pretty much all the information we were getting was old by the time we got it. I found out later that the Irish police had him for a bit, but they're on a different system and he was never actually convicted over there, which would have helped. For us, it was a case of waiting for him to make a mistake.'

As 2002 ran itself out, Castro was no closer to capture. Eastgate revisited the file only to add new crimes. British Airways reported that he seemed to have stopped using them entirely but the credit card companies were still calling. They knew the name but it was arriving too late and masked from view, often as an extra cardholder or in another form that slipped below their radar.

'Everyone was just hoping, really,' says Eastgate, 'and then it came.'

It was January 2003 and Castro was caught.

'I got a call from American Express to say that he'd been found and banged up in Canada,' says Eastgate. 'Some Internet company had tipped off the Toronto police and they'd got him at a posh hotel. He'd been using an American Express card so the Toronto Police Service had gone to them for evidence and they came straight to me. I told British Airways and everyone else who, of course, said, "Great, let's nick him."'

Amid the jubilation, Eastgate was quick to tie down the opportunity. He takes his glasses off as he tells me about this, the call that was to be the conclusion.

'I called the Toronto police,' he says carefully, 'and told them the situation. I told them to ring me up when they put him on the plane, whenever that eventually was, because I wanted to be there to meet him.'

It must have been a good day at Heathrow, I suggest. Eastgate shrugs, raises his palms,

'He was nicked. That was that.'

CHAPTER SIXTEEN

So, Canada. Are you getting bored of prisons? It does get repetitive – the mental torture and the dreaming of better days. And now we have to go to another one, Toronto's Don Jail. Like me, you don't really have much choice in the matter.

Detective Danny Bell was in charge of the hotel bust and he wasn't going to give me a chance to get away, especially after I wound him up with a couple of well-placed jibes. He was a little terrier of a man and made sure there was no suggestion of bail, turning up at court and regaling the judge with an impressive demolition of my character. He also seemed convinced that I was travelling on a forged passport.

I was an interested spectator, particularly when he laid before the court the wealth of information he had received from Expedia, the Internet travel provider I had used often. After the hearing, when I had some time to myself in the back of a sweatbox on the way to the Don, a few things straightened themselves out.

Expedia had shopped me to the Canadian police.

Expedia had also shopped me to Declan Farrell, which was how he had managed to find me in my Dublin hotel room at 5 a.m.

Which meant that Expedia and Declan Farrell had been working together against me.

Which meant that Declan Farrell and the Canadian police

would now be working together against me. The first sign of that was the fact that they were certain my passport was fake – they knew that Declan Farrell had the original.

That was all I knew for definite but there had to be more going on than I could see. Other airlines, credit card companies, the British police, I had no doubt that they would all be on their way to the party.

It was an intimidating and worrying situation, but these things are always relative. It's hard to be intimidated and worried about something that may or may not happen when you find yourself in the Don Jail. I had been toughened to a degree by the British nicks but it was immediately apparent that this was to be an entirely different incarceration experience.

After changing into an orange jumpsuit before a watching guard I was put into a holding cell with a group of vagrants. As we stood there one of them pissed on the floor, contemplating the rest of us defiantly as he did so. I looked at the guard in astonishment but he was pretending not to have noticed. Then they called my name and I tiptoed around the puddle and onwards to my new home.

The landing itself was a large hall ringed at three sides with wire fencing and then a row of cells down one flank. Behind the wire at one end was the screws' control station and a table from where they would observe the goings-on. For large parts of the day the screws and prisoners would remain on either side of the fencing. From their post they could view the whole landing and also keep an eye on a small gated-off area where inmates could shave.

Along the fence that ran opposite the cells were dotted three phones and beyond it was a passageway from where the screws could observe the cells and their inhabitants. In the middle of the landing was a recreational area dominated by long steel tables with benches attached.

This was all not too dissimilar to the British nicks I'd been in, but at the other end of the landing things got a bit more curious.

In a row along the back wall were the sinks, toilets and showers. A free-standing wall had been built to screen the area from the landing, but somewhere down the line it had been decided that privacy was something prisoners didn't deserve, so large windows had been set into the wall as a countermeasure. Therefore while you showered, or sat on the toilet pondering life's great conundrums, you did so in full view of the prison unit outside and all the visual glories that it contains.

The cells ran the length of the landing. The two nearest the guards were occupied by a cadre of Portuguese Canadians who effectively ran the landing and I rapidly realized how important their role was. The respect and fear they inspired meant that the other inmates kept themselves in reasonable check and in return the screws allowed the Portuguese to handle the food distribution at meal times.

Some days, the screws would leave us locked up all day but open the cells of the Portuguese so they could collect the food and bring it round. The Portuguese were also the main source of contraband in the prison, especially for tobacco that was like gold because of the blanket ban on smoking in the jail.

When we were allowed out of our cells – and some days we would be out for hours at a time – there was very little to do other than use the phone or sit chatting at the tables.

People had *nothing* in that prison. There were guys who had been in for years and they would have a single photo of their family and maybe a couple of letters, it was that hard to keep anything else from being swept up in the regular searches.

The screws' paranoia was justified. The Portuguese might have kept my landing in tight check but elsewhere in the prison there would be regular incidences of extreme violence. A favourite trick that I was told of in my first few days at the Don was for inmates to smuggle chicken bones out to the exercise yard – a small area surrounded by thirty-foot high walls that we would occasionally be granted access to – and sharpen them on the concrete walls. These would then be thrust into faces, necks or, if you were lucky, buttocks in a friendly process known as *shanking*.

The layout of the landing at the Don created an atmosphere of constant pressure and distrust that was apparent to me from the start. There was no escape from the screws' eyes. Not only were you forbidden to visit the toilet in your own company, the cells resembled the cages of a zoo.

They faced the landing through a huge barred gate that would open and close electronically at the whim of the screws, with the regimental timings of the British prison system soon seeming a lifetime away. During periods of extended lock-up they would stay resolutely closed and food would be passed through a small gap at the bottom by the Portuguese.

Within the cell there was a bunk bed which was narrow with mattresses that felt like damp wood. Built into the rear of the cell was a sink and toilet contraption and a small desk was tacked on to the other wall. The remaining area, the stone ground that sat between the bunk bed and the desk, well you'd think that this would just be the floor wouldn't you?

When I arrived in my cell on the first day I muttered a

greeting to the two guys that were already there, looked around the room and then looked back in confusion at the two other prisoners. The floor, it emerged, was where I was to sleep. There had been no mistake, the Don was critically overcrowded and that was that.

On my first night in prison in Canada, the first night in an indefinite stay, I curled up on a thin mattress on the stone and tried to sleep. The sadistic prison rules stipulated that the third man in had to sleep with his head next to the toilet rather than the bars. The smell was overpowering. I wrapped toilet paper round my face to try and take away some of the edge but it seemed to permeate through me and that night I dreamt about being submerged in a sea of sewage.

The next day I found out how close the dream had come to reality. The toilets in the Don were notoriously unpredictable and often overflowed without warning. That morning it transpired that a guy a few cells down from me had woken up in the middle of the night with a faceful of shit and piss. He had been taken to the medical wing to get checked over because, in panic, he had swallowed some of the waste.

Jesus Fucking Christ. Canada was supposed to be a civilized country, a healthy nation that projected an image of natural beauty to the outside world, and here I was in danger of waking up covered in my cellmates' shit. Going to prison I could accept, but this was another proposition entirely. Driven by disgust I cornered what looked like a relatively approachable screw and explained I was a young foreign national here on remand for a minor fraud crime, and awaiting assistance from the British embassy.

That evening I was moved to a two-man cell to share with a young car thief called Ned who immediately christened me Scottie. I was pleased with the success of my Embassy line, but for now I was busier getting depressed. When I was in prison in the UK I had always been aware what stage the legal process was at and I'd had the relief of speaking to my mum and reading British newspapers. In Canada I would be snatched from my bare cell and sent to court for meaningless sessions that always ended with me back in the sweatbox, back to the Don.

Detective Danny Bell had worked with Expedia to present a pretty solid case against me. I had taken Expedia for nearly $30,000 – a bill that they'd apparently been unable to pass on to the credit card companies, which seemed to explain their involvement in the case. Now American Express had got in on the act, chipping in claims for a fair few quid themselves and making Danny Bell even more determined in his anti-bail stance. The case was strengthening and I was convinced that the united front against me would have by now stretched to some unknown British authority.

When I wasn't going back and forth to the court, talking to Ned about the intricacies of car crime or taking a scenic dump, I was getting increasingly frustrated with my foreign prisoner status. The phones in the prison could only be used to make collect calls within Canada and to phone home I had to persuade a senior screw to take me to the office. It cost my mum a fortune in reversed phone charges and the screw would sit listening to every word. I made a couple of awkward calls like this and then gave up.

There was also no way for me to get hold of prison money. There was little to spend it on but I could see that it would make things a lot easier if I became a customer of the Portuguese. They had been eyeing me warily since I arrived and I needed the icebreaker of hard cash.

It was a combination of these areas of concern that left me in a particularly foul mood one day when yet another court visit had made me late coming back for lunch. The

Portuguese had left my food with Ned but while I sat eating it at one of the tables a particularly unpleasant screw started dispersing the inmates back to the cells.

As the others wrapped up their phone calls and card games, I continued eating my food until I realized he was standing beside me. I looked up and saw an ugly face, twisted with years of bitterness and conflict.

'Back to your cell,' he said.

'Can I just finish this?' I asked.

'No.'

'Can I take it with me?'

'No.' He stared at me with that repulsive face, and gave me a smirk. I don't know if it was the court and the not knowing, or not having money, or not being able to use the phones, or having my life dictated by this offence to humanity. Either way, it was enough for some Battlefield to break through.

'Why don't you,' I said loudly, staring deep into his stupid, barren eyes, 'go and fuck yourself?'

Time seemed to slow as inmates stopped and turned to us with mouths hanging open in surprise. The screw was moving towards me and then I was being lifted and pushed into the fence. I could hear people running and then I was being lifted again and carried by pairs of arms out the hall, flat on my back as if I was floating while the inmates shouted from their cells.

The Hole at the Don is the nadir, the deepest cut of my prison time. They said I was there for two days but if someone told me today that it was two weeks then I would believe them. A small room without furnishings or light, it was a hell like no other I have ever experienced. For the first few hours I lay unable to move in the arm and leg restraints they had fitted to me on the way from the landing to the Hole. Finally, two guards came in, silently removed them and left me some water. Other than one more cup of water at a future point, this was the only form of nutrition or human contact I had in my period in the Hole.

Locked up in the dark, my other senses strengthened. There were times when I doubted that I was alone in that room, but I couldn't decide if the scratching was vermin or my imagination. I tried to sleep but it was hard with the panic of the blackness and the freezing stone floor. I was forced to busy my mind and, as I pushed myself to find some positive outlook, it produced some unorthodox results.

By the time I staggered out of the Hole and back to the landing, I had a couple of plans to make my stay at the Don a little easier. The experience had also raised my profile amongst the other inmates and when I was led back into the hall the Portuguese called me over to their table. I was apprehensive but my fears dissolved when the head of the gang handed me three large bags of crisps.

I thanked him and made to walk back to my cell, but I would hardly get a few yards before other inmates approached and pushed sweets or cartons of juice into my arms. I became quite emotional at this display of kindness and when I finally reached my cell and Ned produced half his lunch, neatly carved and ready for me, I had to stop myself from breaking down and hugging him. Instead I talked him through my first project.

The Canadian legal service might have appeared a strange beast, but one standard it bore was the sharing with the defendant of all court papers. This had turned up some crackers including Danny Bell's notes regarding my arrest. I still have copies of them. See, for example, this exchange:

DB: Where did you get all these credit cards?

EC: I know more about credit cards than you do (suspect has a smile on face).

DB: No doubt you probably do, but I am not the guy sitting in handcuffs.

EC: I should have known better, what happened at the front desk.

DB: What happened at the front desk?

(no reply)

I was also given a copy of a very cosy letter from Expedia to the Toronto Police Service, detailing their great appreciation of my apprehension and confirming that it was a fraud investigator in their Seattle head office who had sent Bell and his team to wait for me in my room at the King Edward.

More importantly, amongst the notes that Detective Bell had found in that room had been my usual emergency stock of credit card details from the UK. As sharp as ever, he had recognized these for what they were and added them to the submission to the court.

In my cell, therefore, I had photocopied versions of some live credit card details. In the permanent night of the Hole, the possibility that they offered had come to me. All I needed was someone on the outside, which was where Ned came in. He sat on the edge of his bunk looking a little guarded as I tried to break my proposal down.

'Do you,' I asked, 'have someone outside who could do a favour for us?'

'You can't escape, Scottie,' he said in astonishment. 'This is the Don.'

'I know that, Ned. They just have to do a little job for us. I'll pay them, but it's a little bit dodgy. Do you know any-one that would be up for it?'

'*Anyone?*' He laughed, 'How many do you need?'

The next day Ned called his girlfriend and got her to read out the collect call numbers in Canada for the major credit card companies. He whispered them to me twice each and that was them secured. I then walked over to the Portuguese and asked them for their bank details on the outside, which after some explanation they happily gave.

The final step was my calls to the credit card companies, where I passed security and explained that I was on holiday in Canada and had suffered the theft of my wallet and passport. Was it possible to have a small advance sent to a Western Union? This was an option that an operator had once offered me when I made one of my Elliot's uncle calls, and his Canadian counterparts were working from the same script.

The transfer was agreed and I set a test question with the operator for them to forward to Western Union. Ned then alerted an associate roughly the same age as the cardholder and the two of us waited for his friend to pick up the money and pay it into the account given by the Portuguese. A few days later one of them came round to our cell during lockdown. He slid the two trays under the bars and, without looking up, whispered that the money was in.

Soon Ned and I were comforted by the contraband and respect of the Portuguese and I turned my attention to my second ploy: finding a free phone route through to my mum. After a few trial runs and some subsequent adjustment, my method settled into a formula that gave me pretty spectacular results. This was the journey of those calls:

1.   I called the Canadian collect line for American Express, whereupon I would immediately ask to be transferred to a different department.

2.   I would then react with surprise and explain that I was a British

cardholder, waiting to be transferred to the British American Express office in Brighton. They would apologize and put me through.

3. I would tell the adviser in Brighton that I was calling from American Express in Canada. I was trying to get hold of a relative of a British account holder who had been the victim of theft in Toronto. For some reason I couldn't get through to . . . and I would read out my mum's mobile number. Ah, the adviser would say, that's because it's a British mobile number. And then, more often than not, the phone would ring and my mum would answer.

It wasn't an easy way to phone home, and sometimes it would take a few attempts, but there was something deeply satisfying about the calls being generously picked up by American Express. On the days when the screws would let us roam free of our cells I would sometimes be on the phone to my mum for hours on end. Occasionally, she would get a little harassed and explain that she really had to go.

'It's been three hours, Elliot,' she would say apologetically, 'I've got to catch the shops.'

I would allow her to leave, but first she would place a speaker beside the phone and turn it up. While she walked down the aisles of the supermarket in Battlefield, Radio 1 would blast out of the speaker and I would stand in the Don listening to the music and trying to remember the names of new bands.

These developments made my time in the Don bearable in the weeks leading up to sentencing, but I was still terrified of a further spell in there. When the day came, Detective Bell and his many backers put together a thorough portrayal of me as a dedicated international fraudster, but the decrepit nature of the Don worked against them.

So bad were Canadian prison conditions at the time that

the authorities had decided prisoners would serve only a quarter of their sentences so long as they behaved themselves whilst inside. When I was sentenced to a year, the effective sentence was three months, almost exactly the term I had served on remand. At the conclusion of my sentence, the judge announced, I was to be deported back to Great Britain. The message was pretty clear – Canada didn't want me. Well, that was just fine with me.

My lawyer hadn't been able to find out when I was being deported exactly but on one of the court documents I found a name and number of someone at a government agency. It appeared they were handling my case and luckily the office had a toll-free number. I didn't want to cause trouble, but I had to find out what was going on and so I waited until the phones were quiet and went over.

I asked to be transferred to the name that I had and adopted the stiffest of upper lips and a posh English accent, partly for protection and partly through high spirits. This was going to be a short, simple call to give me a date and nothing more. The man picked up.

'I am telephoning,' I explained, 'from the British Embassy. We should like to be apprised of the situation regarding Elliot Castro, whom I believe you are deporting.'

'That's right,' answered the man in an amiable enough voice. 'We're sending him back on Friday, leaves Toronto 8 p.m., gets into Heathrow 8 a.m.'

Friday was in two days. I felt dizzy with delight – I would be in Battlefield by Saturday night, making things right with my family and forming plans. I said what I said next with little thought. It was a glorified sign-off, something that could have come in any other form of words. Luckily, *luckily*, I chose these:

'Excellent, excellent. And, um . . . is there anything else?'

'Ah,' said the man, and I could picture him scanning down the file. 'Well, no, other than this Detective Eastgate at Heathrow Airport.'

My breath caught and my legs felt soft under me. Who was this? *What* was this?

'Eastgate?' I managed meekly.

'Yeah, we've got to contact him, let him know what flight we put Elliot Castro on,' the man continued, oblivious of the horror he was creating for Elliot Castro on the other end of the line. Friday's flight had turned in the blink of an eye from a doorway to freedom to an entrance to an unknown hell. I took a deep breath and sprung into action.

'Ah, yes, Eastgate, I have that here as well. Look, old boy, why not let us sort all that out? I need to speak to him anyway, to give him the flight details.'

The pause was maybe a second.

'Sure, why not?' he said. 'One less thing for me to do.'

Friday came. I woke up sweating in my bunk. It was only now, with everything behind me apart from my departure, that I realized how long I had been here. The unpredictable daily challenges had at least kept time rolling along, but now I was freed from the host of minor concerns that life in the Don created.

I tried to think back to the King Edward Hotel, and to the next hotel that I would be checking into, but it was no use. It was Heathrow Airport, and what would be there, that was controlling me for now. I said my farewells to Ned, who told me that the two of us would drink whisky in Scotland sometime.

As I passed through the landing I waved to the Portuguese, who raised their fists in response, and then I was back down in the processing unit. Two members of the Immigration Service picked me up from there and took me to the airport in a van. We talked about Scotland, the Don and credit card fraud and they even gave me $20 to spend in the airport.

I decided to keep it and the three of us sat at the departure gate until the flight opened for boarding. When it did, the two of them marched me up to the desk and handed a flight attendant a large envelope. They then walked with me down the gangway and waited until I was on the plane, at which point one of them shouted, 'Hurry back,' and the three of us laughed.

I settled into my anonymous economy seat and the questions came like they had been doing since the moment I hung up the phone two days previously and saw that the handle was slick with sweat.

Who was Detective Eastgate?

How much did he know?

Would he be waiting for me at Heathrow?

An elderly woman from Wales sat down beside me and we started chatting shortly into the flight. She was pleasant and talkative, fresh from a trip to see her grandchildren, and it was just the distraction that I needed. The conversation, some sleep and several complimentary drinks managed to get me through the flight but as soon as our descent to Heathrow was announced the alarm returned.

I had a flash of thought and leapt up from my seat, striding quickly down the aisle to find the steward the Canadians had dealt with at the gate. He was looking pretty knackered as he stacked the food trays, and took a moment to recognize me.

'I'll take the envelope now, please,' I said.

He looked wary and leant this way and that to try and spot a more senior colleague. I took a step closer, my voice a little softer.

'Just give me the envelope. Please. The Canadians … they said for me to ask you for it.'

He looked satisfied at this transferral of responsibility and pulled the package from a gap in the plane's fittings. I took it in my hand but he didn't let go, and when I looked up I realized that I hadn't fooled him.

'Good luck,' he said genuinely.

I thanked him, but I was rattled as I returned to my seat. He must have known what was waiting for me after landing. You only need luck if you've been dealt a bad hand to begin with. I ripped open the envelope and found my passport and various official papers that I stuffed into my jacket.

The plane touched down and I said goodbye to the Welsh lady, explaining that I had to wait for some luggage. It's funny, but I was desperate that she should not see me arrested. The other passengers filed off until I had no choice but to follow, and I walked down the gangway with my head swimming.

I rounded a bend in the walkway between the plane and the terminal and found myself heading straight for a doorway where a policeman stood. It was enough for me to lose any final hope, but then I was level with him and then I was ten yards past him and then I was on the escalator. I couldn't believe it. I was free.

With my hands shaking, I handed over my $20 at a bureau de change and looked, dismayed, at the meagre pounds I got in return. I didn't even have the train fare to London. I had to get out of Heathrow somehow, though, and so I hitched a lift on the Heathrow Express to Paddington, hiding in the toilets the whole way to avoid the conductor. From there I spent what I had on the tube fare to Victoria, where I once again retired to the toilets on the Gatwick Express.

At Gatwick Airport I went and found a phone. I was going to have to ask Mum to buy me a flight back to Glasgow. It was a credit card phone and I pulled the papers from my pocket. My hand came back out holding the ticket on which I had been deported. I was about to discard it when I noticed the credit card details on the receipt. The numbers with which some Canadian civil servant had banished me from the country were listed pure and unedited. It was only right, surely, that they paid for this call.

CHAPTER SEVENTEEN

I arrived broken back in Battlefield. Physically decimated from my time at the Don, I was left feeling exhausted by normal life and struggling to keep down any food with a hint of richness. My body seemed to ache permanently and I spent long nights lying awake in my bedroom.

The mental trials of the fugitive played on my mind. Even when I arrived back I had made the taxi driver go to the door for me and press the bell. It was only when I saw my mum standing peering into the street that I knew it was safe. As the days passed and my body refused to catch up, I was left with the painful awareness that each minute I spent at home was borrowed.

This Eastgate would know where I lived. It was a matter of time until he would also know that I had slipped his Heathrow trap. I was under pressure and then I was under more. Nearly a week into my return, I waited until everyone had gone out and then stole through to the living room and settled beside the phone.

I needed to find out who was after me, but that wasn't just it. I was looking for an excuse to stay. I didn't get it. At three famous card companies I asked to be put through to their security divisions and explained that I was calling from the Serious Fraud Office.

'I'm just looking into a suspect named Elliot Castro, and wondered if you had anything on him.'

And back they came:

'Yes.'

'Yes.'

'One moment . . . yes.'

They thanked me for calling and told me to keep them informed. I promised to do so and sat contemplating what these short conversations had meant. What they suggested for the long term was pretty miserable and so I concentrated on what they meant I had to do now. It was pretty clear and I reached for the phone once more to make my more accustomed round of calls.

A couple of days later the cards came to signal my departure and I stood in the hall with Mum and Dean. My mum looked drawn and older and Dean flicked his eyes away from mine. Usually he would ask me questions with loving admiration but this time he just kicked his foot against the wall and pushed his hands deeper into his pockets. I hugged my mum and walked to the door past the entrance to the front room. Inside, my father sat with his side to me, smoking a rolled cigarette and looking straight ahead.

Naturally choosing to give Heathrow a wide berth, I flew down to Gatwick with an open mind. I hit a few bureaux de change and then dallied around the terminal for a while before opting to join Virgin Atlantic's massive Boeing 747–400 to the Bahamas. I dropped several thousand pounds to sleep the entire way there in upper class.

It was a wise decision. If you're ever depressed – maybe you've been stealing credit cards and you have an English detective on your tail, say – then I would recommend Nassau. At first I thought the friendliness and easy patois of the people were suspicious, that I was being set up like I had been in so many schools and prisons for a dramatic switch to hostility, but no punchlines came.

I booked into a sprawling den of luxury on Paradise Island, an outcrop dominated by resorts, casinos and a positive glut of cabaret shows. Ringing this fantasy world was the whitest sand that I had ever seen, running into water that I couldn't believe was natural. That first day I spent lying on a lounger staring at the water or reading a brochure of what lay beyond.

In the evening I was still besotted with the sea, and the Bahamian archipelago that it held, when I befriended a young American couple in the hotel bar. I saw them exchange a smile at my enthusiasm but rattled on regardless, and the three of us seemed to click.

Mike was an oilman whose convention in Nassau had just finished and his wife Jane had flown out from Texas to join him. They had Scottish ancestry, accepted the hotel consultancy line and shared my interests of travel and cocktails.

It might have been the swaying palms, the margaritas or the tinny sound of cabaret drifting through the warm air, but we got along brilliantly. At some point in the evening the two held a whispered conference then turned to face me. The next day, they explained, they were heading out on Mike's father's yacht for a short cruise and would like me to join them.

My first thought, naturally, was that I had run into a couple of swingers but in fact they were straight up. The next morning they came and woke me early, then the three of us made our way down to the harbour. It was slightly awkward, with the drink wearing off and my usual wariness around people in normal conditions kicking in, but the minute we got to the boat all my misgivings vanished.

It was forty feet of beauty, a gleaming testament to excess lolling gently in the water. Mike and Jane bounced aboard like they were stepping onto a bus, and I followed like a kid on Christmas morning. We passed by the cockpit and down some steps into the boat's body where Mike flung a hand to his right.

'That's yours, man,' he said.

I pushed through the swinging door and found a cabin full of dark wood and mirror, and floored with carpet. I dropped my bag and went back up to the deck where Mike was pressing buttons here and there and Jane was setting herself up to sunbathe.

'This is ... amazing,' I said, and Mike smiled warmly back at me.

'Yeah, we're going to have a good time,' he answered, handing me a beer. 'You ready for Toto?'

He meant the Tongue of the Ocean, a huge trench to the west of Nassau where the ocean floor falls away into a colossal ditch thousands of feet deep. I was, of course, engrossed by the place and Mike was happy to indulge me.

I was hopelessly excited during the journey and spent most of it trying unsuccessfully to impress Mike with some Sea Cadet terminology. When we approached the Tongue I clambered round to the boat's bow and stood transfixed by the patch of darkened water that stretched to the horizon.

We sat bobbing on the waves seventy feet above a spot where the world's floor falls away. I had encountered this place, and others like it, one night in Logie. *Tongue of the Ocean, the Tonga Trench, the Mariana Trench*. However, that had been under slightly different conditions – beneath my duvet, reading by torchlight.

'Pretty neat, huh?' said Mike, appearing at my shoulder and shielding the sun with his hand.

The next few days we sailed amongst the cays and shallows of Exuma, Cat Island, Long Island and Rum Cay. We would glide between them aimlessly, stopping at any cove that took our fancy along the way to swim and snorkel amongst the coral and the rainbow-coloured fish. In the evening Mike would drop our anchor, Jane would cook stew and I would mix the cocktails. Then we would sit on the deck and tell stories with the sky full of stars above us.

It felt like we were the only people in the world, and a lifetime away from Battlefield, credit cards and this man called Eastgate. It was impossible for me to worry about such matters when I woke up in the morning and could spot the distant island of San Salvador, where Christopher Columbus had first found the New World.

Back in Nassau I said a heartfelt farewell to Mike and Jane, who were flying out that evening. I gave a worthless promise to get in touch and was a little dejected as I walked back to my hotel room alone. The surroundings kept me there for another week, however, and I developed an infatuation with the pirate Blackbeard who had also used the Bahamas as a refuge from his hunters. I took every Blackbeard tour I could and gave the guides a solid working-over for information on this dastardly ruffian.

All in all, my Caribbean adventure was a trip that filled me with confidence and conviction, reminding me of the rewards of the life that I had chosen to compare with the recent suffering it had brought me. The most important moment of the whole trip, however, came just as it was about to end.

I arrived at the airport, checked in and then retired to the bar. It was a flimsy little affair set down near the gates and with a view of the runways, and there were few other drinkers there. I sat on a stool next but one to a plump man reading a paper. His serious demeanour was slightly offset by his aloha shirt and fishbowl cocktail and I was still in my holiday approach of all-out attack in these situations.

'Some place,' I said, but it was a terrible opener because he looked with little agreement around the bar and so I quickly doused this situation with, 'the islands, they're amazing. I've been out on a boat . . .'

That was enough. He'd been sailing himself and we swapped routes, winds and memories of Toto. I gestured to the barman and he cheerily deposited another round of drinks. As he left I turned back to my new friend.

'They're so friendly,' I said. It wasn't a question but he answered me.

'It's because of money.' His voice was simple and I saw some more of him emerge. Behind the sunburn there was skin smooth with breeding and a thick watch wrapped round his wrist. He sipped his drink in a dramatic pause then expanded.

'The locals get the tourist money but there's a lot more behind it. There's the money you do see,' he gestured out to the airport mobs, 'and a lot more that you don't.' Another sip. I was nearly sliding off my stool when he finally turned back to me and finished it off.

'The islands,' he said, 'are full of offshore money.'

I knew more or less what he meant but I was entranced by the moment.

'What's that?' I asked him.

He laughed and reached for his drink again. 'Money that people have,' he told me, 'that they're not supposed to have.'

Gatwick was cold and threatening and I decided to retreat to the anonymity of London. I booked into a chain hotel in the West End and got to work on getting me some new cards. It was one of the first calls I made, the one that brought the Lieutenant's card. I didn't know about his background until the card came through – I'd asked for a Mr Smith and it hadn't come up in the conversation.

It was one of the card services that didn't offer the duplicate card on the account (for a nephew, say) without all sorts of authorization. I would be out of this hotel within days, however, so I ordered a replacement card in the account holder's name instead. Might as well give it a go, I thought with my remaining Caribbean optimism. Then the next day the card came through and I saw the *Lt* where the *Mr* should have been.

I called the card company to check my details and the young man read out my full title with a definite tone of respect. This was too good an opportunity and I absent-mindedly asked to check the credit limit.

'Fifty thousand pounds,' confirmed the man and I turned to look for my jacket.

A few years before this, in another life, I had sat in the lounge at the Keppenburn Unit in Ayrshire and read a profile of a company called Gieves and Hawkes. They were a tailor's based at No. 1 Savile Row, the 'jewel in the crown' of that famous street, the article stated. They had dressed the world's royalty and rulers for 200 years and also had a firm military tradition. They had made the uniforms of Lord Nelson, the Duke of Wellington and the *Bounty*'s Captain Bligh. And now they were going to make mine.

Standing in the musty store, with the royal warrants on the wall and oil portraits all around, I felt like a returning war hero. An old man stretched a tape measure across my back as we ran through some military small talk. The invasion of Iraq had started a couple of months previously and we spoke of the possibility of me seeing some action out there.

'It's a terrible business,' muttered the old man, 'that bloody Bush, he's made a right mess of it.'

'I've been speaking to some of the chaps,' I said, looking distant and affected. 'They say it's hell out there.'

'Well,' he said encouragingly, 'at least you'll look the part.'

I felt a bit bad then, I promise I did, at this nice old man trying to smooth the fears of a war-bound rookie. But I was also pretty excited about the uniform, which was to be ready the following morning. From Savile Row I wandered round to Bond Street and the Watches of Switzerland store that I had lusted after from afar.

Many times I had stood outside, transfixed by the banks of gold and silver, but this time I walked straight in and called over a sales attendant. I asked him to talk me through the Rolex range, explaining that I was a Royal Navy lieutenant home on shore leave and looking to buy myself a treat.

For maybe the twentieth occasion in the previous two years, I stood and nodded as a salesman offered the particular pull of each member of the Rolex family. Once again I tried a number on before selecting a watch and explaining that I would be back the next day to collect it. The difference was that, this time, I intended to return.

The following morning I was at Gieves and Hawkes for opening. The uniform was superb and I told them I was going to change into it now as I had a formal lunch to attend. I put my other clothes into a briefcase that I had bought the day before and emerged back into the street. I looked both fantastic and ridiculous and got a bad case of the giggles as I walked through the morning shoppers.

I composed myself and slipped back into Watches of Switzerland. The same sales attendant was there but he didn't recognize me until I dramatically removed my hat, at which point he fairly darted around the showcases to get to me. The Rolex I took was at the lower end, a couple of grand's worth, but it was an enthralling moment.

As he passed the card through I didn't feel even a flicker of doubt. Even if the card was rejected, the uniform hung between myself and any chance of discovery. In the void before the receipt printing, he slid the box over the glass to me and I put it with the rest of my worldly possessions in my bag.

From Bond Street I took a taxi to Euston station and then a train to Manchester. I settled into my seat and prised open the box. It was the heaviest stamp I had yet received of my upward trajectory. I pulled up the embroidered sleeve of my jacket and let the watch slip round to flaunt its origin to the world. I practised scratching the back of my neck or adjusting my hat in such a manner so as to display this emblem of excess.

With the uniform and the glinting watch, I was a force to be reckoned with on that train. I was on the up and up and ready to take Manchester by storm but unfortunately one half of the dream pairing was rendered redundant that evening. I booked into a nice hotel in Deansgate and ordered some takeaway food, after which I made my usual security calls to the bank using a merchant code from a bar in London.

My Lieutenant card had been cancelled, an event probably triggered by the item hanging from my arm. *Bollocks*. I needed the card to compliment the uniform, and remove any doubts about my fresh-faced complexion. Without it I was just what I was – an over-enthusiastic twenty-year-old in fancy dress.

I made the reluctant decision to decommission my uniform and also decided to incorporate a new twist into my methods. It was infuriating that a card with such a high credit limit had been taken from me so swiftly. There were two strong possibilities – either the account holder had checked his balance or he had received his monthly statement from the bank.

From that point on when I was ordering a card I would always find out the statement date. If possible, I would push it back further in the month and I would also check the method of payment that the account holder used. Where the account was set up to be paid by a direct debit, I would alter this to cheque payment which could buy a few more days before my activities were detected.

Deflated at my dishonourable discharge from the Senior Service, I threw myself into the new task of locating a base. With Expedia and other websites off limits, I was spending a lot of time at hotel receptions and having to produce ID at every stage. Together with the slight phobia I had understand-ably developed of opening hotel room doors, this had made me consider alternative arrangements.

I found what I needed in Manchester itself, namely the Ellieslea Serviced Apartments. A serviced apartment sounded just my kind of thing and I went inside for a look round. The woman at the desk showed me to a stylish little one-bedroom apartment that was furnished expensively and could be accessed by an unsupervised lift. It was a perfect bolt-hole, and right in the middle of town.

Back in reception, I was told that the apartment would be cleaned every day.

'Also,' said the woman, as she gathered her forms together, 'we offer a full package which gives a linen and reception service.'

'I'll take it,' I said confidently, and then delivered the little touch that had come to me on the way down the stairs.

I took a step closer to her and made my voice quiet and trusting.

'Just to let you know,' I peeked over my shoulder for lurking enemies, luckily there were none. 'I am a Royal Navy officer and will be staying here on official duties. However . . .'

Her hand had poised on the paper as she looked up at me through her reading glasses.

'. . . the official line is that *I am not here at all.*'

She frowned. 'What do you mean?'

'Well, if anyone asks.'

'Who would ask?' She wasn't taking the piss, she was just asking a perfectly reasonable question.

'Anyone,' I answered lamely. It was a good idea, I just hadn't thought it through properly.

'How many keys, love?' she said, as she battled admirably against laughter.

I settled into my new home quickly. During the days I would be back wandering around Manchester before returning to my apartment after lunch. Enjoying the novelty of having a kitchen at my disposal, I would watch daytime cooking shows and then rush down to the supermarket and try and re-create the dishes with varying success. In the evenings I would collect card details and work on my new memory trick.

The incident in Dublin, where I had magicked those card details from somewhere within me, had revived my awareness of what my mind was capable of. What I worked on now was something I had first done when I was younger to remember capital cities: I had given each a symbol or object. Paris had been the Eiffel Tower, Madrid a big, bright sun, and so on.

Now I took the block of data I would gather for each card and give it a piece of fruit. With practice came perfection and soon I was able to hold up to a dozen sets of information in my head and bring them forward individually at my willing. It made things cleaner and easier, with not a scrap of paper to incriminate me.

Also by now I was becoming increasingly familiar with each bank's security methods. HSBC was the great untouchable, with its unhelpful insistence on passwords at every turn. The Scottish banks I found approachable, and a couple of the large English ones, but it was dealing directly with the credit card companies that was my greatest love. Amongst those friendly ranks was of course the magnificent American Express, the company that was flying me round the world and paying for my phone calls when I got caught.

Between the apartment and the Internet café next door, I was amassing information by the day. I was engrossed in the process that I found both exhilarating and exhausting. This in turn created a need for release, and it arrived one night in spectacular fashion.

The Internet café was close to closing and I was aimlessly surfing while I decided on my nocturnal plans. I chanced across the Royal Navy website. I had enjoyed my short naval career (particularly the commemorative watch that it had produced) and was therefore overjoyed when I saw the opportunity to resurrect it that very evening. At a Manchester hotel, the Navy were holding a fundraiser for the Sea Cadets. It was a cause close to my heart and I thought it only right and proper that I graced them with my attendance.

I went back up to my apartment and got gloriously drunk, then put on my uniform and got a taxi to the hotel. My twisted self-belief echoed back to me standing as a young boy in the school corridor and wrapping my father's tie around my neck, ready for my teacher act.

I arrived just after everyone had finished dinner and

marched grandly into the room, shaking any hand I could attract and dishing out unorthodox salutes at every opportunity. People looked at me in confusion, very few others seemed to be in any form of uniform.

For maybe two drinks (it's a little hazy) I stuck it out, arrowing into conversations and leaving small confusions throughout the room. Even in my jumbled state I could feel the eyes falling upon me and I made a retreat, pausing only to sweep round and give an extended wave from the door as the top-table brass nudged each other and squinted in my direction. It's only now, looking back, that I can see the very real chance that I got the wrong hotel.

Such incidents, clearly, were symptoms of an encroaching boredom during my month in Manchester. To rectify this, I decided to make a return to Chile. There were several reasons – I had enjoyed my time there, I needed to visit the airport's bureaux de change after over-using those in the city centre (I was still fearful of the challenge of banks), and a month in one area had given this jet-setter a pair of itchy feet.

As always, I had been keeping in contact with my mum since leaving Battlefield but there had been no conversations with my dad. Although I wouldn't have recognized this at the time, perhaps the biggest motivation for me to go back to Chile was to have a reason to talk to him. I thought that he would replace his doubts about me with excitement and possibly pride that I was undertaking the trip, but when I told him he just said, 'Do not embarrass me in Tocopilla.'

I was stung and angry, probably more so because I knew why he said it. He suspected to the point of certainty that his son was pursuing a corrupt lifestyle. Why would he want this shame conveyed to anyone, let alone his extended family?

The greatest embarrassment, of course, would be getting caught and we had a mutual interest in that not happening.

I flew from Manchester to Paris to Madrid, for a start, confident that this would dodge any arrangements that the mysterious Detective Eastgate or others might have made. At each airport I dashed round the bureaux until I had enough cash to last a year in Chile if need be, and then binned most of the cards at Madrid.

I arrived in Chile protected by the safety of a few cards in my name, a pocket full of money and a head full of fruit.

This time I was the sole representative of the émigré Castros and so my time in Tocopilla was scheduled like a royal visit, with endless people to see and respects to be paid all over town. I stayed with my grandmother and spent the evenings with her and my uncles before going out with some of the younger ones to the bars and clubs.

Previously I would have revelled in my position as the foreigner being paraded round the relatives. The attention and the focus would have been food and drink for me, as I played a role somewhere between a missionary and the Man from Del Monte. Yet it felt strangely unfulfilling, and I was overcome with the falsity of my position.

I didn't work for a computer company, as they all thought and repeated to each other in appreciation and pride. I didn't even have a job. What I did fill my time with was something I could share with no one, no matter how good I was getting at it. This concern came from nowhere and I managed to swamp it with tall tales and bottles of Escudo beer.

After a week in Tocopilla I returned to Santiago for a few days before heading off on another epic, fractured journey to Manchester. By the time I got to Paris I had been going for over a day and booked myself into the hotel nearest to the airport for a sleep. I was just about to drift off when there was an eruption of electronic noise from deep in my bag.

When I pulled out my phone I was confused on two counts: first, the fact that I had so many messages; second, that they had come through only now. My phone was supposed to have worked in Chile, and had displayed the symbol of a local operator whilst there.

Something had gone amiss but what was important now were the messages themselves. Once again I had returned from Chile to a disaster related through voicemail. All the messages were from the management at Ellieslea. The card that I had left to pay for my serviced apartment during my absence, despite being fresh and several weeks from a statement date, had failed.

The messages progressed from airy requests for alternative payment, to talk of changing my locks, to darker mentions of contacting the authorities. I was furious, particularly with my failure to have received these calls in Chile and nip things in the bud at an earlier stage. I had clothes and various possessions in the apartment but, even more, I had been eagerly awaiting my return to what just about passed as home.

I still flew to Manchester the next day, as I harboured the thought of going back to the Ellieslea building and attempting to talk things through with the people there, but I hope that I was never considering that seriously. Instead I checked into a cheap Travelodge motel while I considered my next move.

I wanted somewhere low key but immediately regretted it as I sat in the room and looked with scorn at the surroundings. The plastic kettle on the wooden tray, the horrible green carpet, the ceiling yellowed with cigarette smoke. It felt like another cell but at least here I could leave and that's what I did, showering and then heading into town. The agitation over the Ellieslea situation, the lack of sleep and the fact that my pockets still bulged with holiday money combined to send me racing through the Manchester streets in a mission of self-destruction.

I went to bar after bar where I bought rounds for people who didn't want them and spoke to people who didn't want to speak to me. I drank double rounds, combining cocktails with shots of tequila and sambuca. Sometime in the wee hours of the following morning I stumbled out of a club and managed to rustle up the Travelodge's address for a taxi driver.

If I were to try and tell you what happened next un-assisted, then it wouldn't add up to more than some mushy memories. Luckily for you (though not, of course, for me) I have court records to help. What I did was this:

I staggered into the hotel bar where I found that the card machine was unmanned and that the supervisor's card had been left beside it. I swiped through the supervisor's card and selected the Refund function. I then swiped through my card and refunded myself £2,100. I then went to bed.

Do you think that's stupid? Is it more stupid than this?

The card that I refunded the money to was also the card that I used to pay for my horrible little room. Therefore, in the morning when they inevitably saw what had happened, the first thing they did was to check the card details against everyone staying in the hotel.

*

Do you think that's stupid? Is it more stupid than this?

They didn't twig to what had happened until late morning, and it took them a further few hours to match the card to myself and notify the police. When the police came to my room it was early afternoon. *Too late*, you would probably imagine, but you would be wrong. I forgot to set an alarm, and was sleeping off the booze when they came knocking on my door.

CHAPTER EIGHTEEN

I've had some bad hangovers but there's nothing that quite compares to sitting in the back of that police car as it eased its way out of that Travelodge car park. My head thumped, my body was clammy, and my mind was a black hole of self-hatred. Far beyond the catastrophe of capture was the way that I had brought it on myself.

It was over. Ireland, Scotland, Heathrow, soon the news of my capture would arrive in fax machines and inboxes. The charges against me would start to grow and everything that I was going to have and do had been struck off in an instant. My run had ended just when I was threatening to break free of such irritating concerns as capture and risk. My technique was improving by the week and I even had this new idea that . . .

But it didn't matter now. I was supposed to be a high-flyer, an international man of criminal mystery leaving the authorities trailing in his wake, and I'd blown it all in one night. I'd gone out with a whimper – lying drunk in a £45 hotel room like a delegate at a sales conference. A petty thief. A joke.

I was so dispirited that I didn't even bother trying to explain my actions to the police. I mumbled my way through the interview and even accepted remand without disappointment, such was my conviction that the end had been reached. Even when the van door swung open to reveal Lancaster Farms I saw this not as a coincidence, rather a cheap trick by the police who were yet to reveal their awareness of my fugitive status.

In the prison I struck up a loose friendship with the guy next door to me – a relaxed soul who was having marijuana smuggled in by his girlfriend through an ingenious method. Soon I was spending my days in a stoned haze in my cell, only coming out for meals and meetings with my lawyer. I had told him to expect new charges but each time he came he only had the Great Travelodge Robbery to discuss.

I couldn't understand why things were moving so slowly. I dared not believe that I was going to slip away again, but in the deepest depths of weed-induced dreams I was starting to picture myself walking through airports, or along white Caribbean sands. In daytime prison reality, however, I was here for a long time to come.

After a few weeks my trial date was set and the police had still not played any of their many aces. There had also been no mention of anyone called Eastgate. The night before my court date I didn't sleep, spending the long hours walking from wall to wall or staring through the bars at the clouds. They would be waiting for me, I now knew for sure, outside the court.

After a brief hearing I was given a sentence of four weeks that matched my time on remand and so I was free to go. Only the Travelodge, the swiping of the card, and my previous British convictions had been mentioned. I walked uncertainly from the room and stood with my lawyer in the corridor.

He was a duty brief, anxious to get to his next case, but I tried desperately to extend our conversation because of what I knew was my imminent arrest. Finally, he managed to free himself with an exaggerated look at his watch and a hurried, 'Well, good luck!'

I was left alone looking at the rectangle of light that led to the world. I felt strangely detached as I walked towards it, my helplessness leaving me resigned to any outcome, and passed through into the street.

It was one of those rare quirks you can get in city centre afternoons – where people's movements have become weirdly synchronized to create a vacuum that lasts for seconds. I walked outside the court and there was literally nobody there.

Right, it's time for me to bring out the big one. I've been looking forward to it.

Since my time in the Don, something had been stewing inside me. This escape, and the undeserved second chance that it gave me, was all the motivation I needed to develop my thoughts into a new technique. In the end it would move me up a stage, and then some stages more. It would make me virtually invisible, and would give me access to more money than even I needed. It was beautiful, and slick and easy. It was something that I will call

The Wire Transfer Scam (WTS)

Look at everything that I have done so far and you will see where the WTS came from. There is the hotel phone trick, and the familiarity with the luxury hotel market. There is the confident adoption of identities, and the knowledge of the security arrangements of the credit card companies. There is the love of money, and there is the move that I pulled in the Don – using Ned's friends to pick up cash and deposit it in the account of the Portuguese.

If you take all that and my criminal dedication, then add

the Data Protection Act, you are pretty much there. All that remains is my decision on the train from Manchester to Glasgow that I was going to do more than I had ever done before, and that I was never going to be caught again.

My determination was sealed when I got back to Glasgow and made those same calls from the Serious Fraud Office to the card companies. Elliot Castro was still a man in demand. Whatever police cock-up had let me get away was too amateurish to be repeated and so it was up to me to drive myself beyond their reach.

In Glasgow I did a trial run on a man from London who was staying in a £400 hotel room. It worked, but I knew how it could be improved. A few days later I did it again in a hotel in Birmingham on a Welsh businessman staying two doors down the corridor. A couple of days after that I did it in one of London's most famous hotels on an American man staying in room 83. It worked. It was ready, and it was perfect.

Let me go through that again a little more slowly.

The first time I did the WTS, on the man in Glasgow, I used my hotel phone trick to get his card and personal information. Fortunately, he was a trusting individual and handed over all the information that I needed. I then called his card company and explained that I was the gentleman concerned, in Glasgow on business, and had suffered the theft of my wallet and passport.

I was understandably distraught, lying on my bed in Battlefield and speaking quietly so my parents couldn't hear, and wondered what the company suggested I do. The sympathetic woman at the other end proposed that I take a cash advance set against my account, which they could have ready for collection at a wire transfer operator within a couple of hours.

Now a wire transfer operator could be a bank but it

could also be a newsagent, chemist or just about any small store that fancies making a few extra quid. These are commonly known as cash offices and it is their proliferation that led many to criticize the major failing of the wire transfer service. Not me though.

If the wire transfer operator has no CCTV then the whole process becomes pretty much anonymous and designed only for transactions where the two parties know and trust each other. As I agreed wholeheartedly with the woman's solution, I had finally realized that the wire transfer service left a considerable opening for someone like myself. In the Don it had been a cheap trick, but now it was time to find its true potential.

We are going to be dealing with the WTS a fair bit from now and, for fairly obvious reasons, I don't want to be too clear on some points. Therefore, I am going to refer to all wire transfer operators as WTOs. They could have been any manner of businesses, large or small, but for the purposes of the book they are all going to be WTOs. OK, let's get back to it…

So far so good, and I passed security and agreed upon a £1,000 advance. What, I wondered, were the security arrangements for collecting the money? This was where things were a bit blurred in my masterplan. In Canada there had been only a test question to set, but that had been a foreign setting and a much smaller amount of money.

Here in the UK, I was fearful that things would be a bit stricter. But that's where the Data Protection Act came in.

'So,' I said carefully, 'what information will they have of

mine when I go to pick up the money, so I know what I will
need to give them?'

'Oh no, sir,' she said. 'Because of the Data Protection
Act we can only pass on any information that we first agree
with you.'

'Good,' I answered genuinely.

It meant, in effect, that I was setting up their security
for them. The process was that I would agree a password or
security question with the card company and they would give
me a reference number. Only these two pieces of information
would then be required at any WTO to collect the money.
After all, all my ID had been lost in the robbery. The only
other detail they required was a physical description of the
cardholder, which was generously supplied by E. Castro of
Battlefield.

I picked up that first £1,000 from a WTO in Southside
Glasgow. It was the first time I had collected such a sum away
from the effortless world of bureaux de change but even then
I wasn't particularly nervous.

This new approach left little behind. There was no card
sent out to an address, no list of establishments where witnesses could be sought. At no point was my name ever given
– all they had was a possibly audiotaped phone call and a
possibly videotaped appearance at a WTO.

Their window of opportunity for spotting some discrep-
ancy was down to only an hour or two, from the phone call
to my collection of the payment. The only other slight concern was getting enough information from the original cardholder. By the time I was running further trials in Birmingham
and London I had countered both these areas.

Firstly, I began calling WTOs in between agreeing the
payment with the bank and going to get the cash. If the card

company representative had been male then I would have noted his name and would present myself as him. If not, I would give a fabricated name and position within the card company's global services team. I was calling, I explained, to check everything was OK with a payment I had authorized.

If there *was* a problem then the WTO would have no reason not to share this with the card company, therefore when they confirmed the payment I had only the time between that second call and my arrival in the WTO to worry about. Considering the second call would be made from the nearest phone box to the WTO, that was not a particularly pressing concern.

The second point, the need to obtain a full complement of security information, was even less of an issue. It was more of a hassle than anything – if someone was suspicious I could do what I had always done and hang up and try again. But I managed to smooth this out as well, by phoning people who were actually staying in the same hotel as me.

This wasn't just a touch of mischief, rather the fact that (as you have seen) hotel receptions would commonly have all sorts of useful information lying about. The better the hotel, the more relaxed they would be and the more information I would be able to memorize or grab. If someone calls from reception and starts off by slipping in a room rate, home address or morning newspaper order, then it is fair to assume that they *are* calling from reception.

In Birmingham and London it worked superbly, with the latter cardholder even registering a complaint with me regarding housekeeping that I listened to patiently and promised to address in the morning. That wasn't the best thing about that call though, to the American man in room 83. The best thing about it was that I was staying in room 85. When I called him from my untraceable mobile, via the hotel operator, I could hear his room phone ring.

Generally speaking, the more expensive the hotel was, the higher the credit limit on the card and the higher I could go for the advance. It was perfectly acceptable, for example, to request £5,000 for a businessman staying in a £600 suite and needing to entertain clients the following evening. It was an upward spiral, and it had soon carried me away.

It was more money than I had ever seen. I would ask for it at the WTO in £50 notes and at night would pull it out in bars and watch the staff's eyes light with envy and disdain. Suddenly I was spending money at a higher rate than ever, and was doing so with the utter confidence of a man parting with his own cash. There were no cards being swiped and nervous checks of escape routes. It was paper folding, the glorious anonymity of soft notes that had passed through so many hands before.

My act now perfected, it was time to take it on the road.

As you know, I had always been drawn to scenes that spoke of luxury and lavishness. It was why, as a child, I had been rendered immobile behind the grey curtain en route to Chile, struck by lightning on Bond Street as a teenager, and also why I had spent long nights in HMP Hindley dwelling on the follies and spectaculars of ancient Rome. It was also why, I'm a little hesitant to say, one of my favourite films growing up was *Pretty Woman*.

It wasn't Julia Roberts in the bath at the Beverly Wilshire Hotel in Beverly Hills that I took from the film, it was Richard Gere's financial flippancy. I had watched the movie as an adolescent and longed to be the businessman making offers that couldn't be refused, and sending grateful subordinates to Rodeo Drive on my account. It was a fantasy that I had clearly been unable to shake, and the Beverly Wilshire Hotel was the first destination on my WTS victory tour.

I thought that LA and I would come together in a glorious union. It was, after all, where the world's rich and famous came to spend money. Well, now I could do that with the best of them. I placed a limo driver on permanent retainer, hired a phone from the hotel and settled into a beautiful suite. The Pretty Woman Suite was sadly unavailable but my one was just as grand with its chandeliers and hot tub.

I had a bundle of credit card details and hard-luck stories in my head and I would get up in the morning and make the call to the credit card company. After breakfast, the limo driver's first job would be to take me to a local WTO. Then I would ease back into the cool air and the leather and count my money as he drove me on tours of Beverly Hills and the driveways of the rich and famous.

I would have the poor guy drive me twenty or thirty yards between the Rodeo Drive boutiques, just to have the doormen rush out and open the door and passers-by try to pretend they weren't looking at me. Gucci, Louis Vuitton, Saks Fifth Avenue, all the shops that wouldn't let poor Julia in during the movie, opened their doors to me in grateful anticipation. I didn't let them down. Of the thousands I was picking up in the morning, I would sometimes not have enough left to pay for my champagne at night.

I would be forced to reluctantly hand over plastic in the most celebrated LA bars as I tried to make contact with the other people around me. Conversation was useless, centred on the movie industry and the proximity of the person to it. I was a bluffer, a liar, and a fraudster and I realized quickly that I wasn't alone.

They were conceited and self-confident but not in the true way of the rich, with their sheen of self-belief that I admired so much. These people had adopted it as a defence, maybe against rejection or maybe something else. Either way, I didn't like it and as a result I didn't really like LA.

The WTS had shown its international capabilities though, and as I continued to San Francisco it just kept giving. I booked into the Mandarin Oriental because it said that it had the highest guest rooms in the city, and the view down and over the Bay was incredible.

I spent the majority of my time sitting by the window, idly calling the hotel through an external line and asking for other rooms. I wasn't even always writing down the information that the people gave me. It was a period of streamlining and testing different approaches for the hell of it, two hundred feet above the city's streets.

Did you stay in a luxury hotel in the UK in either October or November 2003? If you did then there's a chance that you might have seen me in that manic period after I got back from the States. Maybe you passed me in the lobby or the young man having breakfast alone with his newspaper caught your eye. Perhaps you got a strange call from reception during your stay or, if you were very unfortunate, I may have stolen your money. You'll have got it back, of course, from the bank or card company but that doesn't make it right.

I know that now but at the time, it was hard to see anything objectively. My life became swamped and clouded by the money, which it had become easier to obtain than to spend. I upgraded suites, I bought clothes and jewellery and phone after phone, but still it was there in the morning.

Crumpled in small piles of pink and brown next to my clothes and the empty bottles.

There were days I hit two, three WTOs and I couldn't fit it all in my pockets. I would stuff them full and then the rest would go down my trousers to form £3,000 underwear until I could find a boutique to blow it in.

On a few occasions, my call to the WTO stopped me from collecting the money. Sometimes they would come right out and say that there was a problem, sometimes it would just be something in the person's voice. These were conversations that written down would look innocent. When your life begins to revolve around phone calls, however, you learn that there is a lot more going on than the words.

I was moving on every few days, here and there across the UK and occasionally on shuttle trips to Europe and beyond (including New York again, this time the Plaza). I was scared to go back to Glasgow, especially when my mum told me that the police had started coming round and asking after my health. My father would shout in the background but rarely came on the phone, and even Dean had lost his enthusiasm for my travels and would ask me when I was coming home.

I couldn't tell him what he wanted to hear. Battlefield was too much of a risk at the very point that I was projected into an area of crime that promised me the world. This life of perpetual motion couldn't be continued for ever though, and so I started to look for a compromise that would let me enjoy the money without worrying about my next move.

I often thought back to my serviced apartment in Manchester, and the extended stays in Dublin, with fondness because of the impression of permanence that they offered. I wanted somewhere that was safe to both live and steal, as well as offering a decent night out. I needed a *base*, and this became my chief concern as I moved through Britain's train stations and hotel receptions in the early winter of 2003. But then something far more worrying happened. They changed the rules.

CHAPTER NINETEEN

I wish at this point I could tell you how I had brought the multinational banks and WTOs to their knees. That, faced with my cunning, they had got together and agreed a shift in rules aimed purely at disrupting my activities. That, however, would be ridiculous. What I was taking from them may have had an explosive effect on my life but for them it would have been a fleeting annoyance to a couple of employees in the security divisions.

It was just time, progress and common sense that signalled an end to my new source of funds. I was in a hotel in Newcastle when I found out. I was generously phoning a bank on behalf of a chap who had left his check-in form sitting in the bar. After relating the sad tale of my mugging, and agreeing upon a rather paltry cash advance of £4,000, I made the seemingly spontaneous point that I wouldn't have any ID to show at the WTO.

Would this be a problem? I asked innocently.

'Yes,' she replied, 'it would.'

What? No it won't.

'Em, right. Definitely?'

She sounded understandably irritated. 'Yes sir, I'm quite sure.'

I annoyed her a bit more and then hung up. Maybe it was something specific to that account. I called back with some other details, with the same result. *Something's happened.* I phoned a couple of WTOs suggesting I was from one of the card companies. I explained that I was just confirming that the new system on ID was now fully operational.

'Yes,' they said.

'So my client can't just set a password?'

'No, they need some ID as well,' they said.

It made sense. You're talking about credit card holders, people with some level of resource behind them, who are within their own country. Email, fax, courier services. There was no real reason that these unfortunate businessmen could not produce some ID in a couple of hours. It was perfectly logical, but that wasn't much help to me.

All was not lost. Surely they couldn't have placed similar restrictions on those account holders stricken down with the crime of Johnny Foreigner? Even the most technically literate travellers would come up against local difficulties in producing substitute ID in some areas of the world. Sure enough, a few more test calls established that my much-loved password system was alive and kicking for any account holder mugged abroad.

When I had been thinking about this idea of a new base, it had always been somewhere within Britain's borders. I was never happier than when I was walking down a foreign street with the sun on my back and a pocket full of strange currency, but that was different from living abroad. The Don had also left me cynical about how things could shape up if I was again nabbed overseas. If I didn't move, however, I was going to have to maintain a life of short trips and living from luggage.

But Battlefield squatted in my mind as the home to my troubles. It meant the pain of childhood, the police looking for me, and my worsening relationship with my family. It was strange, but the further I travelled from Battlefield, the more intimidating this seemed to become. I had found that being able to call my mum with a British ringtone, and being just one short trip from potentially walking through the front door, lessened the hurt and loneliness that was starting to flicker in the background of my never-ending tour of duty.

I needed a foreign footing to keep my access to this new source of funding, but I didn't want to live abroad. I stayed another couple of days in that hotel in Newcastle, stewing over my options, until I arrived at something similar to this:

Reasons for Choosing Belfast

1. My last, and indeed only, memory of it was entirely positive. It had been the final stage of my escape from Dublin. And

2. during that escape I had found that you could get the train from Dublin to Belfast and vice versa without showing your passport, and paying cash for your ticket. In other words you could exit and enter the UK without any trace of having done so. Belfast, therefore, gave me a route to WTS money in Ireland while letting me stay in the UK. There was the obvious problem of the fact that in Ireland I was wanted. However, the

3. prisons in Dublin were not too shabby if the worst came to the worst and I had a little plan regarding that. Also, living in Belfast meant

4. living in the UK. The currency was sterling and, both personally and in business, I would be dealing with people of familiar character. This meant, of course, that I was more vulnerable to capture but

5. the physical barrier of the Irish Sea psychologically removed some worry. Above this, I guessed that

6. Northern Ireland's police force was separated from the British

police in most systems. If I got picked up over in Belfast, they would hopefully not be running my name through the same list.

And so I moved to Belfast.

Let's go through the first bit quickly. There was me checking into a standard room at the Hilton in Belfast city centre, then the calls to the card companies from British businessmen freshly robbed of means and ID in Dublin. There were passwords set, and then I was walking through the streets of Belfast, buying a newspaper and boarding the Dublin train. The train crossed the border and approached Dublin, I got scared and we can pick it up there.

It was an irrational fear. There would be no passport checks at the station and Declan Farrell, the Dublin detective who had caused me such problems before, would not be strolling through the station concourse as I arrived. I *wasn't* straying into an ambush, yet I became agitated and hot as the train arrived in Dublin. I chose the details of one of the cards and lost myself in them, adopting the businessman's identity to gain peace from my own troubles.

As I passed through the frenetic station I no longer morphed every male face into that of Declan Farrell. Instead I pictured the elegant hotel room where my victim had been staying when I had called him – the work documents scattered over the desk while he sat with his collar loosened and his hand gripping a whisky.

I walked through the wintry streets imagining the moment when he had been torn from his figures and projections by the ringing of his phone, and then I was replaying the conversation in my head. He was speaking, and now he was speaking out loud through me as I stood in a WTO and said, 'Oh, hello there. I wonder if this is the right place, a terrible thing happened,' in a drawn, English accent.

Everything went fine there, and it went fine at the next one too. I was loaded with euros and chose an old favourite amongst the city's hotels, paying up front for a nice room in a strange name. I didn't have to stay the night, of course, but I wanted to and I'd covered a week's stay back at the Hilton in Belfast. I liked being back in both Dublin and the hotel, and the over-reaction of the train was long behind me.

I also wanted to do something. I could have done it from Belfast, or anywhere else in the world but for some reason I wanted to do it from here. It was as if I gained more confidence by being closer to him when I tried what I was about to try. That makes as little sense now as it did then, but anyway this is what happened in that hotel room in Dublin.

I had a bath. I ate some room service. I checked international time zones. I picked up my mobile, withheld my number and dialled. A man answered.

I said, 'Declan Farrell please.'

As I implied earlier, phone calls are different for me than they are for you. For you they are presumably nothing more than an extension of life, simply conversations that happen to go through wires. You may have noticed one aspect of phone calls though – it's easier to lie. It doesn't matter if your face is flushed or your eyes are full of guilty tears when you're on the other end of the phone. Only your voice can betray you.

I made thousands of phone calls over the years and very few of them were as Elliot Castro. Fewer still were not full of lies. I picked up the handset wanting something and, more often than not, I put it down having got it. Quickly I realized how to go about these calls, these bundles of lies. The most important thing was not the big lies, rather the little ones. They created the environment for me to introduce the whoppers and the requests.

With my calls pretending to be from hotel receptions, it was my wish to confirm the morning paper or the room rate that allowed me to move on to card details. Similarly it wasn't introducing myself as a Canadian detective to Declan Farrell that was important, it was the fact that I followed it quickly with the following:

Elliot Castro – 'Whom I believe you have dealt with in the past.'

The dates of Castro's spell in the Don – 'Not long enough, if you ask me.'

Danny Bell – 'Whom I believe you have been in contact with.'

Expedia – 'Whom I believe you have been in contact with.'

Declan Farrell was his usual relaxed self, agreeing or confirming where needed and making interested mumblings here and there. He certainly perked up when I came to reveal that Toronto's finest were once again holding Castro, '. . . here in the city.'

'Oh brilliant,' said Declan Farrell, his voice sharper. 'How long will you have him over there for? I'd be very interested in getting him back here after.'

'I thought you might say that,' I said, dropping my Canadian reserve into a friendly touch. 'Well, I think maybe in about six months we'd be looking at deporting him. How about I give you a call nearer the time?'

'That would be great,' answered Declan Farrell in gratitude.

'OK, though I would warn you that the wheels turn pretty slow over here on the administrative side.' (*This was an adaptation of a phrase that I had once heard a lawyer use.*)

'Oh don't worry,' laughed Declan Farrell, 'it's the same over here.' And then he laughed a bit more, and then he just kept laughing.

'Is there a problem?' I said sternly.

'I'm sorry,' he said, calming down. 'Now tell me, is the weather nice over there Elliot?'

I hung up. There's one other side of phone calls I should have mentioned before – it doesn't matter how good you get at them, sometimes they don't work. Even then, for some reason I took a little encouragement from the call. After the shock of discovery I too found it pretty funny. I *definitely* had him early on, but I'd clearly lost him somewhere or other. Anyway, that was that little plan screwed but I had to see the situation realistically.

Declan Farrell was an amiable guy who would be fair with me if I was caught in Dublin. As long as I didn't get caught, everything was OK. It was a city of over a million people and I only had to avoid an unfortunate clash with Declan Farrell, Dermot or, God forbid, Dermot's wronged mother. Sunglasses and a cap could help shield me from such a nasty piece of luck.

Actually, I called Declan Farrell again a few months later. I was in the lobby of a hotel in Dublin but told him that I was in France. He seemed to find that very funny and I got quite angry. To add some more evidence I pretended to talk to someone beside me, saying slightly irrelevant things to them in my rusty French.

At this Declan Farrell erupted in wild, uncontrollable laughter. As he gasped for breath he shouted, 'Put the Frenchman on Elliot, put the Frenchman on.' I hung up once again. As I said, sometimes they don't work.

The call might not have gone as planned but the trial run of the WTS had passed perfectly and I travelled back to Belfast in a fine mood. The first thing to go was the standard room as I upgraded to the Hilton's Presidential suite and began throwing my weight around a bit more in the hotel. It was at this point that I introduced my new take on the hotel consultant line.

It had grown a little old, and I wanted something that chimed a bit more closely with the fact that I quite clearly never did a stroke of work. What the indifferent staff of the Hilton were told was that my grandfather had started up a hotel consultancy in America years ago and I had now inherited it. I had been sent to boarding school in Scotland, hence the accent, and if I'm to be honest I don't really have much to do with the business.

'Well,' I would add with a conspiratorial wink, 'I do stay in a lot of hotels, but I don't do much consulting!' And I would laugh and sometimes they'd laugh too, though their eyes wouldn't join in. I thought I was having a little bonding session with those receptionists, barmen and porters but telling someone on a fiver an hour you are a member of the idle rich is never going to be the basis of a friendship.

I nipped home for Christmas for three days of deteriorating atmosphere where my mum and I spoke about Belfast; Dean and I spoke about music and whether I would be moving back at all; and my dad and I spoke only if we were about to collide in the hall. Whenever the doorbell rang I would retreat to my bedroom and crack open the window until I could hear the voice of whoever was there.

I was glad to get back to Belfast, and not just because of the worries I left behind once more in Battlefield. The city had surpassed what I had wanted from a headquarters, and I was looking forward to taking it to the next level. I had made significant inroads into Belfast's club scene, which was good but small, meaning I was starting to see the same faces several times a week. Nods and smiles had become tentative name swapping but things weren't really going to develop while I still had the temporary status of a live-in Hilton customer.

Also, I'd been in the hotel for nearly a month and suspicions would inevitably grow the longer my stay was extended. As January arrived and normal people went back to work, I went and found an estate agent. I told him that I wanted a nice apartment somewhere in the city centre. He took one look at my suit and the Rolex that just happened to be slung below my cuff and grabbed a set of keys from his desk.

We walked over to a building on the corner of Queen's Square and Victoria Street in the very hub of Belfast. As we chatted about the city and my rather unique line of work I noticed that many of the signs and windows that we passed were the daytime incarnations of the bars and clubs I had been circulating through. I was to be living in the sky above them, ready to swoop when darkness fell.

I tried desperately to look nonplussed by the apartment but it was thrilling and new with fittings that looked reassuringly expensive. Winter sunshine poured through the windows that seemed to be everywhere and through a French door we walked to a balcony that looked out over rooftops and down the street below.

'Yeah,' I said, looking around with a relaxed gaze as my heart raced, 'I think I'll take it.'

On the way back to the estate agent's office I was in a stupor, answering his incessant banter with nods and laughs. All I could think about was what was to come next. I paid a cash deposit at his office and arranged a similar arrangement for my future rent before heading back to the Hilton. There I packed up all my stuff into a collection of bulging luggage and shopping bags and ordered a trolley.

By this point my account ran to several thousand pounds and it took the young guy at reception a few minutes to compile. The delay and my trolley attracted a manager I hadn't seen before who wandered over, smiled at me and began reading the screen over the receptionist's shoulder. It wasn't yet time for panic, he was looking perfectly relaxed although the smile had disappeared.

Finally the bill was made and I handed over a card that I had checked less than an hour earlier. There seemed to be no problem and I said a hurried farewell as I began dragging my trolley towards the door. I had gone perhaps five yards when the new manager called out, 'Mr Castro?'

I stopped and closed my eyes, steadied myself and turned. I was smiling but felt queasy.

'Yes?'

'You've been a valued guest,' he pointed at the trolley. 'Let me get the porter to give you a lift in the shuttle bus.'

It was an open, unmasked gesture but I wasn't big on giving forwarding addresses.

'That's OK,' I said with a light tap of my Rolex. 'I'll grab a taxi now.'

*

Over the next week I turned the executive shell of the apartment into a suitable home for a dynamic young bachelor like myself. I wanted to create living quarters that would impress and deceive in equal measures those who entered. It had to tally with my free-spending behaviour, while I recognized it as a vital tool in my long-running (a dozen years and counting) campaign to find some friends.

I made some calls and nipped down to Dublin for the afternoon before returning with the time and money for my project. First I fitted out the kitchen, returning to the flat weak-kneed with massive boxes of pots, pans and crockery. The majority would never leave the wrapping but it felt better to have the cupboards full and capable.

I bought the most expensive linen I could find for the two bedrooms and made the beds prison-style, which was pretty much the only way I knew how to do it. On the walls of each I had flat-screen televisions fitted and left the remotes lying on new bedside tables beside vases of fresh flowers.

I spent a few thousand on art prints that I hung haphazardly around the place, including two vast pieces that I stuck up in the lounge, which was where I really went to town. This was the room that had to sell the flat, and myself, to the outside world and I didn't hold back.

From a nearby music store I assembled an entire DJ rig – desks, mixer and speakers – and set it up in the corner of the room. I started ordering records by the dozen on the suggestion of *Mixmag* magazine, a process that didn't end until everything did.

Every nook and cranny of the room I filled with coloured lamps that complemented the coffee table I bought from Habitat. It was a £1,000 masterpiece, a low-lying block that had light bulbs laid under the glass surface. When I powered it up the lights would flicker and change colour in time to the music. I can see how that might sound a little ridiculous but I can assure you that the effect was impressive.

Over beside the windows I put in a desk and got an engineer round to wire me up to the Internet. I bought a PC and set both it and my laptop up so I could sit behind the desk and feel quite the businessman as I tapped away or leant back and stared over Belfast in quiet contemplation.

Provisions were bought in line with my lifestyle as I filled the fridge with beer, champagne and little else and the cupboards with wine and teabags. I wasn't the most domestic of animals and so replicated the service of my usual hotel environment by booking a local cleaning firm to send representatives twice a week. I gave them keys and told them to come in the early morning, in between my nights ending and the start of my days.

This whirl of activity left me with an apartment that made me excited to wake up in the morning. It was everything that I had wanted, and it was *mine*. I was ready to go and started heading out with even more enthusiasm, introducing myself properly to those with whom I had made initial contact.

There was a bar called Faith directly across from the flat, and I found to my delight that it was the epicentre of the Belfast club scene. I would be in there every evening chatting to the barman Michael or the owner Edna, or frankly anyone who would have me, before I headed on to whatever club was to be the busiest that evening.

One night I managed to insert myself clumsily into a group that I half recognized and introduced myself to one of them that I didn't. Toby, like me, was a businessman and had been sent to Belfast for a few days by his employers. After the work was out of the way he'd caught up with an old friend and here he was, in Faith, telling me how he worked for a Swiss bank.

From then on I skirted close to Toby all evening, getting in the odd question here and there without trying to raise suspicion. He lived in Switzerland with his wife, he told me swiftly, possibly in misplaced fear at my intentions. The night progressed through bars and clubs until I managed to coax them all back to my flat. I opened the door and signalled them through to the lounge with a dismissive flick while I continued to the kitchen.

I was drunk and excited but the euphoria from hearing their appreciative comments as they inspected the place was overpowering. I stood in the kitchen quietly popping champagne bottles as they whispered – 'Look at the table!' 'What does this guy do again?' 'What's a hotel consultant?'

Back through I went, handing out drinks and explaining the workings of both the coffee table and my sadly demised grandfather's business. They made phone calls and sent texts and soon bodies were milling all through the flat as I walked about glad-handing like a campaigning politician.

Try as I might, I only snatched one more period with Toby and didn't get beyond Switzerland's countryside and the lingual mix of the people that lived there. As daylight approached the party shrunk to nothing and I shook a final hand, closed the door and went to my bed.

The next morning I was woken by the cleaner's Hoover and lay running through the previous evening's events. It came quickly and I didn't move past it. *Swiss Bank.* Since my conversation with the man in Nassau Airport I had been thinking about offshore money, secret money. It had not been much more than a natural interest when I had worked with cards and unseen spending but the WTS had changed all that.

Now I had to hide piles of cash on my person and around the flat. It allowed me to spend in confidence but it also left me tense about a cleaning lady or visitor stumbling across a brick of notes in a cupboard. The sense of security that moving into the flat had given me was being threatened and now I thought I might have found a way out. If there were somewhere where I could safely stash the money but maintain quick and safe access, then *everything* would be complete.

That night I went to Faith hoping to see my new friend again. At first I was on my own, talking to Michael and watching the door, but then I saw them come in. I was straight over, buying drinks and slowly manoeuvring myself to sit beside him. I had nothing to lose so plunged into an explanation of my grandfather's business and the capital that I was currently building up. Although the money was legally mine, I explained, I would rather not pay any tax on it if I didn't have to.

Toby looked a little pissed off by this professional request but patiently explained that, as long as the money *was* legally mine, then Switzerland would certainly be the place for me to do my banking. Clearly wanting to wrap this up, he gave me his card and told me to get in touch in a fortnight when he would be back in Geneva.

'Sorry,' he said apologetically, 'but that's the best way of doing it. Bit of a hassle really.'

'Don't worry,' I said in victory, 'I like travelling.'

DC Ralph Eastgate

When I heard that Castro had got away from Canada I was pretty pissed off, put it that way. Later I found out he'd been held in Manchester for twenty-eight days. I didn't know that at the time. A few things could have happened there but the most likely is that for some reason he'd temporarily dropped off the system. Things built from there. American Express came to me in 2003 and said 'this guy's ripping the arse out of us'. He had cards all over the place. Barclaycard, MasterCard, Visa, Amex, he was just going berserk. He was having a right good time and they just started sending me all this information.

I was reading these card statements and thinking *what is he doing*? He was all over the place and spending money everywhere. He didn't drive a car so he wasn't going to get pulled over. He wasn't shoplifting or pulling burglaries so he wasn't going to be nabbed for that, and, as you know, I didn't know what Elliot looked like. You can't go demanding photos in situations like that, you just have to hope that CCTV picks him up somewhere.

I knew he would get caught again eventually but it's hard to tell card companies that. Especially American Express. They were losing a lot of money and they were saying, 'Come on, how can we find Castro?' And I'm saying, 'We're just going to have to wait until he turns up.'

At that point, if you look at the flights he took, what he was buying and where he was buying it, then he was just enjoying himself. He didn't have a drugs habit because you don't fund a drugs habit by booking nice hotel rooms. I'm thinking, *Why is he doing this?*, not, *I can't wait to get the bastard*. I'm looking forward to arresting him because he'll be an interesting guy to meet. The banks aren't quite so romantic about it. They're seriously fucked off.

CHAPTER TWENTY

Article 47 of the Swiss Federal Banking Act of 8 November 1934

1)   Any person who, in his or her capacity as member of a body, employee, proxy, liquidator or commissioner of a bank, observer for the Banking Commission, or a member of a body or an employee of an authorized auditing firm, has revealed a secret that was entrusted to him or her or of which he or she had knowledge by means of his or her practice or employment, any person who has incited another to violate professional secrecy, will be punished by imprisonment for a maximum of six months or by a fine not exceeding 50,000 francs.

2)   If the offender acted in negligence, the punishment will consist of a fine not exceeding 30,000 francs.

3)   Violation of secrecy remains punishable even when the practice or employment has terminated or the holder of the secret no longer works in the banking industry.

***The Numbered Account** (adapted from international banking literature)*

When the account is opened, the name of the account holder and the account number are separated. The banker who is responsible for the account's creation puts all paperwork displaying the client's name and address within the bank's safe. Any person wanting

> access to these documents must follow very strict procedure and
> the bank manager and authorities may only request files desig-
> nated by their number. Swiss banks do not hold registers that offer
> information to match a client's name with an account number.

Pretty boring eh? Not for me though, not for me. When I
read similar information back in early 2004 it seemed that
I had found a country that could accommodate my twin
pursuits of money and crime. Reading between the lines the
friendly Swiss were telling the individual to make their money
and then come to them to look after it. I had stumbled across
a way of completing my own personal circle. I could steal
money from one area of international banking and then hide
it in another.

It seemed impossibly neat and offered so much more
besides. For all my daily communications with their credit
card wings, I had not had an active bank account since my
teenage years. For me banks were the enemy, faceless adver-
saries that stood between myself and the life I wanted to lead.
The idea of being welcomed into one was exhilarating and
made me feel official and genuine.

The new social exposure that I was enjoying in Belfast
meant I had to reinforce and explain my business credentials
constantly to friends and strangers alike. I was doing such a
good job, adding details and background to this new cover
story, that I'd effectively convinced myself as well. The best
way to remember who I was supposed to be had become to
tell myself that's who I was.

Having a bank arrangement consistent with the story
would be the final mental reinforcement of the lie. And the
stronger the lie became in my head, the smaller the truth and

the fear that it held. (Maybe this seems unlikely to you but, I promise, spend a week telling a lie and then see if you believe it. Spend years and it's hard not to.)

So these were all reasons for my pleasure at reading about Switzerland and its convenient take on bank security. As was the fact that I was doing the reading somewhere over France on a plane bound for Geneva. We had come from Manchester and I looked from the window at the flat footprint of southeast England.

Down there was Heathrow Airport and the man called Eastgate. I thought of his files and the phone calls he might be making. It was a light, detached feeling. My arrangements in Belfast had made my life so much cleaner than before and the thrill of company had diverted me still further from the worry that used to plague me. The journey that I was making now made pressure from the police seem distant and dated.

I hadn't left anything to chance in preparing for the trip. In phone calls and faxes I had given Toby evidence that was suggestive but untraceable. I was travelling with an incredibly expensive new wardrobe and various other costly props dotted about my person. There was still concern – he was a bank employee after all, and if he thought something was amiss then surely he would be obliged to notify someone.

Toby had called me a few hours before.

'It turns out today is my day off,' he started, 'but don't worry I'm going to come and meet you with my wife. We'll have a bite to eat then get things sorted at the bank, it won't take long.'

That was unexpected. But I had done enough work on this guy, I knew he was on the level. I boarded the plane anyway and now here I was, closing in on Switzerland and what it could offer me. Back in Belfast my flat was spotless and safe. The knowledge that I had entrusted to the computers had been cached on encrypted drives, notes and credit cards had been binned and my holiday outfitting had decimated the oversized wad of notes in my drawer. On my person I had nothing that could in itself incriminate me. If it was a trap then they were at least going to have to work for their money.

Toby was at the airport with his wife and by the time we had arrived at the restaurant any lingering concern had gone. They missed England and we talked easily about travel, foreign life and homesickness. Over coffee, Toby pulled out the forms and asked me to add what information I chose to. He had correctly predicted that I was looking for a numbered account so a lot of the form was labelled *not applicable*.

I didn't want to look too suspicious and so asked a few questions here and there as I filled it in.

'This . . . isn't illegal is it?' I even asked innocently at one point, and he assured me that it was all above board to my obvious relief.

After the paperwork was over we drove into Geneva with the two of them pointing out various sights to me until we were in the city proper and pulling up in a side street. Toby's wife announced she was off to have a wander around the shops and he led me along the pavement and then suddenly through a huge wooden door.

It had to be a mistake. Whatever this place was, it certainly wasn't a bank. The building was old and immaculate with vast oil paintings on the wall and a floor of marble. It was also totally silent. *A trap.* But no, the door remained unmanned behind us and Toby was smiling at an old waiter who walked towards us.

'Coffee, tea, a liqueur?' he asked.

'Nothing for me thanks, Urs,' said Toby as he started to edge away. He looked at me. His eyes were calm, his face easy and soft. 'I'll be back in a jiffy, have anything you want.' He turned round and walked towards another heavy door. He was either telling the truth or he was very good indeed.

'Water, please,' I said to the old man in the three-piece.

As I took a seat in some delicate antique arrangement I relaxed and saw that I had been right to trust Toby. It was certainly a bank of sorts. Behind a desk there were a couple of blonde female heads looking down at hidden screens, and I could make out a fading, inscribed *Banque* in one of the huge windows.

The front doors opened again and it was now that I saw this place for what it was. The couple who entered were at the fading end of their lives but they radiated the quality of their past existence. The woman's deeply tanned face was mostly hidden by oversized shades and her slight body was wrapped in a fur that brushed the marble as she slunk along beside her man.

He wore the permanent half-smile of someone who knew that eyes would fall upon him and the blazered uniform of the rich that I had seen throughout the world. I thought I recognized him from somewhere or other, but looked away so as not to draw attention to myself.

I could hear the couple's conversation with the bank's staff – about the weather, the roads, and the skiing – before the lady slipped some paper from her handbag and handed it to the manager. He took it like a tip, deliberately folding it into his pocket without looking. As he darted off on his errand the two of them came over and sat a few yards from me.

She fingered a thin cigarette from somewhere within the fur and he leant back on his seat and drew his view round to myself. I managed to limit myself to an affable nod and he grinned back, then leant a little closer.

'The perch are wonderful just now.'

I nodded again, this time in firm agreement. I must have misheard him and, thank God, here was Toby waving a bundle of forms. I jumped up and turned to the man.

'Nice to meet you,' I said, and he waved clumsily. Outside I told Toby what my fellow account holder had said and he laughed. We met up with Toby's wife for a drink and she laughed as well, and then they explained.

'Perch from the lake,' said Toby. 'The people that live out here, and have accounts at that bank, tend not to have too much to do with their time. How tasty the perch happen to be that week is one of their major lines of conversation.'

'Honestly,' said his wife, shaking her head in heavy pity. 'Imagine your life boiling down to that.'

'Yeah,' I agreed, but I didn't agree. A life spent wandering round a country like this, visiting a bank like that and with my main worry being how good the local delicacy tasted seemed to me a pretty attractive proposition. Conversation was slowing and I said my goodbyes, picking up my bag and heading off to find my hotel.

I had gone with Expedia's top recommendation for the city, without utilizing their booking system of course. It gave me an impish pleasure to follow their picks and they hadn't let me down on this occasion. My room had a view across low buildings to Lake Geneva and I changed and made my way down to the waterfront. I had seen the famous Jet D'Eau fountain before but it looked more impressive now than it had ever done in Logie.

In the rue du Rhône I dawdled and spent in the boutiques before returning to my hotel and requesting a table at the best restaurant in town.

'It is very difficult,' drawled the concierge with a look of disguised contempt, 'to say which restaurant is the best.'

'All right,' I said with a bright smile, 'just go for the most expensive,' and his contempt was no longer disguised.

I was good for a tip though, and he got me a table at a majestic place near the waterfront where the waiters almost broke into a jog when I caught their attention with an arched eyebrow or some similarly ridiculous mannerism. I was lost in the fresh backdrop that Geneva offered. To me the other diners were people like myself – success stories brought here by a common love of money and how to hide it. This new sub-culture that I had won membership of was perhaps my most impressive yet, I resolved as I chewed on my perch.

The buzz lasted through that evening, at the restaurant and then the hotel bar, and into a dreamy sleep. In the morning I had some *rosti* for breakfast and then caught a taxi to the airport. I bought some magazines for the plane and spent the journey adrift in the travel features. It was not until Manchester Airport that I was finally drawn sharply back to reality when I turned a corner in the terminal and saw a familiar face.

It was James McLean, the solicitor who had battled so manfully to persuade others that I wasn't a stethoscope-wielding deviant three years before. He was sitting alone at a café table and immediately his face moved in recognition. As I walked over I could see him looking at my suit and luggage, but I couldn't read his reaction to it. We shook hands and told each other that we were fine and then the conversation moved obviously to where we were going from here. James McLean was going to London for a case while I was going to Belfast on business. The talk was drifting towards a hollow and I pounced.

'I'm not doing any of that shit any more, the fraud and that.' I sounded childish and desperate and he was left weighing his response.

'OK,' he said in a flat tone. He was smiling, trying to reassure me that it didn't really matter but that just made me tense still further.

'I'm *not*,' I continued imploringly. 'I'm working for a computer company.'

'*OK*,' he said again, adding a nod as he willed me to stop. Sweat grew on my brow and my cheeks burned as I said a muddled goodbye and wandered off to the airline desks. On the plane I should have been thinking about Switzerland and the rue du Rhône, about perch from Lake Geneva and the Jet D'Eau, but I thought only of James McLean and his failure to believe me.

It frustrated and pained me, but I couldn't work out why. He was a genial guy but what did it matter if he thought I was a criminal or not? There were plenty of others who believed my cover and would accept my financial wizardry as fact. Whatever the reason for the annoyance, a glass of wine and the approaching lights of Belfast helped me regain my self-belief. After all, this was me nearly home.

Let me tell you about the friends I made those first few months in Belfast. I've already mentioned Michael and Edna from Faith. She ran the bar as well as promoting club nights in Belfast while Michael was the regular barman. Together they offered me ready-made company ten minutes from my apartment, knowledgeable conversation about music and a heads up on upcoming Belfast events.

Then there was Brendan, my good friend whom I met early on and who would be with me until the end. I first saw him sitting in a corner at a party nodding to the music with a hat pulled down almost over his face. When he noticed me he looked up with big Irish eyes and asked me what the fuck I was looking at. He was a wild young guy who nearly matched my own subversive dedication and had a pretty off-the-wall sense of humour. He called me the Rocket Man. I called him Brendan.

Other than that there was a crowd of goodtime characters who came from various backgrounds. Kieran did a bit of this and a bit of that, Caitlin did very little other than try to find the money for nights out, Dominic was a part-time decorator and full-time boozer, and so on. There were probably a few dozen names and faces that I developed links with to some degree or another.

This may seem a little surprising, my sudden ability to form and sustain amicable relationships with other people, but it has to be framed by the life that I was living. As the spring of 2004 arrived, I was Belfast's greatest nightcrawler.

Monday you would find me at a gay night called Forbidden Fruit where the punters danced to bad music and tried hard to pretend it wasn't Monday. **Tuesday** night was student night at Thompsons nightclub and hundreds of drunken students rolled about the hot club spilling their £1.50 drinks on my £300 shoes. Undeterred, I'd go back to Thompsons on **Wednesday** for R'n'B and then on **Thursday** I'd be off to the Kremlin.

The Kremlin was, and for all I know still is, Belfast's main gay club. It hid its light firmly under a bushel with an anonymous entrance that you would pass by if you didn't know to look twice. My love of house music had by now fully taken hold and on **Friday** I would go to the student union club called Shine to see big-name DJs brought over from the UK for the night.

On **Saturday** I would manufacture a team together and embark on a crawl round the weekend bars and clubs. Saturday was good because I could buy champagne without looking like a prick. And then it was **Sunday** and the week would complete with me back at the Kremlin, moving enthusiastically on the Red Square dance floor.

Despite my acknowledged problems in holding down friendships, the timetable that I was following almost forced acquaintances onto me. Throw in the permanently available status of my flat for afterparties and I was a relatively attractive proposition, bar the questions and over-excitement.

Soon my new pals would be visiting at all times of the day. Many had defaulted on most of life's traditional concerns and to them it seemed that I had done the same. I tended to be always available and at this stage that didn't appear strange. I still needed time to myself, however, as I worked nearly as hard as I played.

Constant Internet access had proven a further help. In the hotel calls, which were going out in heavy batches every couple of days, I now had to lay my hands on even less information. From the Royal Mail website, I could get a postcode from an address or vice versa. From the British Telecom website I could get phone numbers from addresses, and from the web I could get any business address I wanted with plentiful background information. With a good percentage of hotel bookings being made on corporate cards, this was invaluable.

Because WTS money meant trekking down to Dublin I took the decision to begin ordering cards again as a supplementary source of funding. Perhaps it was lazy but it seemed to me that the whole point of this new life was an attempt at normality and that meant limiting the danger of the Dublin day trips to one every couple of weeks.

For plastic with high credit limits and far-flung statement dates I would order duplicate cards in my name, usually portraying Elliot Castro as a nephew or stepson to explain the differing surname. Sometimes I would register my flat address with the card company as the main account address and then call back once the card had arrived and change it back to the original. On other occasions I would offer a reason for the despatch to Belfast. There was no great worry there though – the blizzard of cards that had been sent to Battlefield over the years without detection had shown the lack of risk involved.

Even if cards had to be ordered as replacements in the names of the cardholders themselves I would occasionally let down my guard and do so if they were worth the hassle, such as corporate cards with corporate credit limits. With all this going on, cards came to me in a steady stream across the Irish Sea, sourced from Britain's finest hotels.

Everything else would be used to generate WTS money, which I began to send in wired chunks to Geneva, leaving me to use the fake cards and some cash in Belfast. With this being my *barrio*, I used cash anywhere that my face was known.

The Swiss account built steadily northwards while in Belfast I continued happily to spend my way about town. I was alert and secure. I practised my fruit trick regularly, muttering my way through the identities in the shower or the back of taxis, and most afternoons I would be stood in a Belfast store passing security questions as the apologetic assistant relayed them to me. I backed up extra information on my computer but it went each day with the evening encryption and I now had three phones to operate from – one for Mum, one for friends, one for credit card companies.

With business and my social life booming it was hard to drag myself away from Belfast. The first time I did so was really through habit and the wish to make a journey that I had been unsuccessful with once before. I had built up a decent pile of cash in the flat even after a round of Swiss despatches and decided to catch some early sun. I had read about Dubai's seven-star Burj al-Arab hotel in the paper and when I got there I could see how it had got its ranking.

I've probably been in hotels that have had as much money spent on them in one way or another, but none that has ever matched the Burj al-Arab for being quite so blatant about it. There was a reception desk on every floor, butlers everywhere you looked, and so much gold it became almost jarring to see a fixture made of anything else.

I was in one of the smaller suites, but even then it cost nearly £1,000 a night and it was a fair old wad I slid across the marble to the surprised receptionist. It might have looked a little crude to pay for a stay there in used notes, but the alternative was possible capture. My profession may have meant taking the odd chance, but the gamble of having my hands chopped off wasn't a bet I wanted to place.

It was an unspectacular few days. I enjoyed being back in the world of well-heeled travel after my voluntary with-drawal from it, but missed the bustle of Belfast. The other guests were mostly old, fat men with statuesque young women and so there were few opportunities to find company to latch on to. I drank cocktails, read books and thought about Belfast until I was back there.

The second trip I took was more personal. I had con-tinued to drift from everyone in my family apart from the steady presence of my mother. It had got to the stage that I would call her mobile number ahead of the house phone so as to avoid the criticism of my father and the neglected hurt of Dean. With Mum I managed to talk a lot about a little. We would tiptoe around my latest lucrative IT work before relaxing into discussion of travel and Battlefield.

I couldn't bring her to Belfast in case she bumped into one of my friends and the two had an ugly conversation where several of my lies collided. I managed eventually to persuade her to come and meet me in London for the night. This was exciting – not only had I not seen my mum for a while but it was also a chance for me to demonstrate the progress I had made through life's hard knocks.

I had to demonstrate to her that all the earlier trouble was behind me, and to do so I booked two rooms at Claridge's Hotel. I had stayed there once before, a couple of years earlier, and thought that it couldn't fail to impress. I reserved her a flight to Heathrow, explaining that I had air miles from some scheme or other, and sent her a ticket for the Heathrow Express to Paddington.

She was slightly put out that I wouldn't go to meet her from the airport but I explained I was flying into Gatwick and there just wasn't time to get over to Heathrow. I thought that was a preferable version to the fact that there was a detective at Heathrow keen to arrest me for widespread credit card fraud.

I *did* fly into Gatwick but with half a day to spare before my mum's arrival in order to give me the chance to set things up at Claridge's. I decided to take a suite for myself and a superior double for Mum, making the executive decision that I would appreciate it more, and paid in cash for the stay.

In the suite I lay on the four-poster and surveyed the grand scene. The shades were drawn so I rolled over and flicked the light switch but nothing happened. I picked up my phone and called Mum but she must have boarded the plane because it went straight to voicemail. I was about to leave a message when there was a sharp knock at the door.

It didn't matter how long I'd been doing this or that I'd paid cash, that knock still made my breath catch in my throat and my body seize. There was a pause, and then another knock and this time the handle turned.

'Yes?' I produced as the door opened fully and a butler entered the room with his body bent deferentially.

'Mr Castro, how can I help you, sir?'

'I'm sorry?' I was baffled and instantly suspicious that this could be an unorthodox police manoeuvre. The butler gave the slightest gesture to some area over my shoulder. I turned and saw nothing, and then I saw the switch that I had pressed.

'Ah, sorry, mate, I thought that was the light switch.'

'Of course,' he said with over-played patience and reversed his way out the door.

I lay back down, breathing hard. There was a new anger in my relief. I had created safety and an existence over in Belfast that I shouldn't be wagering on the suspicions of one hotel employee. It wasn't *worth* it. But this trip was, and it had to go according to plan. If I were to write the script of my arrest in the most evil manner possible, it would involve being arrested with my mum.

I had a drink from the minibar but continued to fret. What unnerved me most was the fact that, despite paying in cash, I had used my real name when booking in. I hadn't wanted to chance someone calling over with a fake surname as the two of us walked through reception. But now that looked like an error and I had worrying visions of the hotel receiving a phone call and helpfully confirming my presence.

It was too late to change the booking name, but I had an idea that offered a cover and also a light-hearted touch that would help ease my mind. I slipped on my Hugo Boss shades and went down to reception where I hovered in the background until I caught the front desk manager's eye. He answered my jerk of the head immediately and listened attentively as I spoke in a hushed pitch.

'I don't know how this happened,' I said, 'but someone

just called here asking for Mr Castro and was put through to my room.'

He was waiting for me to say more but I didn't. He opened his mouth and closed it again. I continued.

'I was supposed to be staying here incognito, someone should have told you.'

'Ah,' he said in relief. 'Of course, I can arrange that. What name will we use?'

'I'm sorry?'

'What name have you told people to ask for?' This caught me on the hop but I was in a good mood.

'Mr Pinocchio,' I said. 'Use that.' He didn't flinch.

'Certainly, sir,' he snapped and spun away.

I walked over to the lift and laughed out loud as the door closed behind me. I had another drink in my room and then dialled Claridge's from my mobile phone. There was no Elliot Castro staying there. I waited, drank my drink, and then redialled.

'Mr Pinocchio please.' A pause, then my room phone rang both beside me and through my mobile and I laughed again. I called for Mr Pinocchio as I walked through the reception, and again from the taxi to Paddington, using American accents and important tones. It helped distract me from the anticipation of Paddington and my mum.

I found the right platform just as the train arrived. She was wary and taut at first but in the taxi back over to Claridge's I opened her up with stories of some of my recent travels. She gripped my arm as we walked back through the lobby with her shoes clicking on the famous chessboard marble floor. The manager walked round his desk to meet us.

'This is my mother,' I told him.

'Lovely to meet you, Mrs Castro,' he replied, and tightened instantly at his slip. He turned to me but I diffused it.

'Have there been any calls?' I asked.

'Yes, several,' he replied. 'We put them through to your room.'

'Very good, thank you,' I told him and led Mum over to the lifts. I caught her face in the mirror sneaking a warm look in my direction but when I looked back she hid it. I gave her the key to her room and told her to leave her bag and come straight back down to meet me.

We walked the short distance to Bond Street for the beginning of one of my great fantasies. It was one of the dreams that had helped me through prison time or nights in low-rent bed and breakfasts – taking my mother to the riches of Bond Street and telling her to choose anything that caught her eye. I had imagined her grateful and proud face together with the appreciative smiles of the female staff as I announced to all-round rejoicing that money was no object.

In reality, I almost had to bully Mum into the shops, let alone get her to choose anything from them.

'It's a bloody rip-off,' she scolded as she squinted at the racks of finery. I pleaded, begged, and assured her that I could afford anything she wanted from a recent work bonus and finally she relented.

'Well, I suppose *that's* quite nice,' she would say, which is an Aberdonian's way of showing excitement, and I would thankfully gesture over to the sales staff. By the time we got back to Claridge's she had a decent collection of bags and I sent her off to prepare for dinner. I had wanted to eat at Gordon Ramsay's restaurant at Claridge's but it was fully booked, even for the cryptic Mr Pinocchio.

Instead we went to a ludicrously priced restaurant round the corner, where we had a rich meal and talked about the family, and Battlefield, and pretty much anything other than how I was in a position to fund this whole expedition. Mum spoke little and then not at all, hanging her head over her plate and sending up only brief answers.

I tried to regain the atmosphere by stumbling into a clumsy, humorous anecdote about a recent IT conference that I had attended but my mother looked up abruptly and I trailed off.

'Don't,' she said, and I could see why she had kept her eyes from my view.

CHAPTER TWENTY-ONE

It was late morning but no one was going home. Under the white canvas sails that formed the patchwork roof, the crowd moved together to the music that seemed to come from all around us. Huge fans sent out funnels of cold air above our heads but the heat was a constant, cloaking force.

There was Kieran. I raised my bottle of water and he lifted a fist back as he danced. His eyes were heavy and mine probably were as well. I couldn't see the others but I wasn't really looking for them. The music switched again as the DJs bent over their decks and cranked out what was keeping me and everyone else here.

The sun was rising and started to threaten through the gaps in the roof. This place was going to get hotter and at some point soon people would start to drift away. I didn't want them to because I wanted everything to continue – the night, the club, this miraculous existence. I looked for Kieran again but now he had gone, probably to sit on the terrace. That was OK though.

It wasn't a hard decision to go to Ibiza. By the summer of 2004 I had immersed myself in the world of house music with my usual zeal. I spent a lot of time during the day practising on my decks and had made my first tentative steps into the world of DJing. Edna had allowed me to do a couple

of evenings at Faith and a guy called Seb had let me play a
few nights at the Magennis's club he ran.

It was a small place above a traditional Belfast pub of
the same name. (The pub would make the headlines in January
2005 when a Catholic named Robert McCartney was mur-
dered there in a barfight, allegedly by members of the Pro-
visional IRA. When I read about it in prison, I can't say I was
entirely surprised.) Although it wasn't the slickest place in
town, however, I wouldn't have been anywhere else in the
world the night I stood behind the decks at Magennis's for
the first time.

When the place emptied and Seb came over to invite me
back the next week it was one of the best things anyone had
ever said to me. As I was reeling from the news he landed the
knockout,

'I'll give you one-twenty for the night, is that OK?'

'One pound twenty?' I answered. Of course it was OK, I
wasn't expecting cash and hardly needed it, but surely this
was taking the piss a bit? I wasn't too sure what DJs got paid
but I had imagined it would be enough to buy them a pint at
the bar.

'A hundred and twenty,' he laughed.

I was going to be *paid*. The next day I went and opened
an account at a well-known bank, filling in a form without a
single lie. A few more days and it arrived – the first bank card
I had ever legitimately possessed. The feeling reminded me of
the day that first courier opened our gate in Battlefield. This
time, though, both the name on the card and the account it
controlled were mine. I inserted the honest card at the very
front of my wallet, blocking out the less worthy ones behind
it.

I was a paid DJ and I took my new profession seriously, buying piles of records and scouring the listings for

any famous DJ that was coming to Belfast. Fergie, a Northern Irish boy who had gone on to work on Radio 1, was well known in the city and I was delighted when I was introduced to him. He was very knowledgeable about music and I loved talking to him about it. Occasionally he popped up at parties at my flat.

It was a time of possibilities. In Geneva, my account was growing alarmingly and I harboured new daydreams – of opening a club or setting myself up with some palatial pad in London or New York. And then some of the Belfast mob said they were going to Ibiza and I signed up immediately.

They told me which flight they were catching and I told them I had found it fully booked – there was no way I would be joining them on a charter plane full of stag parties and screaming kids. Flying first class to Ibiza, however, isn't so easy as it sounds. The only service I could find involved a mammoth hop, skip and jump from Belfast to Manchester to Barcelona to Ibiza. The fact that my journey would take eight hours while their plane took three never crossed my mind; neither did the fact that my unusual route cost nearly £1,000 while theirs cost £90. I would be on the right side of that grey curtain, that was the important thing.

The last leg from Barcelona to Ibiza was full of rich and interesting people in the front section. There were DJs and models and the young guy beside me told me he was the son of a famous rock star. I didn't even bother to tell him about my grandfather's hotel consultancy business, being too busy straining my eyes for the first sight of Ibiza. Eventually it loomed up from the Mediterranean expanse and the plane dropped towards it.

Not only was I travelling expensively to a new setting, I was doing something novel and thrilling – travelling with friends. Well, sort of. They were staying in a tourist block

near the water park at Playa d'en Bossa while I had called the
hotel of the celebrated Pacha nightclub a few days earlier. I
had made a booking in the name of my work colleague Mr
Castro, paying using a credit card that had arrived in Belfast
a few days before.

The reason for this rather awkward booking was a
conversation amongst my friends in a pub a few days before.
They had been talking about the Ibiza drug situation and how
it wasn't worth trying to take anything there with you. I
deduced that any airport searches would also pose questions
over any obscene amounts of money in high-denomination
notes.

One way of getting my wad down to a respectable size
was to handle the hotel costs separately, hence the call and
the booking on a card. To remove any doubt, I then sent a
fax complete with company logo the day before I left to the
hotel confirming Mr Castro's arrangements. It was a cute
trick, one that I would only ever perform once more.

From the airport I jumped in a taxi to the Pacha Hotel,
where I was given a neat little room with a view over the
marina to the ancient fortifications of the Old Town. I was
just over the road from the nightclub that I had been reading
about in magazines for years and everyone in the lobby
looked like I should know who they were. I showered,
changed, went out and that was pretty much me for a week.

Ibiza was similar to New York for me in that I seemed
to get caught up by some unseen momentum. Every night we
would visit one famous club after another until it got to the
stage that I was never sure of the time or where on the island
we were. At some point I would flag down a taxi and retreat
to the hotel for a few hours but the minute I woke I would
be up and in the shower again and then back on my mobile.

I only remember periods of it now, but that morning

dancing under the sails at the DC10 club shines the brightest. It was a culmination of the nights, the excess and the setting. I was there with Europe's decadent youth, and I was there with my friends.

I had money under my mattress in one of the island's hippest hotels and I had a fortune sitting over in Switzerland. Back in Belfast I had credit cards, an apartment and even the suggestion of a job. I had, it seemed in DC10 as the sun finally sliced through the roof's spaces, everything that I had ever wanted.

It was days after returning to Belfast that it happened. I was in bed when I heard the door open and someone walk into the flat. They walked around the place slowly, unsure and exploratory, so I knew that it wasn't the cleaner. I was overtaken with alarm and was hurriedly getting dressed and thinking about the load-bearing capabilities of my drainpipes when I heard the footsteps come to a stop outside my bedroom door.

With desperate confidence I walked over and pushed it open.

'Oh, hi,' I said in relief. It was Carol, a nice girl who had taken to coming by during the day. She didn't answer. There was something ... she looked *frightened*. As if in reflex she glanced towards the half-open main door, and then down to the floor in front of it.

I followed her gaze and saw the envelopes. The uncertainties of credit card processes and the postal service had produced an unintentional glut. Four padded bank envelopes sat face up, showing their differing names but matching addresses. I had never thought about this, about how it might look to others. Now I knew. I tried a surprised laugh but it emerged dry and nervous and Carol turned silently and slipped out into the hallway.

That day I destroyed anything that could have been of any evidence to the police, and wiped my phones and computers. *Was this enough?* I should have been packing my bags and leaving, but that wasn't something I could even consider. Carol wasn't answering her phone but then Kieran called and said that he was with her and a couple of others. His voice sounded artificially restrained; there was anger behind it.

I met them in a bar and put in one of my finest performances. Maybe I had exaggerated my business credentials, I conceded early, but this was all I was guilty of. In reality, I had a wealthy uncle who bankrolled me. It was his name that Carol had seen on one of the envelopes. Two others addressed to me and the final one addressed to a Mr Smith were all junk drops.

It was plausible to a degree but there was a hell of a lot of circumstantial evidence that pointed to my true calling. For the small kangaroo court that sat round the table listening to my pleas, they must have been matching this against the Rolex on my wrist and the lifestyle they had witnessed. In the end, they just about took my word but I could sense that some were not fully convinced.

It hit me pretty hard even though it shouldn't have. What these people thought of me was irrelevant as long as they didn't go to the police. I should have walked out of that pub delighted I had stalled them for long enough for me to get my stuff and put some miles and oceans between Belfast and myself. Yet I walked home drained and ruined from the experience.

I couldn't leave Belfast because it felt like I had nowhere to go. The police had been round to the house in Battlefield a couple more times to try and tease some information from my mum. Anywhere else just offered extended solitude and empty days. Once that would have been my aim but now I couldn't help compare it to Belfast and it came back looking false and wanting.

I decided to stick it out and over the next few weeks I managed to get the majority of those who had heard the mystery of the letters back onside. Kieran even accepted my invitation to move into the spare room and I enjoyed having some instant company when required, though I was sure to be the first to check the mail in the mornings.

With my DJ career making slow progress, life got back to being somewhere near enjoyable. I became more careful and orderly with my more established line of work, but this new efficiency soon presented a problem of its own. I had stopped sending money to Switzerland because, frankly, the size of my bank balance scared me. If anything were to happen to the account the loss would be devastating. As a result, I had a stash of money hidden around my bedroom that was proving impossible to shift.

Soon there was so much cash that I was feeling uncomfortable in the flat and I decided it was time for action. I stuck all the money in the bottom of a duffel bag and covered it with clothes. To my wallet I added an American Express corporate card in the name of Chad Smith. The American Mr Smith had happened to be staying at a well-known London hotel the week before and, somehow, had then lost his card in Belfast and needed an emergency replacement sent to the apartment he was staying in.

For corporate blockbusters like this one, as I mentioned earlier, I had stopped trying to wangle duplicate cards in my name. These cards had substantial credit limits and strange transactions would sometimes not be picked up for over a month. I also had an idea that might allow certain large transactions on a one-off basis.

With these possibilities on offer it wasn't worth letting such a card slip away by pushing for too much. As long as I had the personal information, and the fruit it came with, then I was happy to be any old Mr Smith.

Armed and dangerous, I flew to Edinburgh and booked into the Glasshouse Hotel and my favoured room 81. I was there for four days and, as you may remember from way back, I spent £42,000. Here's how I did it.

Rolex – £12,110 That opening afternoon in Edinburgh I walked along George Street, the shopping jewel of Edinburgh's New Town, and into the jeweller's Hamilton and Inches. The room was long, carpeted red and with grandfather clocks and chandeliers amongst the glass cases. I had seen it before but only on the company's website and it was even grander than I expected.

This didn't worry me, though; I was ready to go. I attracted a sales assistant and explained in a reserved American accent that I was here on business and had to buy a retirement gift for a colleague. The assistant took me under her wing and talked me through their range, but I knew exactly what I wanted. Slowly, slowly, through questions and measured enthusiasm, I pushed her towards the Rolex Oyster President.

It was a target that I had been aiming towards for years, a heaving piece of gold that made me ache with desire. I managed to limit my admiration to a level consistent with my high-flyer status and told her that I would be back the next day. On the walk back to the hotel I called American Express and passed security as Chad Smith.

I explained to them the same story – that the following day I was going to be buying an expensive watch for a partner's retirement and I wanted to ensure that the card would pass without problems. The lady there confirmed that would be fine and put a note on the account to expect the transaction. My idea had worked.

The following morning, a little bleary from the previous night, I phoned Hamilton and Inches as I walked once more along George Street. Luckily, the same assistant was working which smoothed my way even further and I told her to start wrapping the watch. When I got to the shop I explained I had a car waiting round the corner to take me to the airport so unfortunately, no, I didn't have time for a coffee. Instead we chatted about America while she wrapped the watch beautifully for the lucky retiree.

The card went through without a murmur, as Mr Smith's company dropped £12,110, and soon I was thanking her again and stepping out into the sunshine with the box in my hands. I started down George Street but I could hardly feel my legs and when I saw the sign for the Opal Lounge I sneaked down the steps.

The Opal Lounge – c. £5,000 I had read about the Opal Lounge in the papers after it had hosted the after-party for the MTV Awards the previous year. It was a dark and sleek bar that ran from the street through into various back rooms. I took a table near the front and ordered a glass of champagne and some lunch but in reality I just wanted the waitress to leave me alone with the box.

As soon as she had left I tore the wrapping off and pulled the watch out. I looped it over my hand and fastened it tight, turning my wrist upwards so the light caught the gold. So thick and pure was the gold that there were hall-marks on each section.

'Wow.'

The waitress was back, holding my glass but transfixed by the watch. She looked at me in open wonder.

'That's beautiful.'

'Thanks,' I said. 'Yeah, it's nice.'

From then on she would loiter as long as she could at the table and I could see her discussing me with the other staff. It might have been a misguided piece of flirting, but I enjoyed it nonetheless. This was clearly an establishment where extravagance was properly appreciated.

After an afternoon nap then a pricey solo dinner I returned to the Opal Lounge where I rapidly pulled in a small entourage of suits. They had been drinking since the offices had emptied and couldn't help but be attracted to this new-comer with his Rolex, high-end champagne and a better suit than any of them.

The girls preened and whispered about my watch while the guys wanted to talk about what I did while they sized up my threat to their status. Hours passed and more people came and went in an onslaught of alcohol, cigars and tales about my grandfather's business daring.

Every so often a bar manager would steal up and whisper in my ear. The number kept getting higher and higher and his tone more urgent until one time I turned towards him so my new friends couldn't see. I pulled open my jacket and lifted the wad just far enough.

'What anyone wants,' I said to him, 'anything at all.'

He smiled wolfishly and backed away and then there would be barmaids coming to see me every few minutes. Bottles of champagne and trays of cocktails came and went with ever-increasing frequency and I used any split in conversation or company to order more, more, more. Then the music stopped and the club was closing so I went and found the manager.

The tab was around five grand but I had seven with me so I still had a bulge and possibilities as we spilled out onto the street. One of the guys said he knew a dealer where we could get something to keep the party going and I told everyone to get into taxis. We travelled in convoy to a desolate council estate where I followed the guy into a flat.

Inside newspapers and porn mags lay all over the front room and I stood with my sleeve yanked down over my new watch, watching my companion haggling with the skinhead dealer. We left as quickly as we could and then led the merry band of cabs back to the Glasshouse where I bribed the night porter to look the other way as we all trooped up to my room.

Harvey Nichols – c. £11,000   The last person left my room in the mid-morning and I had a few hours of troubled sleep before waking up hot and nervous. I showered and then tidied up, wiping down the tables and piling the party's various remnants into plastic bags. I emptied my pockets and pulled out what was hidden behind the bed to form a pile on the duvet. I still had so much left.

At Harvey Nichols I quickly attracted the attention of a personal shopper, a guy called Stewart. He had attended to me on a couple of occasions before, but this time was more serious as I attacked the store with a vengeance. I worked through the men's department, stacking clothes for myself, and then went to the ladies' floor. Here I spent a bit more time selecting clothes and accessories until Stewart was struggling to keep check.

I went and had lunch alone in the store restaurant while he compiled my spoils, and then met him at the till. There was a row of bags over a metre long and a bill of five figures. I paid cash, thanked Stewart and returned to the Glasshouse where I laid out those purchases I had made for myself. I chose a light suit, new shirt and a thin tie.

It seemed a long time ago that I had stood in front of a mirror at the Glasgow Holiday Inn and seen myself in that first stolen suit. When I looked now, in the limestone majesty of the Glasshouse bathroom, I saw myself as others would. I wore these clothes the way that they were supposed to be worn – as if they were the most natural choice in the world.

I clipped all the prices from the ladies' clothing and crammed it into a single bag. Leaving the hotel I turned left and walked through the evening crowds towards Princes Street. The Edinburgh Festival was in full swing and tourists swarmed around the centre's streets as I passed through and made for the Balmoral. As I passed him by on my way to the restaurant entrance, I didn't even look at the hotel's doorman.

The maître d' scuttled towards me.

'Table for two, Castro,' I said, and he led me onwards to a window table. I thanked him and took the chair facing the door. He peeked at the bag but I pushed it under the table, imagining the flourish with which I would produce it. Then I was hit by the thought that this may cause too much of a scene and pulled it back to sit at my feet. The contents had begin to spill over the top, spoiling the surprise, and I was trying to squeeze them back in when ...

'Hello, Elliot.' I looked up and saw her, standing with her handbag tucked into her side and her other hand in her pocket. I felt caught and vulnerable with my hand still in the shopping, amongst the clothes that I had bought for her with stolen money.

Sotheby's — c. £7,000 By the last day of the trip I was succumbing to anxiety. I had received huge highs in the days before, some of the best that I had ever had, but they had come with a new reflex. Before I would have been left cruising for days on achievements such as these, but now they would be followed with an emptiness that echoed with withdrawal and guilt. Smaller victories – the hotel, the meals, the tipping – didn't raise a flicker of enjoyment any more.

The meal with my mum had gone badly. She had been fine when talking about home and the family, but I could see a fear when she looked at me that I had not seen before. In the phone calls since London she had appeared to accept what I told her about my fictitious IT career and I had viewed it as progress. Now I could see that what it had actually been was defeat.

It was only after she left, and I almost physically forced her to take the bag of gifts, that I realized we had only talked about the past. I knew what that meant but I wasn't ready to confront it yet, not when I had time in the day and thousands in my jacket. I walked down George Street and there was a doorway that I had never spotted before, belonging to the famous auction house of Sotheby's. I had long meant to visit the branch in London and hadn't realized that they were also in Edinburgh.

There were a fair few people milling about the entrance so I strolled on in and found to my delight that there was an auction in progress. I went and registered at the desk and was handed a numbered card that I took with me through to the auction hall. It was filled with a happy crowd of elegant ladies and gents bearing an alarming amount of tweed.

I had to stretch to see the lots as men in overcoats hoisted them next to the auctioneer. The first few were old oil paintings that simply wouldn't have worked amongst my flat's current art scheme but then the two men lifted up a beautifully carved wooden table.

It was Scottish Jacobean, explained the auctioneer in his solemn tones, and the bidding kicked of at £2,000. It was a fiery little contest between half a dozen bidders but it came down to who had the deepest pockets and luckily they belonged to me. I was so absorbed with the number waving and the flip-flopping lead that when I finally won I wasn't sure how much I had paid.

Over at the desk they revealed that I had committed nearly £7,000 of my hard-earned savings. The man filled in his form and then looked at me over his half-moon glasses.

'How will you be paying sir?'

'Cash,' I said politely, 'and I need it delivered to Belfast please.'

Miscellaneous – c. £7,000 That makes about £35,000. Throw in the hotel at roughly two grand all in and you're left with £5,000. And yet when I was in the taxi to the airport the next morning I had just £200 left in my wallet. That shows what happened to me during these bursts. I lost all concept of reality and spent money with something approaching anger. The result, it appears, was nearly £5,000 in four days spent on odds and ends.

Food and drink were ordered on price, the higher the better. Taxis were caught at every opportunity and I would tip anyone who would accept it. It didn't matter what I was buying, as long I was doing so regularly and significantly. Maybe I knew that I would only be calmed, and my thoughts cleared, when it had all gone. Back in room 81 at the Glasshouse, as I sat in the taxi to the airport, was a pile of unopened CDs, unread books and clothes with the labels still intact. There was also, it later turned out, a significant receipt.

As we left the city behind us I looked at my new Rolex Oyster President. It was a glaring statement, signifying the position I had longed to be in for so long. I had been obsessive in my quest to get to this life and now I knew that I had made it. I won't lie to you, the main effect that had on me was entirely positive. I saw the way that others looked at me now and could see their natural retreat in the face of what I represented. Those who *did* belong in the world I had been chasing now saw me as equal and legitimate. I felt satisfied and I felt vindicated.

But behind it there was something else, and it was growing.

CHAPTER TWENTY-TWO

Con artists, swindlers, tricksters, charlatans, confidence men, and impostors. They're all over the place. You see them in the movies, romantic but flawed, and you see them pulled out and defamed in reality. Pick up the papers and they'll be there – a car salesman who gave a granny fifty quid for her Mercedes, a couple of pyramid scheme sellers, some guy who had housewives stuffing envelopes for 50p an hour.

They're all over the television in the shows where there has to be a baddie. Turn on some preaching consumer show and they'll be destroying some crooked estate agent or plumber through hidden cameras and the gift of opportunity. Switch to one of those daytime disasters where the audience round on the halfwit guests and you might stumble across a builder called Bill who declares himself a transvestite.

He'll sit there in a loose wig and lipstick and say that he's never been happier while his wife cries and screams, 'It's not *you*, Bill, you're living a lie!'

These people are not what I was. The car salesman, pyramid men, envelope tyrant, estate agent and plumber, they do their swindling and then go home to families and proper lives. If the police were to come knocking then they might end up fined or facing directorship bans, with the law misty for these specimens with one foot in society.

They are 9-to-5 fraudsters – diluted imitations of what I was, who live diluted versions of the life I had. Bill the builder can go home, take off the fancy dress and say it had all been a terrible misunderstanding. He certainly isn't living a lie. None of these jokers do. I, on the other hand, did.

For me there was no knocking off at the end of the day and re-entering the world of the straight and narrow. I lived amongst my lies every moment I was awake and then they would rule my sleep. Every sentence I spoke for over four years had been calculated and examined before it left my lips. It didn't matter if I was in a bar, a courtroom or a jail cell, I was controlled by the need to protect my lies and myself.

They defined the way that I spoke, looked and walked down the street. They told me where to go and what to do when I got there. And when I was living happily, as I was in Belfast, they seemed to feel that they had to intervene. Beneath the surface contentment, they would begin to pick away.

The longer I stayed, the more damage the lies did. When I was zipping around the UK, or off on some foreign ramble, it was easy to bring out the same stories to eager faces night after night. It became less satisfying as time went on but there was no great challenge in making these people, and sometimes myself, believe in what I was saying.

For those with whom I spent any length of time it could grow demanding. There were a dozen daily touches that they could pick up and form doubt from. As time passed the reality of my position would present more and more incidents that would make them question what I was telling them. And then something would be started that couldn't be stopped.

It wasn't specifically the spying of the credit card envelopes by Carol that was causing me problems in Belfast, it was what it had led to. Now that people had heard the first whispers of suspicion they were viewing me in a new state of wariness. Kieran moved out of the flat after a few weeks of deteriorating atmosphere and others were clearly cooler towards me. Away from the false, alcoholic environment of bars and clubs there was a gap growing between myself and the majority of those I had enjoyed a closeness with.

The pressure continued to build and my only real refuge was the DJ shifts that I hunted down tenaciously. Standing behind decks in a dingy club and earning legitimate money in return for legitimate work was my leave from what lay back beyond the club's doors. No one could query me there and no one could see the Rolex Oyster President, wrapped loyally round my wrist in the shadows.

But these gaps in my torment were temporary and soon I reached a point that changed things again. I was drinking alone at the bar in Faith when a couple of friends entered, saw me and left. Michael noticed my dismay and he looked genuine when he stopped drying glasses to ask, 'Are you OK there, Elliot?'

'No,' I said. 'Not really.'

He was finishing his shift and the two of us went up to my flat where we opened beers and sat down in my lounge. Again he asked if I was all right and this time, with little thought, I answered, 'I'm into, well, I do a bit of fraud.' He looked spectacularly unaffected.

'Fair enough,' he said. And that was that. He could have pushed me for anything with the state I was in but he just let it slide.

The next day I woke panicked. *Why did I do that?* I spent a day of going over every detail – running through the worst possible outcomes, then the best, then back to the worst. I had to see what damage I had done and that evening I went down to Faith. Michael greeted me in his usual friendly way and didn't look concerned when I suggested he grant me some form of *omerta* on my revelation.

He had told Edna. That was OK, I had expected it.

'What did she say?' I asked sheepishly.

'She laughed and said that she kind of thought you might have been,' said Michael. 'She didn't want to know any more but said don't use any of that money in here.'

'Right,' I said.

Although events could have taken a far worse course this situation was a significant blow. The news that I was a fraudster just seemed to have confirmed prior doubts. I could see now that amongst the fluctuating responses of distrust from my previously solid social circle there had been one reaction consistently absent. Surprise.

The detailed pictures of foreign companies and high-powered consultancy positions had not been real to either party. For me it had been cover for my financial means and companionless state. For the people I had gathered around me it had provided convenient sand in which to bury their heads in order that the relationship might work.

'Connorree,' roared the driver, 'Connorree.'

'Yeah,' I shouted back above the air pulling through the open windows and the overworked engine. I was utterly, utterly terrified. The guy was driving like a fucking lunatic and two yards to my right was one hundred feet of nothing to the Mediterranean. The road swayed left and right as it hugged the cliff that ran above and below.

'Connorree,' he shouted again and I could see his mouth open and close with a laugh that was carried away with the wind.

It wasn't supposed to be like this. The journey was meant to be the calm before the storm as we raced along the Côte d'Azur. It was the destination that generated the adrenalin but I hadn't planned for this driver. I had told him I was going to the casino at Monte Carlo and he had put that with my Scottish accent to form this double act of screaming Sean Connery's name and demonstrating his own piece of Bond driving.

At the casino, I hoped, lay my salvation. I needed to get it back. The buzz, the charge, the *reason*. Whatever it was. I had turned in desperation to this new theory, this new line in sedition. I was going to become a gambler. I had never gambled before and now, as I sat in the taxi and tried desperately to stop myself from working out what 140 kph was in miles per hour, I hoped that it would be what I was looking for. If nothing else, it had taken me away from Belfast.

The skies over the British Isles had been particularly grey that morning and as we weaved our way down the hills into the heart of Monte Carlo I was enraptured with the sun and wealth on view. I got dropped off at my glistening hotel (one last Expedia pick) and was in and out in five minutes.

My suits in Belfast had all been crumpled or smoky and I wanted to look my best for a night at the most famous casino in the world. In the Metropole shopping centre I found a tailor who fashioned me an outfit that he insisted would make me a worthy visitor to *le casino*. I had dinner in my room and then prepared for my daring arrival into the world of jet-set gambling.

The suit was a little tight, it pulled across my back and was somewhat snug around my thighs, but other than that I looked pretty respectable. I picked up a white envelope and took out €10,000 in large notes. I placed the stake money inside my jacket pocket along with my passport. I was ready,

ready like Joseph Jagger had been in 1873 when he became the man who broke the bank in Monte Carlo.

I walked through the vibrant streets towards the casino, which was picked out with spotlights and behind a square of green and fountains. Up those famous steps I rushed and into the rooms where I boldly passed through to the high-roller area that I had read about over dinner. I showed my passport and paid an admission charge and then I was in amongst the action, ready to follow in Jagger's famous footsteps. I hope, I remember thinking, that they don't think I'm a pro and eject me on the spot.

An hour later I had lost most of my money and was in a bit of a bind. My trousers seemed to be getting tighter by the minute, I was practically welded to the stool and sweating badly. The other gamblers were an impressive-looking bunch that stood at the table coolly flicking their chips about with manicured hands. I was hot and heavy-handed as I randomly piled my chips on the felt in a desperate manner.

As the wheel spun I would grow almost delirious with fear even if I had only a few chips on the table. Combined with the fact that I had no strategy and it felt as if my legs were on fire, this left me an increasingly distraught sight. The croupier must have seen some real wrecks on the other side of his table, but even he looked worried and asked if I would like a glass of water.

It was the final insult. I peeled myself from the stool and walked back through the casino with my trousers sticking to my legs like the lower half of a wetsuit. I drowned my broad selection of sorrows in the hotel bar and woke up the next day in reflective mood. Gambling, with its constant battle against fate and violent swings between euphoria and despair, was clearly not the ideal pursuit for a fugitive living on stolen money.

Well, that was that. Deciding to make the most of the sunshine I got up and headed into the city streets. From the marina I followed the winding roads uphill as they became steeper and steeper. The gradient became so challenging that there were occasional elevators to take you from one street to the next, and I was tiring badly when I finally made it to the fortifications set into the hillside.

When I turned back, it was as if all of Monaco was laid out before me. I sat on the ancient stone and watched the boats silently carve white lines through the water, in front of the packed marina and then the clutch of apartment blocks. This was another home of the private banking world and, like Geneva, it wore its riches well.

I don't know why when I was sitting on that wall I didn't think about moving permanently to Monaco or somewhere similar. OK, so I'd miss out on a few DJ shifts and would have to leave the apartment and the life. But I would have been safe.

These thoughts just didn't arrive and instead I concentrated on Belfast and what state of affairs would be awaiting my return. I could see no option but to go back and wait for fate to catch up with me, whilst I did nothing to stop it from doing so.

Back to Belfast and back to the bleakness. That was the final diversion, I'm afraid – Monte Carlo and the tight trousers. Now I have to take you through another trench of despair and I'd better start with the money.

What I didn't mention earlier was that after Edinburgh and the £42,000, things started to go a little askew on the fraud front. From that peak I slowed into a voluntary decline fired by fear and exacerbated by apathy. There were fewer hotel phone calls, fewer cards arriving at the flat, and practically no trips down to Dublin. I had started using the WTOs in Belfast instead for a less demanding routine – the unloading of the Swiss account.

I could not motivate myself to create funds when I had so much there. There was no longer any enjoyment in the technique, no challenge and thrill of victory. Instead the process began to feel artificial and vulnerable and I would be hit by a novice's panic of capture at every stage.

'OK, no problem,' I would say and hang up whenever I hit any kind of obstacle. The phone went down and usually stayed there until I chose once again to line up ten grand from Switzerland, wired to a WTO or even straight into my once-innocent Belfast account. Previously I had thrived on hitches in my phone trick and welcomed them as tests through which I might improve my technique. Now simply I swallowed hard and surrendered – 'OK, no problem' – and turned to the easier option.

By rights, I should have been at the pinnacle of my self-belief but instead I began to regard the fraud with a genuine dislike. More than anything, I think my newfound agitation was due to my knowledge that the next involvement I had with the authorities was going to be final and crushing. I was very reluctantly starting to lift my horizons to spy at the future and what I saw was so terrifying I tried desperately to block it out.

I no longer travelled because I didn't want the pain of return. Money still passed through my hands like water but it did so through habit and not enjoyment. Unless I was DJing, I began to stay in the apartment alone most nights. I would watch DVDs relentlessly and when that eventually bored me I'd sit at my antique desk surfing the web.

I spent a lot of time looking at property around the

world and planning escapes that I would never make. Hours were wasted evaluating anonymous apartments in Ibiza or cabins in Topanga, up in California's Santa Monica Mountains. But I would never be able to buy any property without the risk of capture. Sometimes I would look at employment websites but I would never be able to get a proper job.

These epiphanies were gradually squeezing some clarity into my outlook and I could see the trap that the fraud had formed. It was supposed to have given me a life and a future that I couldn't have otherwise had. Instead it had taken my future from me. I had taken my future from myself.

The short term wasn't looking too promising either. I was bleeding the Swiss account dry and what was going to happen then? Meanwhile, conversations with my mother were becoming harder, and those with my father were unbearable for us both. He could not get beyond urging me to take care while my awareness of his embarrassment of me left me sharp and unresponsive. When I spoke to Dean I found his voice had steeled and deepened. He was an adult himself now, but I still saw him as the kid who had walked with me through the dust during that first trip to Chile.

On those nights I did venture out into Belfast I would find that I had lost another friend, or was unwelcome in another bar or club. I was down to Michael and Edna at Faith, Brendan and a couple of others.

At the beginning of November I made two moves amidst the doom. The first was to invite Brendan to move into the flat. I thought that some company might help as I tried to decide if it was the city or my return to a lonesome life that was causing this certainty of catastrophe.

The second was another trip, a decision I made with little enthusiasm but for the faint hope of some inspiration from the past. I hardly had the money to make it but I had got hold of another couple of cards from another couple of Mr Smiths, one of whom was staying at my old friend the Balmoral Hotel. And so one night I booked a flight to Amsterdam and went to bed. In the morning I called the airline and found there was a problem with the booking. I couldn't even get myself on a plane any more.

The other card. I went and got it and decided on Edinburgh, booking a flight and then room 81 at the Glasshouse. They knew me there, of course, but I would fax them from Edinburgh airport just in case. I powered up my computer and grabbed a logo from a website, dragging it across to a document that I quickly worked into a suitable cover sheet.

I was relegated to one card and what little cash I had in the flat. There would be a way, there always was, of releasing some funds when I was over there. Maybe through gift vouchers or something similar. The cards in my wallet were duds but I still had some active identities stored amidst my churning thoughts.

This extra work meant I didn't have much time to play with so I threw on a suit, packed quickly and got ready to leave the flat. At the last minute I wiped the computers then walked out. I didn't have a last look about or anything dramatic like that, but then again why would I?

It was Friday, 5 November 2004.

CHAPTER TWENTY-THREE

'I got the call from Scotland to say he'd been nicked – he'd been buying Harvey Nichols vouchers, he's staying at a posh hotel, he's got a Rolex on his wrist. That's my man. And then, well, he nearly bloody got away again...'

DC RALPH EASTGATE

For a long time, the end didn't look like it was going to be the end. At Harvey Nichols the policeman led me outside to his partner and a half-hearted interrogation. They didn't need to ask questions at this stage though. David Smith's card, which had started the sequence that led to their presence, had been quickly located in my wallet.

I explained with little enthusiasm that David Smith was my uncle. It didn't seem to register, partly because it was such a weak cover story and partly because their attention had drifted to my wrist.

'Nice watch,' one of them said as the other lifted his radio and called for a car.

They took me to Gayfield Square police station, just round the corner. As you might recall, I had been there before when I had first tried to join the guest list at the Balmoral. The desk sergeant frowned at my face then chuckled when he read the name.

'Ah, Mr Castro,' he said, 'I remember you.'

I didn't answer him, just emptied my pockets of the cards and money. They sent me to a cell while the two coppers went off out again. I was fairly confident that they were going to the Glasshouse Hotel, the likelihood of which made me squirm with embarrassment. I was correct, but I didn't predict what unfolded when they got there.

Evidently, I had been a cause of in-house gossip at the hotel. I suppose a young man who seems to have lots of money for doing very little, and flits through reception laden with shopping, would raise some interest. I thought that the looks in the lobby, and the smiles and questions were signs of awed deference. In fact, they had been sourced from suspicion.

My last visit to Edinburgh, the great blitz, had not gone unnoticed and neither had the Hamilton and Inches bag. After I had left, the cleaner had found the receipt for my new Rolex and the story of the £12,110 watch had quickly done the rounds. Now that same watch was in a plastic bag under the care of the desk sergeant.

The police couldn't believe their luck. When they reappeared and called me into the interview room they were smirking and teasing like a couple of naughty schoolboys. 'Your watch,' they said. 'Let's talk about your watch.' With the vouchers, the Glasshouse bill, and now the Oyster President the charges were creeping towards £15,000.

I didn't say a word, refusing comment while I tried to calculate my position. They had already mentioned that I was to appear in court the following morning. It was now a matter of time. The longer I was in custody, the longer other people had to realize where I was. Without doubt, my only chance of escape was to be granted bail, but that prospect was receding by the minute.

The next day at Edinburgh Sheriff Court it disappeared entirely. My bail application was dismissed out of hand and I was sent to Edinburgh's Saughton Prison on an initial ten-day remand. As I made my way down the steps to the holding cells I felt an unexpected serenity. I was back in prison, and back waiting for confirmation of my complete collapse. Once again, others were determining my fate and it felt like a temporary relief after the constant turmoil of recent months.

At Saughton I lucked out with a solo cell and so only had to rub shoulders with that prison's large junkie population during exercise. As they stumbled about with their light green skin and twitching jaws I stood in a corner, looking up at the Edinburgh sky and wondering when this Detective Eastgate was going to make his move.

When I spoke to my parents I was in a tricky position. Do I play down the situation and tell them only about the current charges, so giving them some hope, or do I prepare them for what I knew must eventually come to light? In the end I told them what I believed – that this was it, the final call I would make to them with the prison beeps and the news that I was again under lock and key. My Dad alternated between shouting and asking me questions I had neither the means nor the phone credit to answer. Mum said little, which was worse.

Nine days went by. Early on the morning of the tenth the screw who banged on my door had a message to deliver with my wake-up call.

'You're needed today,' he shouted.

'I know,' I said, but he'd already gone. At court I was to discover the full charges that I faced, and I fully expected to be meeting Detective Eastgate at some point in the very near future. I lay on my bunk waiting for the next knock as time lagged. Every footstep on the landing sent a nervous rush whirling through me as the day's multitude of possibilities fought for my consideration. Every eventuality was analysed while hours passed and I had lunch and returned to the cell. More hours. Late afternoon and the second knock came.

I followed the screw down to be processed. Instantly I realized that something was amiss. This wasn't the area I should be in; this wasn't the form I should be signing. It was all impossibly, unimaginably, gloriously wrong. I filled in the form with a shaking hand. The duty officer directed me to a side room where I changed back into my own clothes. I returned to reception to retrieve my possessions and then I was walking through a door and then I was walking down the street.

Someone, somewhere, had cocked up badly and I knew what had happened because of the form I had just signed. They had somehow failed to appreciate the importance of getting me to court today, where I had to go to either have my remand extended or further charges laid. Now it was too late in the day, the court was closed and there had been no choice but to release me direct from prison on police bail. It was a one-in-a-thousand chance that had left me dazed, confused and nearly free outside the gates of Saughton.

I stood contemplating my unlikely liberation. There were cars driving past, there were lampposts and even a public bus groaning towards me. There were two policemen . . . Oh fuck, there were two policemen. It would have reminded me of Lancaster Farms, if such a thing had mattered.

'Hello, Mr Castro,' said one, and the three of us turned towards their car that straddled the kerb with hazard lights blinking in tribute to the public highway. A cock-up there may have been, but elsewhere the wheels had turned and these two policemen had been despatched to pick me straight back up. As I digested all this in the car I could see only one explanation.

'Are these Edinburgh charges?' I asked. At first I thought they hadn't heard me, then one turned his head reluctantly.

'England,' he said tersely, and that was enough.

I was taken to another Edinburgh station and another holding cell where I fell asleep. Then there was a banging and it was morning and the screw told me that the English police were here for me. I sat up on the bed and tried to compose myself. If this was Eastgate, as I expected it was, then I wanted to be careful in this first meeting. As my vision cleared, something occurred. The window was frosted and dirty but it still showed me that it was dark outside. The duty officer returned and I asked him the time.

'Two.'

'In the morning?'

'Yep, now move your arse and if you need to piss do it now because they won't stop the car.'

I thought it was impressive that Eastgate had travelled through the night to nick me. It was considerably less impressive that he had come by car. The guy works at Heathrow, you'd have thought he could get a plane. I dressed and pissed as advised and was led through to reception. Two uniforms, messengers sent to collect me.

We got in the car and drove through the dead streets towards the motorway. Their accents were northern English and matching, it didn't tie in. I asked them a few questions and tried to mask my reaction to the answers. Once again, Britain's creaking and tangled legal system had caught me by surprise. There was no Eastgate, and there was no Heathrow. I was going to Manchester to face charges of parole violation. I pushed for more, and the long journey and the quiet of night seemed to leave them relaxed and open. What they told me was that there was no more.

I sat there in the blackness and wrestled with events. It

had been nearly two weeks since Harvey Nichols and the
capture that had seemed to represent the latter stages of my
criminal career. I had accepted my incarceration on the basis
that it involved a final reckoning. Now that inevitability had
become foggy as another flimsy piece of police bungling had
left me adrift, unsure and – though I hardly believed it – with
yet another chance of escape.

Escape? I couldn't, surely not. The problem was that, for
the first time, escape almost scared me as much as capture.
I no longer knew what either would bring. But let's not get
carried away here. I might have been ready to face Eastgate if
he appeared, but I wasn't going to go asking for him. If there
were a way out, then I would take it, even if I didn't know
where it might lead.

We arrived at Manchester's Bootle Street police station
in a grey rainy dawn. I was booked and told to ready myself
for court that afternoon, then a duty solicitor came and took
me through the charges. They were minor – parole violations
from my last Manchester sentence that I had taken little
notice of at the time. They *could* lead back to prison although,
handled well, might not.

My solicitor, perhaps not surprisingly, did not seem to
have total confidence in the strength of my case. Of course,
this was not exactly the trial of the century but there's always
a chance with these things and I was hoping a barnstorming
performance in the courtroom might just present me with
the greatest escape of all. It was pretty clear that he was
here to fulfill his role, presenting my case to the panel of
magistrates in as efficient a manner possible, and not much
else.

When we got to the hearing, things went pretty much as
I had feared. I looked on with increasing apprehension as the

three magistrates and my solicitor talked in mystifying legal-
ese. There was no pause in the process where he was allowed
to add some colour to the half-hearted defences I had offered
him in interview. With no mitigating circumstances to call
upon, my case appeared to be sliding inevitably towards a
textbook resolution.

I stood up. Everyone in the courtroom looked at me.
Following their reaction, my solicitor turned also. When he
saw what I was doing he looked as if he were having an
asthma attack. I concentrated on the magistrates. They were
lay magistrates – pillars of the community who had taken on
the position for reasons rooted in respect and responsibility
no doubt – and so more approachable than the full-timers
who were firmly bound by etiquette.

'May I say a few words?' I asked, and after a whispered
exchange they gave their assent.

I started by explaining my absence from the missed
social work appointments (I had no idea what exactly I'd been
doing instead, but could take an educated guess that it was
more fun, and more expensive, than the alternative) that had
brought me before them on the charge of breaching the
probation agreement under which I was released from my
most recent spell at HMP Lancaster Farms. I described how
my non-attendance had been unavoidable on compassionate
grounds, and then went on to discuss at considerable length
the new leaf I had gratefully turned since my last release from
prison.

That last touch might appear risky, but in fact it was a
strategy based on logic. I had calculated that, although the
Edinburgh business was technically ongoing, there was no
procedural reason that the magistrates' panel would have
been informed about it. As far as they were concerned, it was

entirely feasible for this young parole violator standing before them to be explaining his successful DJ career and the priceless rewards of a life of honesty and virtue.

When I finished they had a whispered conference and then the chairman spoke. 'Well, Mr Castro,' he said with a warm smile. 'It appears that the gods are smiling on you today . . .'

A £350 fine. I led my gibbering legal adviser from the room. As we walked downstairs hope swelled once more. My impromptu speech and its result had returned some confidence and energy as I coolly planned my next steps. I managed to ignore the building buzz of escape and focus on the logistics.

I was going to have to go somewhere when I left here. There was so much else that was going to have to be dealt with and addressed but for now I had to find somewhere to do it. I would go home, that was what I would do. There were risks but they were worth it. I would go home.

We turned the corner to the desk and two policemen rose immediately from their chairs. Two policemen. How many times have you read that now? I had never run from the police. All those times when they sent two men, they could have got away with one. But it had always been two. And it was two that had waited down in the depths of the courthouse, shooting the breeze about this and that as I chanced and charmed the magistrates upstairs. My hope teetered briefly, right up to when they spoke.

'Mr Castro, we're apprehending you on behalf of the Metropolitan Police.'

The Metropolitan Police. London. Heathrow. Eastgate. Finally, finally, we had reached the end. My body seemed to give way. I followed them to the car on empty legs and when I got to the station's cell I lay down and slept. There was nothing now

– no long shots or outside chances. It was done and, as everything exited my thinking other than that certainty, I felt as if I had been washed of worry. I found sleep without dreams or nightmares for the first time that I could remember and when they woke me they had to shout and prod. I rolled my weary body and looked up with shattered eyes as they said,

'There's someone here to see you.'

DC Ralph Eastgate

After what happened in Edinburgh I wasn't taking any chances so I flew straight up to Manchester when they told me they had him. I'll tell you a story. I got to the station and they went off to get Castro. I'm waiting for this amazing, powerful fraudster and they bring me back this fucking kid. He looked tired and scruffy. I said to the desk sergeant, 'You've got the wrong geezer here,' but they checked and told me it was definitely him.

So I walk over to him and I say, 'Hello, Elliot, I've been looking for you for a while.'

And he turned round to me and smiled and says, 'So have a lot of people.' That's when I knew it was him.

You know, I liked Elliot pretty much from then on. He made me laugh on the way back. I had flown up on a first-class ticket but the captain wouldn't let me take a prisoner in first class and we had to go through the back. So we're stuck at the very back of the plane with our knees up under our chins and all Elliot can say is, 'This is outrageous.' He told me to make sure I got a first-class meal because of my ticket. I told him to shut up but he was banging on, telling me I'd paid for a first-class meal and I should get one.

You can't speak to prisoners when it's not on tape so all I said to Elliot was that I was a nice guy and if he didn't fuck me around then I wouldn't fuck him around either. He said that he wanted to be honest with me and tell me what he'd done. We got back to the station and got him in an interview room straight away.

What we did was get him to admit to a few sample charges at this stage. Then we could have him on remand and get everything together. That's what happened and then Elliot went off to Wormwood Scrubs. From his point of view it was a chance to get various reports and assessments done for the sentencing.

For me the work really started there and I had to pull all the offences in and see what I could do. There was a lot that had to go out the window straight away because I just didn't have the jurisdiction. There was a shedload of stuff in Eire but that had to go. Any offence committed in North America, we couldn't touch that. I could do him for flights in and out of Heathrow but not the legs that missed out the UK.

So I'm immediately chopping stuff out, but when you have as many offences to play with as we did then you can afford to lose some. Of course we didn't have everything that he had done but we still had hundreds of offences to go on. It's horse trading, I suppose, that's the best way of putting it. Elliot would come in with his lawyer and we'd just start going through the list.

It was a long old process but there were a few laughs. Sometimes we'd come to a flight or a hotel and Elliot wouldn't be able to help himself. He'd start smiling away to himself right there in the interview room and say, 'Let me tell you about that one.'

CHAPTER TWENTY-FOUR

Here we go, the final leg. And Eastgate. Ah, Eastgate. I smile now, thinking about him and what he did. It's hard not to be impressed. When I walked through to the waiting room I knew straight away which one he would be. As the others talked and laughed he stood there like a signal amongst them – straight-backed and possessed of the same easy confidence that I had spent long years striving for.

At first – in the waiting room, then the police van on the way to the airport – things were a bit strange between us, as if we were both waiting for the others to go so we could size each other up in privacy. Once the Manchester police had dropped us off we walked into the airport and he stopped me.

'I'm not going to cuff you, Elliot,' he said with a smile, 'but then you're not going to run are you?'

'No.'

As we made our way through the airport, with Eastgate flashing his plastic and taking us through back corridors and blank doors, I tried to gain a picture of what he had. He couldn't discuss much but he let a couple of things slip that confirmed that he had plenty to be getting on with.

Canada wasn't mentioned, which was a relief. He couldn't add any charges for the move I'd pulled to dodge him, but if he'd held any malice then it would make things a lot trickier. A policeman scorned can be a dangerous proposition, but Eastgate seemed to be labouring under nothing but contentment.

On the plane he declared that he would be honest with me and I answered that I would return the compliment. I said it as a reflex but, as I fell silent once more in the cramped economy seat, I realized with surprise that I had meant it. With this came relief. I was fascinated with the prospect and the unburdening that it offered.

For the rest of the journey I chatted away to Eastgate while he laughed or shook his head and tried manfully not to respond. Giddy with nerves, I must have looked like an over-excited kid. At the station Eastgate had initially been convinced that I was the wrong man and any disappointment he'd felt would only have been enhanced by my high jinks on the plane south.

Once a lawyer had arrived to advise me at Heathrow police station, Eastgate produced his sample charges. They were largely flights and I admitted them without hesitation and, frankly, without much choice. He would have descriptions and witnesses behind these, if not CCTV and still photos. This was an exercise to get me on remand while he threw together a master list of offences. From the first few charges, I could see that this wasn't a project he would be tackling alone. The airlines and card companies were ready and waiting.

So Eastgate went off to sort things out at his end and I went off to do the same at mine, with accommodation generously provided by the remand wing of Wormwood Scrubs Prison. Compared with some of my back catalogue of prison terms, conditions weren't too bad in there. Though I didn't have to, I took a cleaning job to fill my days as I tried to banish the ever-present concern of sentencing.

I was pleading guilty, that was a no-brainer. I had my

reasons for doing so but it was also not a fight that would have been worth taking on. Eastgate was busy, speaking to card companies, airlines, Declan Farrell, the Canadian police. Every time I saw him or received a visit from my lawyer there would be another pile of charges. Sometimes there would be a surprise in there, a wink from the past that I had forgotten about and I would enjoy detailing the trip or evening to who-ever was in the room.

(I should say that, obviously, Eastgate did not have everything. Equally obviously, I'm not going to elaborate.)

I was evaluated by a psychologist, which was a nice distraction from scrubbing toilets. She was a friendly woman who put me through various simple tests and probed about a bit in my jumbled childhood. I knew what she wanted to hear but I tried to be as honest as possible, though I couldn't help myself from lightening the mood on occasion.

All documents sent between the card companies and Eastgate had to be copied and handed over to us and several showed scrawled notes from the company's security people to Eastgate. There was 'well done' and 'great news' and a suggestion that 'Castro has been a problem for some time'. I pinned that one up in my cell. *Castro has been a problem for some time.* I managed to make my mum laugh at that one, eventually.

Clearly, this flow of charges had more sinister repercus-sions. My lawyer had started by talking about a possible one- or two-year stretch, but as the charge list grew she upped this to four or five. Sentencing kept being delayed as more charges were unearthed and my lawyer bargained hard from a position that everyone knew was weak.

Towards the end, when we had hundreds of charges in front of us and damning summaries from credit card com-panies and airlines alike, she stopped making predictions entirely. The maximum sentence, I was told but wished I hadn't asked, was ten years. There was very little possibility of me receiving that, she said. *Very little.* That was presumably supposed to cheer me up.

I prepared my parents as best as I could for a lengthy sentence, and tried to placate them by matching it with an assurance that this *really* was going to be my last time inside. At first this was understandably met with the jaded observation that this was not the first time I had set my stall out in such a manner. Over the five months of remand, however, I managed to drag them on board. First my mother, then my father bought into this latest promise, and that was the best moment of those five months.

Prison was just prison for me by then. Like all regular boarders, it was boredom and not fear that told me I was back behind bars. I was polite and chatty with the screws and the other prisoners, going about my cleaning tasks robotically as I thought of sentencing, undiscovered crimes and occasionally some distant city or nightclub.

With my case to be considered in a crown court, I was appointed a barrister who started visiting in the weeks before the case. He was a young, confident guy who impressed me greatly, even if he became distinctly less forthcoming when I brought up sentencing.

What he was impressed by was the psychology report, which had by now been returned to us. I must say I'd been a little tickled by it myself. From memory, I was said to be a young man of superior intellect who slotted into the IQ level of the top 7.3 per cent of the British population. My non-verbal reasoning was superior and my vocabulary well above average. If I sound a touch boastful here, well, forgive me, but this is someone for whom school report cards had seen any achievement tinged markedly with despair.

Even more rare than my intelligence results had been the findings of a memory test that the psychologist had subjected me to which I, unsurprisingly, remembered very well due to the misused talent that it confirmed. I was given a list of 40 items and told to try and memorise them. The first time round I remembered 13, above the average of 10.9. One and a half hours later, at the end of the session, the psychologist asked me to try and recall the items again. The average at this later stage drops to 9.2. I hit 14.

The barrister was astounded and told me this was quite a talent. I agreed but added that this talent was one of the reasons that I was sitting talking to him in a cell, a point that he enjoyed. He was also surprisingly taken by my exceptional ability at playing the trumpet – a skill I had revealed to the psychologist. When he dallied over this I found it hard not to laugh but he insisted gravely on the possible significance. 'Something like that shows a willingness to learn,' he said. 'You never know, the judge might play one himself.'

All in all, he might have been asked to flog a dead horse, but he was clearly going to do it thoroughly.

The date came through and I was told that, this time, there would be no delays. I phoned my parents the night before and spoke to them each in turn. My mum wished me luck and told me to hold my head up high.

'Take what's coming to you, Elliot,' she said, 'and then you can look forward.'

My father was tense when he came on. The conversation was jumpy but civil and then he grew a little louder.

'This has to be it, Elliot,' he told me. 'This *has* to be *it*.'

'It will be, Dad, I promise.'

'OK,' he said, 'then good luck.'

I knew I wouldn't sleep that night. I thought about my parents and the sense of unity, however loose, excited me, as did the new life that it pointed towards. Perhaps there really could be another course for me after all. But first I had to find what lay between myself and my future.

I sat up in the bunk and reached for the court notes once more. I flicked my lighter and turned the pages in the half-light. Names, transactions, places. Running my finger down the pages I followed myself around Britain, over to Belfast, down to Dublin, back to Heathrow and from there to the world. I saw the shops, the restaurants and the bars and I remembered the clothes, the people and those wild rounds of drinks.

My finger grated as it pressed down the lighter's switch and then there was the slightest hiss as the flame wilted and died. I lowered the notes to the stone and lay down in the bunk, my body slightly crooked so I could straighten my legs. I thought about Chile, and the long road to Tocopilla. I thought about the Beverly Wilshire Hotel and the chandeliers. I thought about the floor of the lobby at Claridge's and the dark sheen of the Tongue of the Ocean. I thought about New York, Sydney and Battlefield. I thought about my mum and, sometime close to morning, I even fell asleep.

I was knocked up early by the screws and taken first to the office, then over to Isleworth Crown Court. There I was put in a cell, where I tried to read my notes or sleep and didn't manage either. Five hours I was in that cell, which vied with my spell in the Hole at Don Jail for the closest I have come to torture. Finally, the door opened without warning and I was taken upstairs and into a modern courtroom that had attracted a few curious onlookers to go with the official personnel.

I caught a glimpse of Eastgate but was more interested in the woman sitting near the front. She was the court recorder, an appointed journalist who fed news agencies with anything of interest, and she was scribbling away as the judge entered the room and took his place at the bench. I was troubled by the court recorder's presence but had to ignore it and zero in on the judge.

When you're in that position, standing waiting for another person just yards away to take your life and twist it one way or another, it's hard to stop yourself from going a little crazy. You want to shout out with promises or pleadings, or clamber over the wooden barrier to get closer to this man who holds years within his grasp that had once belonged to you. You want to shake his hand, touch him, transmit to him what you want him to say.

I adopted my usual hangdog demeanour as the prosecutor embarked on his summary. Here I got a break. This was perhaps his third or fourth case of the day and his enthusiasm was obviously waning. He took the room through the charges and the basic summary he had been provided with in a neutral, official manner, without any extra detail or rhetoric.

Other barristers could have painted a picture of me as a habitual offender whose prison history had served only to encourage him towards ever more outrageous crimes. They could have gone through my adventures in technicolour, shocking the half-empty courtroom with dastardly deeds and criminal cunning. Instead, he trailed off into legal murmurings and then sat back down. I'd have been disappointed at such a lacklustre depiction if it hadn't been distinctly in my interests.

I could see that the court recorder was struggling to hear what was going on, and registered some pleasure there. Later I would find out that she had hung about and got more precise details from the prosecuting council at the end, in a piece of efficiency that would have unfortunate consequences for myself.

My barrister did a good turn, portraying this day as the great finale of whatever it is that I had been doing, and whatever the reasons behind it.

'My client,' he announced gravely, 'has reached the end of the road.' It wasn't the most difficult of observations, but it wrapped his address up nicely.

With the speeches over, the judge was handed some documents. He had seen some of them before, while others were only official scraps. Amongst them was the glowing psychology report but it wasn't the report that I could see in his hand. It was something else, a small piece of paper written by an author I guessed immediately. This was what he read as everyone stood waiting – me to find out how long life would stand still, and everyone else to find out when they could leave.

Letter to the Court

11 April 2005

Your Honour,

I am writing to you as you hold our son's future in your hands. May I first state that my husband and I are under no illusions as to the gravity of the offences our son has committed. Elliot knows of our disappointment in him. He accepts that his way of life cannot continue for his own sake.

We cannot explain Elliot's actions although I can say the following. We are a loving family and have always shown Elliot this. Elliot has not had an easy life, he was bullied a lot at school, and this caused him to become very introverted and his self-esteem became very low.

We tried to rectify this by changing schools several times although I think in retrospect this may have done more harm than good. Elliot always wanted friends but very rarely had any, as by his teens he had already started lying to make himself seem to be something he wasn't.

We know Elliot must be punished for his crimes, and we are aware that he will probably receive a custodial sentence. Your Honour, please help our son. He is not a bad person, he needs help, please be lenient, he is still young and we are here to support him.

Yours sincerely and respectfully,

Mrs Jane Castro

What do you think? Well, this is what the judge thought. He pushed all his papers to the side and criss-crossed his fingers as he spoke with a voice strong and polished through public exposure. He told me that my guilty plea and cooperation with the police acted in my favour. He told me that he had read the psychologist's report and my mother's letter with great interest. I nodded and pursed my lips and felt the tingle of optimism.

'But this is a serious crime, Mr Castro,' he continued, the voice moving fluently into a tougher pitch. 'This,' he opened a hand towards the wedge of offence details, 'is a staggering litany of crime that hints at much more.'

The pendulum was swinging back. I felt nauseous. Then he told me my sentence.

Later both the court recorder and Eastgate would say that I showed no reaction when the sentence was passed. They couldn't see my face though. They also managed to miss the quieter, final comment from the judge, who could see my face just fine.

'Don't get too excited, Mr Castro,' he said. 'You're still going back to prison.'

DC Ralph Eastgate

Two years! Two years he got. I just couldn't believe it. I suppose the judge believed that he wanted to give up the game but even then you'd have expected a far heavier sentence than that. He didn't react though, Elliot. Not a flicker. He must have known that he'd got a right result there, he could have been looking at doing a long stretch, but he just stood there calm as you like.

I got a commendation after the sentencing, which was nice, in a hotel over the road. In the Renaissance Hotel in fact. And then it started, the press and all that . . .

I've never spoken to Elliot since. Why did he do it? I asked him once and he told me, 'Because it was easy.' It was the lifestyle, I think. You know what was incredible? I'd seen all those statements and all the spending and when we caught him he didn't have a pot to piss in. All we ever got back was a Rolex watch.

I think we probably both knew how things were going to end up. He's a clever guy and he must have known that one day he was going to get nicked for the whole lot. You live that life knowing you're going to prison. The reason it took Elliot so long to get there is because he was very, very good at what he did. If you look at the amount of activity going on then you'd imagine this was the work of a well-organized gang. When you add in his age – well, it's unbelievable.

Yeah, he was unique.

JET-SET CONMAN CHECKS INTO PRISON
The Scotsman, 19 April 2005

TRICKSTER'S £70,000 HIGH LIFE
Sun, 19 April 2005

FIRST-CLASS CONMAN
Daily Mail, 19 April 2005

FIDDLE CASTRO
Daily Mirror, 19 April 2005

CATCH ME IF YOU CON
Daily Record, 19 April 2005

DOGGED DC GETS HIS MAN
Heathrow Skyport, 22 April 2005

CHAPTER TWENTY-FIVE

It gets hot here in Battlefield in the summer. I lie in bed and I sweat and I watch the curtain rock so slightly that at first you think you're imagining it. I know it's moving though, because below the windowsill is a line of sunshine and it's twitching in time to the curtain. I've been watching that line for an hour.

When I first got out I was up no later than nine every day. I'd sit and have happy breakfasts with my parents and Dean, then walk Dean up to Battlefield station for his train to college. I'd stand on the bridge and watch him go and then I'd go and run errands for my mum – to the supermarket or the post office or to the paper shop to pay the account.

Now I just don't seem to be able to get up. I've been staying awake late, looking at the Internet or reading, and coming through to my bedroom at four or five in the morning. I don't set an alarm and I don't ask to be woken up. When the day finally arrives for me I lie in bed and think about things. If it's sunny outside, then I watch the line on the wall while I think.

The other day Mum gave me a pile of clean laundry and I lugged it back through here. I went over to the cupboard in my room and pulled open an empty drawer to unload the clothes but the drawer wasn't empty. Inside was a sea of paper – letters, envelopes and brochures from the banks and the card companies. There were statements, pin codes and letters offering me extra credit.

I put down the clothes and passed my hand through the paper, seeing a flash of gold as I did so. It was still stuck to the letter it had arrived on and above it was printed *Credit limit* – £25,000. I stirred my hand back through the pile and found more. Silver, gold, platinum. Old, dead cards that I had never even bothered using. That I had never even needed.

I could have not got caught. If I had stuck to all those rules and standards that I thought up along the way then I would still be out there now. I'd be on a plane ordering from the first-class menu, or checking into a hotel, or on the phone telling lies to strangers. The problem with living like that, though, is that you have to give up so much.

All the money that I stole through the WTS and the ordered cards, and the hotels and the flights and the nights out that it paid for, I find it hard to regret. Maybe that's not the right thing to say but I'm not going to start lying to you now, not when we're so close to the end. I regret the early thieving, the wallets and all the rest, much, much more. They were horrible crimes committed in a horrible time, and I can't think of them without feeling prickly and ashamed.

With my later work I stole from multi-billion companies. That's not right, of course it's not right, but people got their money back and I went to prison. It wasn't personal and prison is not a good place to go. But it's not as simple as that. Ultimately, of course, I stole in some minuscule way from people like you with your bank charges and insurance policies. I have no defence against that. I apologize unreservedly.

What I regret more than anything is what I told you right back at the beginning – the people that I lied to and let down. Frankie in Manchester, Dermot and his mother, Brendan, all those teachers who tried to help, my family (a hundred times over), and that old man in Canada who drove me to the airport. And plenty of others. Maybe if they read this then they'll understand a little more. If not then, well, I'll buy them a pint sometime and try again.

I'm not sure about the title of this book. *Other People's Money*. The money was for spending, nothing else, and I never saw it as other people's money. I saw the money that I created as a route out of my life. I saw it for where it could take me and who it could make me. It turned me into someone else and put me next to people that I had longed to belong with. *Other People's Lives*. That's what we might have gone for, but maybe it's not so snappy.

The story that you've just read has never been told in full before. I've given you as much as I can, as much as certain factors will allow me to give. No one has ever asked for the whole lot and, even if they had, I couldn't really tell them. A fraction of what I did got to the police. A fraction of that got to the courts and a fraction of that slipped out through newspapers. What they ended up with was a story and person that I didn't recognize.

I've got nothing left by the way. No money. Nothing. Now, if I was you I'd read that and think *bullshit*, but there you go. It came and it went and I stopped being able to make it come again. A few weeks after Harvey Nichols and Eastgate, my mum and dad went over to Belfast to fetch my stuff. When they got there the place had been stripped. Somewhere in Belfast someone has a very nice table. And quite right too.

Of course I think about going back, how could I not? Life changes when you have money, no matter what you go through to get it. But I haven't and I don't think I will. The longer I stay straight the harder it becomes to start all over again. The more normality I gather around me, the more I have to throw away. Especially people. The fraud – the lying and the stealing –

detaches more from me each day. By the time you read these words, I hope that it will be far away and foreign.

Before I forget, I can't really play the trumpet.

I get up and out of the bed. I could take the dog down to the river, or go and practise on the record decks in Dean's room. I've been picking up DJ shifts in Glasgow and it's been going well. I can feel the tentative arrival of ambition in this mind that has habitually dealt only in dreams. Sometimes I'll arrive at a club for a shift and someone will look at me strangely, or come over and say, 'Is your name . . .', and I'll say, 'Yeah,' and walk over to the corner to play my records in the dark.

I have a couple of other legitimate ideas but, for now, I'm lucky to have the DJing. You'd be surprised how few jobs there are kicking about for convicted fraudsters without a single qualification. And so my days are often like they have always been, just myself and my thoughts. At some point today, Neil will probably call and ask me more questions.

I walk out into the hall and then through to the kitchen. She's so still I don't see her as my eyes turn away from the sunlight and I move to the kettle. I push my fingers through the handle and am tightening them around the plastic when she says, 'Elliot,' and I turn round.

She's sitting at the kitchen table with the sun behind her. It glows the edges of her hair and leaves her face shaded and difficult. From outside I can hear steel slowly hitting steel but when I look there is just the washing line and the shared green. In front of her, beside the newspaper, a cigarette sits in an old pub ashtray and sends smoke towards the open window. It curls up in a stairway of circles that grow as they go. When they get to the window they pause just for a moment, and then slip away into the world.

Acknowledgements

From the start, I'd like to thank Eoin and Dave at *Maxim* for agreeing that Elliot Castro sounded like an interesting guy to meet. From there I went with an idea and an email to many, many people. Among the few that replied, and the fewer still that replied positively, was David Riding at MBA.

Thanks first to Diana Tyler, who passed my unusual case to David, and then, hugely, to David, whom Elliot and I would like to thank for his hard work and caring approach from that initial encouraging reply. He fielded our constant questions, from Edinburgh and various prisons, with immense patience and guided us brilliantly along the way.

This book wouldn't be in your hands if it weren't for Pan Macmillan taking a brave decision that others, quite understandably, shied away from and we'd like to thank them once more for that. Ingrid Connell, who helped significantly to make that decision and then acted as a supportive and sensitive editor, we would like to thank especially.

I'd like to thank Jane Duncan, Declan Farrell, Danny Bell, Chris McArthur and Helen Cope for their time and assistance. I'd also like to thank Trevor Horwood for his fine copy-editing and both James Burns and Iain McLellan for the use of photos.

The wonderful, and inimitable, Ralph Eastgate was very generous in his co-operation for this book, which would have been a far duller place without him. We would like to thank him again, and wish him and his wife a happy retirement in Draguignan. Elliot will visit, he says, when he has saved up the air miles.

I would like to thank Elliot's loving and welcoming family for their assistance in writing this book. In particular his mother, Jane Castro, for her humour and uncompromising honesty. One of the great surprises of Elliot's story is that he constantly risked being on the wrong side of her.

I would also like to thank my own Jane for everything from invaluable readings to driving me to HMP Spring Hill, and then Elliot and me to the Pheasant Pub in Brill, where we decided to write a book.

I want to thank Elliot Castro. He doesn't know about this bit, I sneaked it in late in the day, because we're both east coast Scots and things like this make us shuffle our feet and look away. But I'd like to thank him. He didn't have to trust me and he didn't have to tell me his story, yet he did both and never flinched from either decision. For that I will be forever grateful.

Finally, finally, I would like to thank my family, for always listening to my stories.

Neil Forsyth, *Edinburgh, August 2006*